A Slip in the Rain

The True Story of the 1967-1972 Toronto Argonauts and the Fumble that Destroyed Canada's Team

by
Craig Wallace

Acknowledgements

Nobody can write a book this detailed without a great deal of help. Thanks to Jeff Dominic and Shawn Lackie at the CFL head office in Toronto. They gave me full access to the league archives and records at no cost to myself. Their help saved me many hours of research and helped ensure the accuracy of the book.

Keith Pelly, the President of the Toronto Argonauts has been very supportive and helpful in every way possible.

I need to thank my wife Bridget who very patiently put up with all my talk about the Argos and never complained when I was "holed up" for hours at a time working away or off to the Canadian Football Hall of Fame or local library for research.

Thank you as well to my three closest friends in the world, Yvonne Chadwick-Whittome, Christine Newman, and Jeanne Albert-Cheng. Yvonne created and maintains the web page I use to promote my writing. Jeanne and Christine were always there with words of encouragement and support that kept me going on this project. Jeanne's husband Nick Cheng assisted me with the final formatting of the book.

Shane Kelley of Hudson Quebec did a wonderful job designing the front and back covers. Her assistance was invaluable.

Thanks to Tom Lawrence of Surrey B.C for tracking down one hard to find photo.

Paul Woods of Burlington, Ontario did a "bang up" job in editing the final draft of my book. Mark Estep of Austin, Texas assisted me in the research and read through an early draft and suggested several changes which I incorporated.

A huge thank you to the players I interviewed. Wally Gabler, Michael Eben, Jim Tomlin, Jim Stillwagon, Dave Raimey, and ball boy Randy Beatty were very generous with their time and answered all my questions. Coach Leo Cahill spent a number of hours with me on the phone allowing me to find out more about the architect of this great team. Coach Cahill also gave me permission to use several quotes from his 1973 book "Goodbye Argos."

And finally a special thanks to three Argos in particular: Peter Martin who invited me to his home for interviews and kindly lent me all of his enormous collection of scrap books and programs that were an invaluable aid in my research. Bill Symons and his lovely wife Trish who allowed my family and I to visit them at their farm for an interview and gave my children a wonderful day that they still talk about. And finally Dick Thornton. Dick was the first Argonaut I contacted when the idea of this book was still fresh and from day one he has always been available to answer any and all questions I had, gave me tips on research and writing and has truly become a good friend.

Foreword to "A Slip in the Rain"

By Dick Thornton

It's amazing how modern technology has changed us all…for better or worse – and it certainly had a positive impact on my life. Let me explain!

A long time ago, an astrologist in England said I was born under a wandering star and this very accurate prediction…led me to a very nomadic existence since I retired from professional football at the end of 1974 as captain of the Memphis Southmen, the WFL's Central Division Champions.

My first real job in the after-life was working in the front office of the Hawaiians, another WFL team. Although it was a fantastic opportunity still being in the game and living on the island of Oahu…unfortunately, the League folded half way through the 1975 season.

Thus, quickly found myself back in Tennessee to accept the Athletic Director and Head Coaching position at Southwestern At Memphis College - the Division III college there. While that too became a great learning experience (my record of 19-9-1 still puts me at the top of all coaches in terms of a 647% winning percentage) I couldn't resist a unique marketing challenge from the very prestigious Coca-Cola Company to join their international team and coach sales people instead of athletes.

Originally based in the States for two years training, was later was sent to the CC-South Pacific Division in Australia for eighteen months and then worked seven more years with CC-Northwest Europe in London, England, travelling constantly throughout the European Continent. My final assignment before taking early retirement in 1994 was directing a Global Training Program for accelerating the development of high-potential managers…which brought me to the Philippine Islands and where I got my first real glimpse of South East Asia.

"A Slip in the Rain"

When I set up my own beverage consulting business, it was in Makati...better known as the business and night-life district of Metro Manila. From this base of operations, it was more traveling to work on special Coca-Cola marketing projects in Korea, the Micronesia Islands, India, Singapore, Malaysia, Vietnam, Nepal and Thailand. Afterwards, I finally came to the conclusion that this part of the world was definitely going to be my permanent home. Toss in additional contracts for other multi-national fast moving consumer goods companies in Italy, Greece, China, Argentina, Chile, Brazil, Mexico and Venezuela and one can easily see why it was impossible to me track down at the time by conventional means. Thus, over the years, I slowly faded away from family, friends, ex-wives, girlfriends, business associates and former teammates.

However, with the technological emergence of computers...that brought with it - Electronic Mail, the Internet, Websites and more recently, the Mobile Cellphone...people's lives, including mine...began to change drastically. So it was in April, 2001 that I came home from a round of golf at Canlubang County Club and found an e-mail from a Craig Wallace in Toronto in my Inbox.

He mentioned that as a youngster, he was a big fan of the Toronto Argonauts during the Leo Cahill era and that he was working on a book describing those exciting yet tumultuous times in Canadian professional football. He was still in the research stage then - with much of his time spent at the CFL office digging through game summaries and hours upon hours at the library reading endless articles and columns during those years from 1967 to 1972. When it came time for some player interviews...Craig felt that since I was one of the more colorful athletes of that period, he typed my name into a Search Engine and up came my Website: www.coachingpoints.com. The rest...as he now says is history.

At first, I eagerly answered his probing questions which elicited incredible memories from the past; especially the 1971 Grey Cup game in Vancouver and with each successive e-mail, a true friendship blossomed.

In November of that year, was making a series of presentations at a Beverage Trade Show in Miami, so on the way home, made a slight detour up to Toronto in order to meet Craig in person and during that visit was also able to catch up with ex-teammates, Bobby Taylor, Wally Gabler, Bill Symons, Pete Martin, Paul Markle and even the team ball-boy, Randy Beatty. Guys I hadn't seen nor talked to in almost 30 years.

In early 2002, Craig Wallace was instrumental in broadening my e-mail horizons even farther. He wrote my biography and got it included on the Legends Page of the CFL Website so via this vehicle, have received well over two hundred messages from fans and friends all across Canada saying basically in part, "thanks for the memories" and to which I've replied to each and every one. Those were real thrills to get such honoured antidotes from the past and would have never known any of this without Craig's help and assistance. So now, thanks to him…I am back 'on-line' with the past - even though I'm living halfway around the world.

Being an accomplished journalist, Craig also gave me the pleasure of the first crack at editing "A Slip in the Rain". I write a regular column for the global magazine, Beverage World…a renowned beverage industry publication and also do a weekly Sunday football column on the NFL/CFL for the Bangkok Post, SE Asia's leading English newspaper.

Thus, concentrating on 'Slip' for almost three months, page by page, it was like going back in time and reliving history. One must remember those were chaotic times within a vast period of change; the height of the Vietnam War coupled with a rebellion against the Establishment. There were demonstrations, assassinations, a sexual revolution that was in full swing, long haired hippies and love beads yet we as 'Double Blue Gladiators' somehow represented a sense of true normalcy to sell-out crowds in a crazy, mixed up outside world.

Found it fascinating to recall many of those magic moments; like when I was traded to the Argonauts in May of 67 and then months later, whipping my former team, the Blue Bombers 53-0 at CNE stadium. To then visualize our slow rise up the ladder in the Eastern Conference, to re-live those fierce battles with the Ti-Cats and Rough Riders and the infamous 'Act of God' playoff game in Ottawa. The culmination being our agonizing defeat against Calgary in the 71 Grey Cup and it's amazing that my interception and the infamous fumble are still talked about…as if it happened yesterday.

Then there were the injuries and bad luck that plagued the team during the entire 1972 season, culminating in that final 'totally uncalled for' management decision to fire Coach Cahill. I left CNE Stadium for the last time nine months later, cut by the new coach and with all my gear dumped in a green garbage bag…facing a very uncertain future. However, I did get some measure of early revenge when I covered the team as a reporter for the Toronto Sun, under the excellent tutelage of sports editor, George Gross.

I am forever grateful to John Bassett Jr. for giving me a second chance with the Memphis Grizzlies; proving the Argos made a big mistake in releasing me and which eventually became the launch pad for me to a very productive, rewarding and exciting lifestyle over the next 30 years.

Enjoy this book on Canada's Team; the true story of the Toronto Argonauts from 1967-1972. Author, Craig Wallace has captured it all with real quotes from the players and media of that era…game by game action – year by year - in a fine, easy reading literary style. Learn about this unique group of individuals, renegades and mavericks brought together and molded into winners by Leo Cahill, a true player's coach – who brought all of us to the 'edge of immortality' but for a 'Slip in the Rain.' It was a team I was very proud to be part of and which will now live on forever…in the hearts and minds of true & knowledgeable football fans everywhere in Canada.

Dick Thornton

Table of Contents

Acknowledgements .... ***iii***

Foreword to "A Slip in the Rain" By Dick Thornton .... ***v***

Table of Contents .... ***ix***

Preface .... ***xi***

One Fall from Grace ***1***

Two Leo Cahill Joins the Argos ***13***

Three 1967 .... ***21***

Four 1968 .... ***47***

Five 1969 .... ***75***

Six 1970 .... ***109***

Seven 1971 .... ***135***

Eight 1971 Grey Cup ***175***

Nine 1972 .... ***199***

Epilogue ***235***

Where Are They Now? ***241***

The Coaches 241

The Players 241

Index of Photos ***247***

Photo Credits ***249***

Bibliography ***251***

For my two lovely daughters
Emily and Erin.

Preface

The pounding rain continued to fall at Empire Stadium in Vancouver as Joe Theismann, rookie quarterback for the Toronto Argonauts, led his struggling offence on the field. The 1971 Grey Cup had so far been an exercise in futility for the usually high-powered Argo offence, and the team trailed the Calgary Stampeders 14-11 with less then three minutes to go in the game.

In the huddle, however, all the futility of the first 57 minutes was forgotten. The team had just got the big break it needed. Star defensive back Dick Thornton had intercepted an errant Jerry Keeling pass, returning it 54 yards to the Calgary 11-yard line in one of the most dramatic interception returns in the history of championship football games. The Argos were now poised on the verge of a Grey Cup title for the first time in 19 years. A touchdown would mean almost certain victory. At worst, they'd kick a field goal and send the game into overtime with plenty of Double Blue momentum. It was all there – ready for the taking.

The offence lined up as 40,000 stadium fans screamed while millions more sat glued to their TV sets. The Grey Cup – that vaunted, circular silver trophy the city of Toronto had been waiting 19 years for – was finally within their grasp.

The Stampeders had already began to feel a sense of panic. They had lost the 1968 championship game in excruciatingly close fashion to Ottawa and been hammered in the 1970 final by Montreal. They were closely favoured to win this one, however, and it was now slipping away despite a superb performance by their defence.

Moisture clouds from the day-long, drizzling rain rose from the helmets of the huge lineman of both teams as they lined up prepared for the final drama – yet the ultimate decision lay in the mind of Toronto head coach Leo Cahill. Be conservative with the running game and play for the tie and a new chance in overtime, or gamble by throwing the football to the end zone in an attempt to win the game right now? There was no hesitation in the mind of Calgary coach Jim Duncan. He ordered his Stampeders to stack the line of scrimmage with nine men ready to blitz. Leo called for a running play. Theismann quickly handed off to sensational rookie Leon McQuay, who crashed through the Calgary line, legs pumping and driving for four hard yards down to the seven-yard line.

The crowd at Empire Stadium waited in tremendous anticipation as the teams lined up once more on second down. Theismann barked the signals and again handed off to McQuay, who scampered to his left this time. The offensive linemen of the Argonauts exploded off the ball, trying to create a hole for their running back to bust through. Then, instantaneously, two things happened. One was the opening of a slight hole with almost a clear path to the end zone. The other was the arrival in that hole of Calgary middle linebacker Wayne Harris, perhaps the greatest to ever play that position in Canada. He was crashing in from the right on another blitz. McQuay cut back inside on the rain-drenched artificial turf . . .

One

Fall from Grace

In November 1966, the Toronto Argonauts of the Canadian Football League were at rock bottom. Not only were they the worst team in the league (and likely all of professional football), they were also a laughingstock in the eyes of their fans and the reporters who covered the team. The bumbling and sheer incompetence of management and players made for a never-ending stream of Argo jokes. Attendance was dropping at CNE stadium and there was no light at the end of the tunnel.

It had not always been this way. The Toronto Argonauts were the oldest professional sports franchise in North America, having been founded in 1873. In the first 30-plus years of their existence, the Argos were a rather informal club. Owned by the Argonaut Rowing Club, the football team was an outlet for club members to stay active when they weren't hitting the water.

Formalized play began in the second decade of the 20th century, and the "Boatmen" quickly became a formidable football team. The official competition for the Grey Cup, emblematic of football supremacy in Canada, started in 1909, and the Argonauts made their first appearance in the final two years later, suffering a 14-7 defeat at the hands of the University of Toronto Blues. The Argos won their first title in 1914 with a 14-2 victory over the same team, and they picked up another in 1921 by defeating the Edmonton Eskimos 23-0 in Canada's first East-West Grey Cup matchup.

It was during this early period that the Argos adopted their famous "double blue" colour scheme, with the dark and light blues of Oxford and Cambridge universities. The team became a powerhouse in the 1930s. In 1932, Lew Hayman came to Toronto from the University of Syracuse, starting a relationship with the Argos that would last close to 50 years. With Hayman behind the bench, the Argonauts won the coveted Cup in 1933, '37 and '38.

"A Slip in the Rain"

A great source of pride for the team and their fans in this era was the fact that this success was achieved with a roster consisting solely of Canadian-born players. Toronto at the time was a team very connected to its British heritage, and the fact that the Argos had no imported American players made the team even more popular.

With the start of the Second World War, the Argonauts' string of Grey Cup championships temporarily came to a halt and they began to join other Canadian football teams by openly and aggressively recruiting top American players. But Canadians were still the key players. When the war ended in 1945, the Argonauts began a run of absolute greatness. Led by the "Gold Dust Twins" – quarterback Joe Krol and receiver Royal Copeland, both Canadians – and coached by Ted Morris, the Argos won the Grey Cup in 1945, '46 and '47.

That last contest was a classic victory that firmly established their reputation as a great "clutch" team. The Winnipeg Blue Bombers battled fiercely against the Argonaut juggernaut until a booming Krol kick for a single point in the dying moments gave the Argos a 10-9 victory. The Argonauts never gave up and seemingly always found a way to win a critical game.

At that point in the late 1940s, the Argonauts were considered by many to be the epitome of professionalism. Everything about the organization was first-class, and the feeling among other Canadian football teams and fans was that you did not want to face the Argos in a critical game. They always seemed to find a way to beat you.

That was proven again in the 1950 Grey Cup played at Varsity Stadium in Toronto, immortalized as the "Mud Bowl." During Grey Cup week, Toronto was hit with a heavy snowfall. The day before the game, groundskeepers at Varsity Stadium decided it would be a good idea to clear the field using a snowplough. One does not have to use much imagination to envision the result of that type of machine being driven on a sodden grass field, and indeed the playing surface turned into a sea of gooey, slippery mud.

While the Winnipeg Blue Bombers slipped and slid all over field, the Argos kept their footing. Team management, in an effort to ensure victory, had found the longest cleats that could be legally worn, giving Toronto players solid footing. Argo quarterback Al Dekdebrun filed down the points on thumbtacks and taped them to his fingers, enabling him to grip the ball better. It all led the Argos, by now coached by Frank Clair out of the University of Cincinnati, to defeat the helpless Blue Bombers 13-0. Again, the Boatmen had found a way to win when it mattered most.

The Argos were back in the Grey Cup game in 1952. Led by quarterback Nobby Wirkowski, running back Ulysses Curtis (who set an Argo team record by rushing for 985 yards) and receivers Bill Bass, Rod Smylie and Zeke O'Connor, the Argos came from behind to defeat Edmonton 21-11. The Argonauts had now won 10 Grey Cups and had never lost the big game to a western-based opponent. The good times, it seemed would never end.

However, they did – and very, very quickly. A black cloud of misfortune suddenly descended upon the team, as if a voodoo curse had been put upon them. The Argonauts slipped in 1953 and '54 and missed the playoffs both years. They had missed before, but never two seasons in a row. The 1954 season was notable in two other respects. One was the debut of Dick Shatto. He was a good-looking blond running back out of the University of Kentucky, whom the Argos had stolen out from under the noses of the National Football League and who would go on to a superb 12-year career with the Double Blue. The other was the firing of coach Frank Clair, who would in later years turn the Ottawa Rough Riders into one of the great powers in CFL history. The coaching was taken over by Bill Swiacki, a well-regarded young coach from the New York Giants who brought in a number of assistant coaches from the Detroit Lions and Notre Dame University.

The Argonauts also made headlines for another reason. A team director by the name of Harry Sonshine, who had been horrified by the team's poor play in 1953 and '54, signed seven top NFL players from the Giants and Detroit Lions to Argo contracts. NFL head office personnel were outraged since those players were still under contract in the American league. After heated discussions between the two leagues, and a nasty court battle, four of the players were cleared to play in Toronto. This was the first major attempt by the team to try to find victory through heavy reliance on American players and coaches. The Argonauts were turning away from their tradition of great Canadians, and embracing the idea that NFL players and coaches would be able to help them win – an idea that prevailed for the better part of two decades, usually without success.

As it turned out, Swiacki and the four NFL players signed by the Argos were not the "supermen" the media made them out to be. The team finished with a record of four wins and eight losses but managed to make the playoffs for the first time since 1952. The Argos upset Hamilton 32-28 in the Eastern Semifinal, but lost a wild 38-36 decision in the Eastern Final to Montreal.

The Argos fell apart in 1956, finishing with a 4-10 record, yet the big news was the sale of the team after the season. The Argonaut Rowing Club made a deal with a consortium headed up by John Bassett, Sr., the founder of CFTO television and owner of the *Toronto Telegram* newspaper. The new ownership did not provide immediate positive results on the field. The Argonauts missed the playoffs in 1957, '58 and '59, ending up with identical 4-10 records in each of those seasons. Swiacki was fired and replaced by Hampton Pool. The black cloud that had appeared in 1953 now seemed a permanent part of the team. The only positive notes in this era were the continuing fine play of Dick Shatto and the move from Varsity Stadium on the campus of the University of Toronto to CNE Stadium, located on the Canadian National Exhibition grounds along the shore of Lake Ontario.

The Argos christened their new stadium by playing an exhibition game against the NFL's Chicago Cardinals. It was thought that a good CFL team would be able to give the Cardinals, who were at best just an average NFL team, a tough game. But the Argos, who were a poor CFL team, were expected to get killed. Toronto shocked everybody (including its own players, probably) by jumping in front 13-1 on a Ronnie Knox-to-Dave Mann touchdown strike and an interception return for a touchdown by Bob Dehlinger off Chicago quarterback M.C. Reynolds. Chicago then got serious and when the smoke cleared, the Cardinals had thrashed the Argonauts 55-26. Not only did they lose the game, the Argos lost four players with broken bones as the Cards outweighed them by an average of 20 pounds per player.

Later in the 1959 season, Ronnie Knox, the Argos' bright young quarterback, declared "football is a game for animals" and walked away from the team to concentrate on writing poetry and acting. That startling news heightened the sense of weirdness now associated with the Argos, leaving fans scratching their heads and wondering what had happened to their highly professional profile of the 1930s and '40s.

Starting a new decade in 1960, John Bassett, Sr., was determined to turn his team around. Lew Hayman was installed as general manager and he hired Lou Agase as head coach. Hayman also signed quarterback Tobin Rote away from the Detroit Lions. Rote was a certified star who had led the Lions to the 1957 NFL championship, and he did not disappoint. Rote shredded opposing defences and the Argos threw a tremendous running attack into the equation with Dick Shatto and young Chester "Cookie" Gilchrist.

The Argos rolled to a 10-4 record in 1960 and first place in the Eastern Conference. The cloud that had hovered over the team since 1953 seemed to be disappearing. The Grey Cup was not in the cards, however. In the playoffs, Toronto faced the Ottawa Rough Riders led by a young Canadian quarterback named Russ Jackson. Coached by former Argo boss Frank Clair, the Riders won the two-game, total-points Eastern final 54-41.

Some fans wrote the loss off as a fluke, figuring the high-powered Argos would be back on top in 1961. Others, however, felt the bad times might return. For one thing, the Argos were not a well-balanced team. They relied very heavily on their three stars: Rote, Shatto and Gilchrist. The defence was erratic, and if Rote was not at his best, the team struggled.

The Argos sputtered throughout the 1961 season. Late in the season they had a mediocre record of 5-6-1. Agase then introduced a unique offence known as the "shotgun," which required Rote to stand five yards directly behind centre and take a long snap. This formation gave him a couple of extra precious seconds to find open receivers, and Rote put it to good use.

The Argos won their final two games with Rote bombing the opposition into submission. They met Ottawa in the Eastern semifinal and Rote fired four touchdown passes as the Argos won 43-19.

The city of Toronto was now convinced the Grey Cup was coming back to "Hogtown" as the Boatmen prepared to meet Hamilton in the two-game, total-points Eastern final. With the "shotgun" offence firing on all cylinders, the Argos hammered Hamilton in the first game 25-7 at home in CNE Stadium. The Grey Cup seemed to be a certainty now. With an 18-point lead heading into the second game, most experts felt the Argonauts would revert to a simple "ball-control" offence. The Argos didn't need to score many points as long as they could keep the ball away from Hamilton's potent offence. With their strong running attack, the Argos should be able to use up a lot of time simply by moving the ball along the ground.

But coach Agase had other ideas. For some reason he stuck with the shotgun formation and had Rote come out firing. Unfortunately, he wasn't connecting very often. The Argos faded throughout the game and Hamilton took full advantage. The 18-point lead vanished as the game neared its conclusion.

In the final minutes, Hamilton was leading 20-2 and the series was tied on points. Then the Argos caught a big break. Linebacker Stan Wallace intercepted a Bernie Faloney pass, giving Toronto a first down at the Hamilton 27-yard line. The Argos' history of grabbing a break in a crucial game seemed to be coming back.

Back in a regular offensive formation, Rote called two running plays to run down the clock, and the Argos then lined up for a punt with 28 seconds to go. The game was in the bag in the minds of all Argo fans. Dave Mann, their magnificent punter, would simply punt the ball out of the end zone for a single point and the Argos would escape with victory – despite their horrendous overall performance. Jim Trimble, the Hamilton coach, put his two kickers, Don Sutherin and Bernie Faloney, deep in the end zone with orders to kick the ball back out if at all possible.

Jay Teitel, in his wonderful 1982 book *The Argo Bounce*, described what happened next:

"Dave stepped forward and kicked. It was his worst punt of the day, a wobbly forty-yarder, but it still carried eight yards into the end zone. It came down to Don Sutherin, who somehow, surrounded by blue-shirts, managed to execute a panicky stutter-step and actually kick it back out. The camera swung back crazily, tennis-style, catching Sutherin's kick coming down just past the 30-yard line into the hands of, amazingly, Dave Mann again, who hesitated, then stepped forward and again, kicked it back towards the end-zone. Dave's second kick landed on the goal line, and bounced into the hands of Bernie Faloney. And Faloney began to run. Faloney ran and ran. For the first thirty yards or so he wove in and out of would-be Argo tacklers at a leisurely, hypnotic speed, so that as he moved up the field, he seemed to be passing the same players twice and even three times. Even when he passed mid-field and there were no Argos left to weave around, he wove.

Faloney took Mann's kick back 111 yards for the touchdown but Hamilton players and fans were soon shocked as that magnificent run was called back due to an illegal block. But the overall damage had been done – the Argos were finished. In overtime, the Tiger-Cats exploded for 28 points on their way to a 48-2 massacre and an overall 55-27 total point victory in the series.

For the first time in their history, the Argos had a playoff game seemingly "locked up" and let it get away. In the coming years, it would only get worse.

The Argonauts spent most of the 1962 season in a daze. They could not seem to recover from the shock of the previous year's collapse against Hamilton. With much the same team as the year before, they finished 4-10, which by now seemed about standard. Lou Agase was fired before the season was finished and replaced by former quarterback Nobby Wirkowski. Agase, who was never considered an "Einstein" in the coaching profession at the best of times – especially after his disastrous decision to stick to the "shotgun" offence in the critical game of the 1961 Eastern final – seemed utterly lost and confused in the games before he was fired. Tobin Rote looked average at best and spent much of the year in a well-publicized feud with Toronto newspaper columnist Annis Stukus. Dick Shatto continued his fine play but it was not nearly enough. Cookie Gilchrist, who was a brilliant running back and a never-ending disciplinary problem, was released and signed with the American Football League's Buffalo Bill early in the season. At year-end, Rote joined him in the AFL, signing with the San Diego Chargers.

The fall from grace continued into 1963, and the Argos' misfortunes multiplied. The misery that began back in 1953 now seemed a permanent fixture. Wirkowski tried hard at the head coaching position and really was not a bad coach (as he would prove in later years at York University in Toronto), but he had very little talent to work with from the start. Would-be saviours such as quarterback Sandy Stephens were brought in, but none was what the team needed to get back on the winning track. In fact, if Nobby himself had decided to suit up, a decade after his playing career ended, he probably would have been a major improvement over the crop of quarterbacks with whom he had to work.

The legitimate players Wirkowski did have were Dick Shatto, still a star near the end of his career; Dave Mann, who continued to excel at wide receiver and kicker; and two key offensive linemen: Danny Nykoluk and Norm Stoneburgh. Lew Hayman also obtained safety Marv Luster from Montreal, which eventually proved to be a very important acquisition. Luster, a former UCLA all-American, had run into difficult times with the Alouettes and been released. Toronto, desperate for anyone who could play, snapped him up and he would become a mainstay of the Toronto defensive secondary for many years to come.

This era also marked the beginning of what came to be known as the "Argo Airlift." It was a simple concept, and never a successful one. The team would lose a series of games and appear to be on the verge of collapse. In a knee-jerk response, Argonauts management would begin cutting players and flying in replacements who had recently been cut by NFL or AFL teams. Argo veterans (the few who survived the chaos of the period) often complained they didn't know the names of many of their teammates on a game-to-game basis.

Linebacker Peter Martin looks back on the days of the airlift:

"I remember 1965 in particular. When we'd lose a game on the weekend, there would be nine or 10 new players in the dressing room on Monday. They'd practise with us during the week, and then on Thursday we'd scrimmage to see who would be on the team for the game on the upcoming weekend. It was complete chaos."

In 1963, with the Airlift in full flight, the team collapsed to a dismal 3-11 record. On Sept. 22, Calgary, a so-so team at best, walked into CNE Stadium and obliterated the Argonauts 50-0. That was and still is the worst defeat in franchise history. It had been only 11 years since Wirkowski led the Argos to their come-from-behind victory over Edmonton in the Grey Cup, but it seemed more like a century ago.

Things got no better in 1964 and the team could only manage a record of 4-10 – again. The Airlift continued to the point where one reporter suggested it would rival the "American bombing of Vietnam" for the sheer amount of air traffic activity.

Around the rest of the CFL in 1964, things were in great shape. The two top teams in the league were the British Columbia Lions, led by quarterback Joe Kapp, middle linebacker Tom Brown, and running back Willie Fleming, and the Hamilton Tiger-Cats with such stars as Garney Henley, John Barrow, Angelo Mosca and Hal Patterson. The Lions would win the Grey Cup that year against the always tough Ticats. The Ottawa Rough Riders, with Russ Jackson at the helm and Frank Clair as the head coach, were a rising power. Montreal was not a great team but was pretty well guaranteed a playoff spot due to the sheer ineptitude of the Argos.

Out west the Blue Bombers, coached by Bud Grant and with such stars as Leo Lewis, Dick Thornton, Kenny Ploen, Ernie Pitts and Ferrell Funston, suffered a disastrous, injury-plagued 1964 season, but had too much talent not to bounce back the following year. Saskatchewan had rising superstars in quarterback Ron Lancaster, wide receiver Hugh Campbell and fullback George Reed. Calgary and Edmonton were also solid. It was only the Toronto Argonauts that looked hopeless. The league was thriving and teams often played before capacity crowds, except in Montreal, which was finding pro football a tough sell after the glory days of the mid-1950s.

The CFL at this time was considered "big league," very close to being on par with the NFL and AFL. It was generally accepted by knowledgeable football people that the best teams in the CFL would be competitive in either the NFL or AFL. In fact, some thought the best CFL teams would beat the best AFL teams if they were to engage in "head-to-head" matches. Salaries in all three leagues were similar, and the Canadian dollar was valued at par or sometimes even a bit higher than the U.S. dollar. CFL teams were able to offer certain players more money then they could make in the NFL or AFL. Teams in Canada would recruit a player and offer to help him find a job outside of football. Because CFL teams did not practise before 5 p.m., players could hold down full-time day jobs to earn extra money. Jim Tomlin, who joined the Argonauts in 1969 from the NFL, commented:

"I knew many guys in the NFL who wanted to play in Canada as you could make more money. I made $15,000 with New Orleans in 1968. I came to Toronto in 1969 and the Argos gave me $15,000 and Toronto got me a job during the day that paid me $10,000. I was making a lot more in the CFL then I did in the NFL."

At the end of the 1964 season, John Bassett, Sr., fired Wirkowski and replaced him with former Saskatchewan head coach Bob Shaw. Shaw was the sixth Argonaut head coach in the past 10 years.

As a fan looking back, it is interesting to speculate at this point. What had really happened to the Argos? Had a member of the team offended a distant witch doctor who, in turn, put a curse on the squad? Had somebody walked under a ladder, broken a mirror, crossed paths with countless black cats? Surely there had to be something almost supernatural that had taken place to turn this vaunted "machine of professional excellence" into a squad of ineptly paid losers. Good teams in other sports had gone through rough times, but never had a squad as dominant as the Toronto Argonauts experienced such a drastic turn of fortunes. The Detroit Red Wings of the NHL and baseball's New York Yankees both fell from lofty heights, but neither ever became such a bizarre spectacle. The Argos had gone from a team that took pride in developing Canadian talent and seldom lost a big game to a team that went all out to recruit American players (most of whom could not perform – at least not in Toronto) and hired coaches who became legendary for poor regular-season performances and occasional playoff collapses.

Shaw's first season in 1965 was definitely not a success. The team failed to improve and in fact regressed – finishing 3-11. It dropped its first eight games that year, was shut out twice in that stretch and lost 36-1 to British Columbia in another game. The 1965 season also marked the final year for Dick Shatto. In 12 seasons, he had been the epitome of class and professionalism for the Argonauts. Upon his retirement, Shatto led the CFL in most career touchdowns, pass receptions and offensive yards gained. Many times during his tenure, he had been the only Argonaut worth paying the price of admission to see. Now he was gone, too. The Argos wasted little time in retiring his #22, and he was inducted into the Canadian Football Hall of Fame in 1975.

Fortunately, the Argos added two players who would play a much larger role in the future during the 1966 season. They were quarterback Wally Gabler, who played his college ball at the University of Michigan, and tight end Mel Profit from UCLA.

Gabler was supposedly a solid, all-around performer and coach Bob Shaw, management and fans were hoping he would be the quarterback to finally bring the team back to respectability and prominence. They had not had a competent pivot since Tobin Rote left town four years earlier.

Mel Profit was something of a mystery. A six-foot-five all-American tight end from California, he joined the Los Angeles Rams in 1964 out of college. After getting injured early in training camp, he was shipped by the Rams to the Pittsburgh Steelers, for whom he spent the entire 1964 season on the taxi squad. Profit quit football after that year and spent 1965 touring Europe. He figured he was finished with pro football, but upon his return from Europe he found he missed the game. Profit returned to North America and signed a contract with the British Columbia Lions. He didn't last long there, however, as he described in his 1972 book *For Love Money and Future Considerations*:

"As soon as I arrived I started receiving suggestions to cut my hair. These came not only from the management, but from some players as well. As it turned out, I became Toronto property before the season got under way, and the management here was too busy trying to field a team to bother about the length of my hair."

Mel Profit quickly became one of the most distinctive players in the league, due in no small part to his size (he was much taller than most receivers of that era) and his long, blond hair which flowed out of the back of his helmet. He also proved to be one of Toronto's better receivers in 1966, hauling in 32 receptions – many in clutch situations. Mel was the first of the "new breed" of athlete to join the Argonauts. He was extremely intelligent, articulate and concerned about political and social matters. He denounced the "cult of the athlete," as shown in a 1971 *Toronto Star* interview:

"Personally, I've never been able to see the glorification of athletes at all. If we are going to glorify someone, why not doctors and humanitarians? Football is entertainment. When it tries to be something more, it ceases to have any reason for being."

With Profit playing a large role, and Wally Gabler alternating at quarterback with veteran Eagle Day, the Argos did improve slightly in 1966, to a record of 5-9. That was their best record since the Tobin Rote era, but they still finished last in the Eastern Conference and out of the playoffs for a fifth consecutive season. Even this modest improvement was not enough to save the coaching career of Bob Shaw in Toronto. He resigned in the spring of 1967 and once again Toronto was looking for a new head coach – one who would finally return winning football to Toronto.

Two

Leo Cahill Joins the Argos

With Bob Shaw gone, the talk in Toronto centred around who would be next victim. Owner John Bassett Sr surprised some when he announced, that the new head coach would be none other than Leo Cahill.

Who exactly was Leo Edward Cahill? Born and raised in Utica, Ill., a small town southwest of Chicago, Leo attended the University of Illinois, making their varsity football team as a guard and linebacker. He was a bit small but a fine player nonetheless, and in 1947 was the only freshman to appear in the Rose Bowl game for Illinois. By his senior year, Leo was voted to the All-Midwestern and All-American Catholic teams.

After university, Leo realized he was never going to play professional football. He enlisted in the Army in hopes of playing for or coaching one of the Armed Forces football teams. That hope was dashed when, during basic training, he was involved in a fight with a sergeant. The officer was severely injured and Leo was facing a stint in prison at Fort Leavenworth, Kan. He caught a break, however, when he was offered a plea bargain: the choice of facing charges and in all probability going to military prison, or accepting assignment to a combat zone in Korea. The Korean War was in full fury at this point, with many casualties, and thus was not a very attractive option. But reckoning that it was better than prison and a dishonourable discharge, Leo decided to go to Korea. He was trained as a medic and spent seven months overseas.

He was honourably discharged from the Army in 1953 and returned to Illinois, where he approached his old coach Ray Eliot for a coaching position. Eliot gave Leo a job handling the Illinois B team or taxi squad. In one year at the helm, Leo showed great creativity and promise, which caused issues with Coach Eliot. Players on the B squad were supposed to be able to immediately move up to the varsity team in the event of injuries. This required them to be well-versed in the plays and formations used by the varsity squad. But being creative, Leo installed a different series of offensive plays and formations into his group's playbook before a practice game against the Ohio State B team. The Fighting Illini B squad, using this unique set of plays, destroyed the opposition that day. The varsity head coach was not pleased. Leo's rationale was simple: he wanted to show Coach Eliot and the staff his own coaching abilities.

Later, Leo allowed his players to exceed their meal allowance at a post-game dinner held at a local restaurant, a breach of the rules that greatly upset the athletic director. Leo defended his decision by saying it was good public relations, plus a reward for his players who had performed well on the field.

One year at Illinois was enough for Leo and probably for the school administration as well. He was eventually offered an assistant coaching position at a small Illinois school by the name of Lewis College, and spent the 1954 and '55 seasons coaching and gaining a great deal of experience, especially in the recruiting area. He also got married and he and his new wife, Shirley, immediately started a family.

In 1956, Leo landed his first major coaching job. He was hired as an assistant with the University of Toledo and spent two solid years there as the line coach before moving on to the University of South Carolina for the 1958 and '59 seasons. He had by this time developed a reputation as a very sound coach with a particular knack for recruiting good players.

Leo made the "big leagues" in 1960. Perry Moss, who had been the quarterback at the University of Illinois when Leo played there, had just been hired as head coach of the CFL's Montreal Alouettes and was in the process of building his staff. Leo had kept in touch with Moss since their Illinois days, and Moss offered Leo a position on his staff in Montreal. Leo jumped at this golden opportunity to move into professional football and happily relocated his family north of the border.

The Alouettes in 1960 were in a transition period. Their glory days of the 1950s, when quarterback Sam Etcheverry and wide receiver Hal Patterson led the most explosive offence in professional football, were over. They staggered into the playoffs in 1960, Leo's first year there, mainly due to the sudden collapse of the Hamilton Tiger-Cats. But their season ended quickly and decisively at Ottawa in the Eastern Semifinal.

Montreal missed the post-season in 1961 but returned to the playoffs the following year due to the sheer incompetence of the Argonauts. But the Alouettes were a mediocre team throughout this period, and Perry Moss was fired in January 1963. In his final act as the boss, Moss told Alouettes owner Ted Workman that Leo Cahill should be the next head coach.

Leo might well have been a good choice. In his three seasons in Montreal, he had developed a reputation around the league as a capable coach with a strong grasp of the Canadian game. He was also very popular with the fans and reporters, for whom he was always available.

In his 1973 book Goodbye Argos, Leo described how he had been considered the front-runner for the head job. "Every time a director came to me and told me that I had a good chance, or I heard that Ted Workman was leaning towards me, it just reinforced all this belief around the Cahill home that a big move upward in challenge, prestige and (incidentally) money was about to happen for us."

Leo was absolutely floored when he didn't get the job. Jim Trimble, the former Hamilton head coach who had taken the Tiger-Cats to five Grey Cup appearances and one championship from 1957 to 1962, was suddenly available and showed a keen interest in the job. When the former Ticat coach threw his hat into the ring, Leo's chances disappeared.

Trimble was hired in the winter of 1963 and Leo had no idea if he was even going to have a job. Trimble took his time making decisions on his assistant coaches. "For weeks I just sat around the office waiting," Cahill wrote in his book. "I was still under contract but that didn't mean anything if he didn't want me. He'd said publicly things like I'd done a good job and was liked by the players and maybe he'd like to keep me on the staff. But he made no decision."

Trimble finally offered Leo a spot, which he quickly accepted, but it was a marriage that was destined not to last. Trimble was like Leo in many ways. Both men strongly expressed their opinions and always had time for the media. (Trimble had been immortalized in the Canadian press for a strange comment he made before a Grey Cup game against the Bombers when he declared, "We'll waffle them!")

Trimble also seemed to radiate a sense of violence. He was a large man and had been involved in a number of physical altercations throughout his coaching career. In fact, he threatened Leo after one bitterly contested Montreal-Hamilton game. This aura of violence and intimidation continued while he coached in Montreal. Leo describes one of the incidents: "We had a couple of disagreements on personnel. I can remember him once asking my opinion on a player. After I gave it he shouted, 'Do you mean to tell me that I haven't been fair with this player? Do you want me to knock your teeth out?' "

The two men managed to co-exist throughout the 1963 season and the Alouettes were able to make the playoffs again, due to another complete collapse in Toronto. However, once they got there they were no match for Russ Jackson and the Ottawa Rough Riders in the Eastern Semifinal.

Things came apart for Leo in Montreal during the 1964 season. The team struggled, and the relationship between Cahill and Trimble became almost bizarre. Leo says there were times when Trimble would offer to drive him home after a game or practice and then abruptly tell him to get out of the car! One time he dumped Leo on the side of the road a mile and a half from his house in the midst of a violent rainstorm.

The end came after a 32-0 defeat in Regina. On the flight home from that contest, Trimble told Ian MacDonald, a Montreal reporter, that the loss – and all the losses that year – could be attributed directly to Leo. MacDonald passed this comment on to Leo, and the following day he resigned his coaching position. For the first time in a long while, Leo was out of a job and out of football.

He was almost broke and had no way of supporting his family. A friend in Montreal who had a printing business gave Leo a job, which helped him make ends meet, but it wasn't much. He knew he was an excellent coach and wanted to stay in the game.

Leo Cahill Joins the Argos

When the 1964 season ended and the Argonauts fired Nobby Wirkowski, Leo quickly applied for the job. But the letter he got back from General Manager Lew Hayman stated that since he had no Canadian coaching experience, he would not even be considered! (This is a fine example of just how badly the Argonauts were being run during this period.)

Leo did get a big break, however, and it was perfectly timed. The Continental Football League, a semi-pro outfit with teams in Canada and the United States, had a franchise in Montreal known as the Rifles that had recently been sold to two Toronto businessmen. They planned on moving the team to Toronto. As they were in the market for a new head coach and general manager, Cahill interviewed for the job and subsequently turned out to be the successful candidate.

Even though the Continental Football League was considered a notch or two above college ball but considerably below professional football, it didn't matter to Leo. This was the opportunity he had been craving. The Toronto Rifles would be his own team. Not only would he coach the team, he'd also recruit players, handle contracts, oversee marketing and run the entire administration of the team.

"In those first weeks I worked 20 hours a day, mostly on the phone. I was mainly responsible not only for the team but for buying equipment, getting practice space, recruiting players and setting up a training camp."

Semi-pro ball did not pay very well, which made Leo's job as a recruiter even tougher, especially when one considers most of the players would be American. (The Continental League used American rules.) He would have to persuade players to move to a foreign country, without offering them big money. A top player for the Rifles could make up to $250 per game but most played for as little as $100 a game.

Still, Leo's first year with the Rifles was a success. The team played its home games at old Maple Leaf Stadium, which was home to Toronto's Triple-A baseball team. One night they drew more than 16,000 fans to a game. Their attendance was usually not that high, yet they seemed to have sort of a cult following among a certain group of local fans.

The Rifles finished the 1965 season with a record of 11-3 (while the Argos went 3-11) and went to the league championship game, where they were defeated 24-7 by the Charleston Rockets. When one considers the challenge Leo faced in persuading American players to come north to play in a minor league, this shows how good he was at assessing top talent and recruiting it.

"That may have been my finest coaching performance ever," says Leo. "I had to do everything and I was able to build a successful team while being able to offer very little money to the players."

The Rifles moved to Varsity Stadium (the Argos' old home at the University of Toronto) for the 1966 season as Maple Leaf Stadium was going to be demolished. They had less success that season, finishing with a record of 9-5 (again the opposite of the Argos, who finished at 5-9) and were defeated 24-14 in the playoffs by Charleston. Leo began to show a strong sense of creativity and willingness to "think outside the box" as a head coach that year. In one game, the Rifles made headlines when Leo had linebacker Allen Ray Aldridge stand on the back of a teammate to block a field goal attempt. The kicker was so unnerved by the sight of this seemingly 11-foot-tall monster that he shanked the kick. The tactic worked to perfection but was soon banned by all levels of college and pro football.

Leo's brilliance as a head coach and recruiter did not lead to long-term financial success for either him or the Rifles. Attendance at Varsity Stadium was at best spotty throughout the 1966 season and there was concern whether the team would survive for the 1967 season. It was not due to a lack of effort by Leo to promote the team, though. The Rifles got good media coverage for such things as Leo's oddly named "Indian Blitz" and his offer to challenge the Argonauts for the city championship. Leo always got the team plenty of press.

The problem he and the Rifles faced was that, regardless of how exciting a product they put on the field, Toronto was only interested in major league sports. The Triple-A Toronto Maple Leafs baseball team had just died and it seemed the Rifles would soon follow suit.

Leo Cahill Joins the Argos

Deeply concerned about the long-term future of his team, Leo had to prepare for the next season all the same. Then the Argos got a big shock. In the spring of 1967, Bob Shaw suddenly resigned and the team needed a new head coach immediately. Training camp was only two months away and speculation was rife among the Toronto media that Leo was a strong candidate for the job. And why not? He was a proven winner in the Toronto area. He had head coaching experience at the pro level, he had CFL coaching experience, he was popular with the fans and media in Toronto and he was liked and respected by his players.

In April 1967, Leo was in Chicago recruiting players for the Rifles when he was contacted by J.I. Albrecht, who was a close colleague of Lew Hayman. Leo knew J.I. from his days in Montreal and that he was well connected though the world of professional football. J.I. got right to the point. He asked Leo if he was interested in the Argonaut job. Leo indicated that he was, indeed. Albrecht said he would call Lew Hayman and set up a meeting between the two.

When Leo returned to Toronto, he met with Hayman, and a few days later he was hired as the new head coach of the Toronto Argonauts. The Rifles were happy to release him from future commitments as their ownership doubted the team would last the season. (In that regard, they were correct.)

In 1965 when he applied for a job with the Argonauts, they seemed not to even know who he was. Now the hopes and dreams of this storied franchise were resting firmly on the shoulders of Leo Edward Cahill.

Figure 2-1: "*Leo Cahill*"

Three

1967

Leo had his work cut out once he took over the Argonauts. He had to assemble a coaching staff, plan for training camp and, most important, try to build a better team – all in just a couple of months. He decided to keep two of Bob Shaw's assistants, Gord Ackerman and Blackie Johnston, and then hired Steve Sucic, who had been an assistant under Lou Agase. (Coaching staffs were not the behemoths they are today – most teams had only two assistants.) Nobby Wirkowski, who was now director of player personnel, was also going to assist when time permitted.

As for players, Leo discovered he had a few good ones in the fold already. On the offensive side of the ball, there was quarterback Wally Gabler, tight end Mel Profit, scrappy Canadian receiver Bobby Taylor, veteran receiver Dave Mann, offensive lineman Danny Nykoluk and aging centre Norm Stoneburgh, who was nearing the end of his career. On defence, the Argos had Marv Luster, one of the finest safeties in football, an outstanding young Canadian lineman in Mike Wadsworth, and two young Canadian linebackers who looked like they had potential, Peter Martin from the University of Western Ontario and Dick Aldridge from the University of Waterloo. Both would go on to have long careers in Toronto. Beyond that nucleus, though, there wasn't much that could be moulded and shaped into a winning formula.

One of Leo's first moves upon taking over was to meet with the players. He wanted them to get a sense of who he was and instill in them a sense of confidence about his abilities. Leo later recalled what he said that day: "When anyone plays the Toronto Argonauts, they'd better fasten their chin straps because we're going to go for broke. We're going to tantalize them on the field and in the papers. We're going to challenge them. You have been a public laughingstock. You've been shot at and missed, and spit at and hit. Now we shoot back."

Leo also knew the team needed a sense of stability. The Argo Airlift had to end. You simply could not keep changing the roster and have any sense of cohesion on the squad. "The Argo airlifts in situations of duress were a joke in the league every year until I got there," Leo says. "The fans never really got a chance to know the players and half the players never felt they should start reading a book in case they weren't around to finish it. So I told the players that once we selected our team, we'd stick with the personnel we had. In my mind, I hoped to make the playoffs that first year by hook or by crook. Then we could make changes. But we'd make them carefully in the quietness of the winter afternoons, not in panic during the season."

But that didn't mean no changes whatsoever. Before training camp opened, Leo made his first big trade. Since he had been on the coaching staff in Montreal, he had always wanted to coach Blue Bomber star Dick Thornton.

A few years earlier, the Alouettes had offered Winnipeg seven players for Thornton, yet Bombers Coach Bud Grant turned the deal down. Cahill knew a versatile player like Thornton would greatly assist in the Toronto rebuilding process. Dick was an all-star defensive back, but much, much more. He could also play quarterback, running back and wide receiver, and handle punting duties in the clutch. In the 1965 Western Final, he had replaced the injured Kenny Ploen at quarterback in the second game and rallied Winnipeg to a come-from-behind victory over Calgary. He then made two great defensive plays in the third game to send the Blue Bombers back to the Big Dance in Toronto. In the Grey Cup, he did double duty at defensive back and wide receiver for the entire second half.

Despite his outstanding all-around abilities, Thornton was now available. The Blue and Gold machine that had won Grey Cups in 1961 and '62, and lost in 1965, was old and battered. Bud Grant had left to take over the head coaching job with the NFL's Minnesota Vikings and it was time to rebuild under Joe Zaleski, a long-time assistant. Thornton, a well-known free spirit, had made a joking remark during an off-season radio interview that made his football future very uncertain. Asked what he liked best about the city of Winnipeg, he answered, "The road leading out of town!"

It was the final straw for Bomber management. They realized that the squad would have to be rebuilt, and with Dick approaching 28 years of age and Zaleski growing weary of his unpredictable behaviour, management decided to put him on the trading block. Cahill immediately seized this golden opportunity, sending three players to Winnipeg in exchange. It was a trade that would help shape the entire Cahill era in Toronto.

What was it about Dick Thornton that caused him to be known as a "free spirit"? Tricky Dick himself describes it best: "I was often misunderstood, but did nothing more than market and merchandise myself as an athlete. Rebellion against the 'establishment' had begun and I was at the front of the line. I ranted and raved about not playing quarterback, had my own fan club, wore white shoes until Grant fined me, painted my name and number on my sports car, gave all the girls I slept with a solid gold pendant with Number 14 etched inside as a lasting memento, even changed my jersey number from 14 to 28 for a couple of games and had to call a press conference to explain why. The answer: I needed to play twice as good! But it was all smoke and mirrors. I made myself unforgettable to the fans, the ladies and the media, and everyone loved it – except for the coaching staff, of course.

"Remember, those were crazy times: the Cuban Missile Crisis and the Bay of Pigs, integration, John (Kennedy), Martin (Luther King) and then Bobby (Kennedy) got assassinated, there was the sexual revolution when the birth-control pill came on the market, we were fighting the Vietnam War, players became hippies with the long hair and we were all wearing weird clothes, there were protests and massive demonstrations . . . it was all these crazy things happening around us. I had to think outside the box and keep doing things differently in order to keep my own sanity."

That being said, there was never a doubt in anyone's mind that when Tricky Dick hit the field, he was all business and one of the game's very best players.

Joining Thornton in the defensive backfield would be another solid addition, the wiry veteran Ed Learn, who was picked up from Montreal. Leo did not forget his roots with the Toronto Rifles, either. Three members of that squad – defensive lineman Ed Harrington (who had played for the Argos earlier in the decade), linebacker Allen Ray Aldridge and quarterback Tom Wilkinson – would also join Leo's band of renegades.

When the Argonauts started training camp up in Aurora, there was a certain amount of curiosity around the city regarding the team. Could Leo turn them into a winner as he had done with the Rifles? Or would the black cloud that had been hovering over the team since 1953 defeat the new coach as well?

Quarterback Wally Gabler liked what he saw in Cahill. "I was really impressed with Leo's enthusiasm and people skills. He was an excellent communicator."

Things started on a positive note, with the Argos winning three of their four exhibition games, which instilled self-assurance and a bit of confidence among the players. However, no team sees against an opponent's best in preseason. The test would come when they began playing for real.

Leo did make a couple of firm decisions based on the exhibition game results. One was that Wally Gabler would be his No. 1 quarterback and Eagle Day, who had played alongside Wally in 1966, would be given his outright release. Day, who had been a consistent winner with the Stampeders, was an ancient drop-back quarterback with very little mobility and Leo knew that was not suitable the offensive package he had installed. He hoped Thornton could serve as the main backup, but learned that Dick had suffered a severe shoulder separation the previous year and his throwing arm was at only about 60 per cent of normal strength. Thornton could play QB in an emergency, but couldn't handle the assignment on a regular basis, so ex-Rifle Tom Wilkinson became the backup.

Leo also planned to emphasize the running attack more this year. In 1966, the offence was based on Wally Gabler running around the backfield looking for open receivers – and when he couldn't find one, running for his life. Leo knew he had to have a disciplined running game to be successful and take pressure off his quarterback. He had a solid back in Larry Ferguson but needed more sheer power.

Just before Bob Shaw left the Argos, he had traded the rights to Canadian wide receiver Jim Young, who was playing in the NFL with the Minnesota Vikings, to B.C. In exchange, Shaw picked up, among others, a young running back with a bad knee by the name of Bill Symons.

Symons, a native of Nucla, Colo., was probably the finest player in the history of the University of Colorado. He had the misfortune of being drafted by the powerful Green Bay Packers in 1965. The Packers, consistently the NFL's best team under Head Coach Vince Lombardi, were loaded at running back with future Hall of Famers Paul Hornung and Jim Taylor along with another great back in Elijah Pitts. Most observers felt Symons would be an early cut in training camp. But thanks to his tremendous talent and fierce "heart," Symons battled non-stop and had a roster spot nailed down, only to see disaster strike. In the final exhibition game of 1965 while returning a punt against the New York Giants, he suffered a catastrophic knee injury that cost him the entire season.

Despite a desperate rehabilitation attempt, the knee would not respond and the Packers cut Symons at training camp in 1966. He caught on with the B.C. Lions, for whom he saw action in 10 games that year as a defensive back and slotback. The Lions figured his knee was shot and were happy to pass on him off to Toronto after the season in the deal for Jim Young.

Leo felt Ferguson and Symons could give the Argos a potent one-two running attack if the offensive line could hold up. A lot of pressure would be riding on Danny Nykoluk, Norm Stoneburgh and the rest of the offensive line. They had to come through for the ground game to be effective.

The first regular-season contest under Coach Leo Cahill was at CNE Stadium on Aug. 11, 1967, in front of 27,142 curious fans. The Argonauts opened against the Montreal Alouettes, the team Toronto would probably have to battle for the final playoff spot in the Eastern Conference, so the game was critically important.

It started off well, with Symons running six yards for a touchdown nine minutes into the first quarter, but after that the offence struggled. Gabler completed only 12 of 28 passes for no touchdowns and had one pass intercepted. The running attack was at best adequate, with Ferguson carrying nine times for 49 yards and Symons picking up 46 yards on 11 carries. Though unable to put the ball into the end zone after Symons' score, the Argos managed to score on a field goal, two singles and a safety. The defence came up with an outstanding effort, holding Montreal to just 25 rushing yards and 350 yards overall. The most important statistic was the score, of course, and that came out in Toronto's favour, 14-7.

Al Sokol's report on the game in the Toronto Telegram said: "If fans came away from this game with a pessimistic view of the 1967 Argos, they must have been looking through the wrong end of their binoculars. While the offence ran (and passed) hot and cold, the defence stood its ground." Sokol singled out linebackers Pete Martin and Dick Aldridge and defensive linemen Dick Fouts, John Vilunas, Walt Balasiuk and Mike Wadsworth for their outstanding play.

That first win was very important for Leo. He had been trying hard to create a sense of team loyalty, and getting off to a poor start could have destroyed all the positive aspects of training camp.

Their next opponent would also be the team's first road trip as they headed west to battle the British Columbia Lions at Empire Stadium in Vancouver. For Mel Profit and Bill Symons, this would be their first trip back to the West Coast since being cut loose by the Lions, and like all players in that situation, they were eager to kick some B.C. ass.

The Argos jumped out in front 7-0 on a three-yard run by Larry Ferguson, but the Lions roared back 14 seconds later when that old Argo nemesis, Bernie Faloney, hit Jim Young (whose rights the Lions had received from Toronto for Dick Fouts and Bill Symons) on a 50-yard bomb to tie things up. The Lions then began to pull ahead and by the fourth quarter they were up 17-11. With time running out, Wally Gabler finally went to work, engineering and sustaining a drive which climaxed with Wally himself slamming into the end zone with 2:29 left.

The Argos hung on to win the closely fought contest 18-17. The running attack was again decent, led by Symons with 70 yards on 15 carries.

Gabler showed excellent mobility, picking up 44 yards on 12 carries while hitting on 11 of 16 passes with no interceptions. Tricky Dick Thornton picked off a Faloney pass for his first interception in an Argo uniform.

Figure 3-1: *“Wally Gabler grimly watches the Toronto defense in action, during the 1967 season.”*

Figure 3-2: *"Wally Gabler sends Bill Symons into the B.C. line, during the Argos 18-17 win over the Lions."*

Also visible, Mel Profit # 75, and Danny Nykoluk #60.

For Leo, the Argonauts and their fans, to come flying out of the gate in this fashion was a dream. The team that had been a joke was all but forgotten. However, some sense of reality had to intrude here. Yes, the defence had been great in the first two games and the offence was solid. But this had all been accomplished against two of the league's weak sisters. The true test of the new Argos was yet to come.

It was at this time that Leo picked up a new running back by the name of Jim Dillard from Ottawa. Cahill was determined to stick with his current players, but felt Dillard had a lot of potential and was bigger and stronger than Larry Ferguson.

Two days after the win in Vancouver, the Argos came crashing down to earth with a loud thud in Edmonton. The Eskimos hammered the Argos 31-10 at Clarke Stadium. Toronto was never in the game. The Boatmen fell behind early and it was 24-3 in the fourth quarter before Jim Dillard scored his first Argo touchdown on a pass from Gabler. The running attack bogged down, with Dillard leading the team with seven carries for 41 yards. Gabler completed just 10 of 22 pass attempts and a single touchdown strike.

Those western swings were tough in those days. Two hard-fought football games within a three-day period, and travelling 6,000 kilometres, will take a toll on any athlete.

After returning home to Toronto, the Argonauts had to go back on the road for the third consecutive game when they took on the Montreal Alouettes at Molson Stadium on Aug. 26. Leo made one surprising roster move before the game, taking Symons out of the lineup to go with a backfield combination of Jim Dillard and Joe Williams, another former Rifle who had moved to the Argos in 1966.

Surprisingly, the Montreal fans were treated to a real shootout. Dillard scored a touchdown on a one-yard plunge and Bobby Taylor hauled in a 15-yard pass from Gabler for another. The biggest play of the night was contributed by Toronto defensive back Jim Rountree, who returned an interception 60 yards for a touchdown. Despite those heroics, the Argonauts were beaten 34-22. Their running attack again did not produce, with Gabler leading all Argo rushers with 55 yards on seven carries. Wally hit on 10 of 15 passes, but for only 51 yards. Obviously there was a distinct lack of a long passing game.

Concern was being raised among Argo fans by now as the running game was not working well and their most effective rusher up to this point was the quarterback. Wally was also not picking apart defences with his passing, and the defence had allowed 65 points the last two games – far too much for a team hoping to make the playoffs.

The schedule-maker was obviously not an Argonauts fan. The team had to hit the road for a fourth consecutive game, this time Sept. 4 against the arch-enemy Hamilton Tiger Cats. Actually, the rivalry was less heated than it had been or would later become. The Argos had been so bad for so long that the Black and Gold didn't consider them much of a threat. The focus of Hamilton and its fans had shifted over the past few seasons to the Ottawa Rough Riders led by Russ Jackson. Hamilton had played in five consecutive Grey Cups from 1961 to '65, beating Ottawa every year in the Eastern Final with the exception of the Argo nightmare of 1961. In 1966, Jackson had finally solved the Rider playoff puzzle, taking Ottawa to the Grey Cup game where the Rough Riders lost to Saskatchewan.

The Ticats were licking their chops at the thought of getting back to the big game in 1967, and they had an outstanding team. The offence was led by Joe Zuger, a tough, underrated quarterback who did nothing spectacular – except win. His top receiver was Tommy Joe Coffey, who by the time of his retirement in 1973 was the leading receiver in CFL history. He also had Garney Henley, one of the finest all-around players in the history of the game, in the starting backfield.

The Hamilton defence was one of the meanest and best in the league, led by defensive lineman Angelo Mosca, who delighted in destroying opponents. Mosca was notorious for his vicious play. In the 1963 Grey Cup game, he rocked B.C. running back Willie Fleming with a late hit that sent Fleming staggering to the sidelines, never to return – a blow from which the Lions never recovered. Joining Mosca up front was John Barrow, another lineman with the disposition of a constipated rattlesnake. Dave Fleming was a brutal, hard-hitting defensive back who made catching any ball a very painful and dangerous occupation for opposing wide receivers with enough nerve to venture into his area, and he also doubled as a very good flanker on offence.

The Argos travelled down the Queen Elizabeth Way to Civic Stadium, desperate to break their two-game losing streak, but it wasn't to be, despite an outstanding effort from their defence. They held the potent Hamilton offence to just 12 points, yet Toronto's own offence could muster only nine and the team went down to a three-point defeat. Gabler struggled again, connecting on only five of 14 passes, throwing one interception and being sacked six times. Under fierce pressure all day, he rarely had time to set up properly and was forced to take off and run on nine occasions. Mel Profit picked up the only Argo points when Dave Mann took a lateral from Gabler and surprised the Ticat defence by firing a 39-yard strike to Profit for the score.

The two teams resumed their rivalry six days later at CNE Stadium, and the Argonauts desperately hoped their long-awaited return home would reverse their fortunes. They did play better, but the result was the same. Toronto went down to defeat 23-15. Without Symons in the backfield, the running attack struggled again. Gabler played better, hitting his receivers on 14 of 27 pass attempts for 153 yards and TDs to Jim Greth and Bobby Taylor, but he also tossed two interceptions. The Argos actually jumped out to an 8-0 lead on the Greth touchdown, but Hamilton pulled ahead in the second quarter and never looked back. On the other side of the ball, the Toronto defence gave a solid effort, holding the powerful Ticat offence to only 359 yards. Dick Thornton intercepted a Joe Zuger pass, and Ed Learn stopped another Hamilton drive with a fumble recovery to help the defence in a losing cause.

It was now past cut-down time down south, and players and fans alike braced for another possible airlift. Argo players began looking around the dressing room, wondering if they would still have a job the following day. Which NFL or AFL cuts would be on their way to Toronto? To the players' surprise, the airlift stayed grounded. True to his word, Leo was determined to stick with his players. He reiterated that message to them, and made it clear that he would not panic. Yes, they had lost four games in a row and were sitting on a shaky record of 2-4. However, in only one of those four games (Edmonton) had they been blown out. They had battled Hamilton, a much better team, hard and had been competitive in both losses to their rivals. There was no reason to throw in the towel yet.

Talk of the airlift was really put to rest the following week when Toronto took on the Calgary Stampeders. Led by quarterback Peter Liske and receiver Terry Evanshen, the Stamps were a strong Grey Cup contender and they came into CNE Stadium expecting an easy victory. The fans in Toronto even seemed to figure the game would be a disaster as only 22,092 bothered to show up.

But it turned out to be a great football game. Jim Dillard was the big story as he rushed for 95 yards and two touchdowns on 17 carries, and fired a 50-yard touchdown strike to Joe Williams on a halfback option pass. Wally Gabler continued scrambling, picking up 67 yards on 12 carries, and hit nine of 14 passes for 104 yards and just one interception. Tom Wilkinson also got into the game, marking his first regular-season appearance in an Argo uniform. Liske was kept under control by the Argo defenders, who intercepted three of his passes, two by veteran Jim Rountree. Ron Arends got the third pick late in the game when Liske took to the air in a desperate effort to avoid defeat. The final score was Toronto 22 Calgary 13.

The Argonauts had now hit the halfway point of their first year under Leo Cahill and were 3-4. They had beaten two poor teams (Montreal and British Columbia) and shocked one of the league's elite (Calgary) in a huge upset. They had dropped one game to a bad team (Montreal), been hammered by a very average team (Edmonton) and lost twice to Hamilton, one of the league's finest. One common thread, though, was that they had battled fiercely in all contests. Their defence had played well in all but the losses to Montreal and Edmonton. Offensively, they had not been very impressive – their running game was at best spotty and their aerial attack was very shaky. Wally Gabler had only four touchdown strikes at this point to go with six interceptions. A wide receiver (Dave Mann) and a running back (Jim Dillard) together had half as many touchdown passes as their quarterback.

Leo Cahill knew in his heart that his team was still not very good, but he refused to admit that to those around him. He consistently told the players they were improving, that they could beat anyone on any given day, and he worked hard at keeping the atmosphere positive on the practice field and in the dressing room. Leo knew the only chance the Argos would have in their remaining games would be to simply outwork and out-hustle their opponents, and hope to catch a big break now and then. They had done it against Calgary by playing with a wild tenacity, catching the Stampeders slightly off their game. They now had to continually provide that kind of effort.

Toronto's next game would be a huge test. The Argos would be heading into Ottawa's Lansdowne Park to battle the powerful Rough Riders. They had been Grey Cup finalists in 1966, dropping a 29-14 decision to Ron Lancaster and the Saskatchewan Roughriders, and were led by perhaps the greatest quarterback in the history of the Canadian game, Russ Jackson

A native of Hamilton and graduate of McMaster University, Jackson had few weaknesses as a player. He could throw passes like laser beams, run like a halfback, hit like a linebacker and was as tough as nails. "Russ was the greatest quarterback to ever play up here," says Leo Cahill. "He could do everything. His only weak spot was his big nose, which got broken a number of times. But that was it."

Jackson had a habit when he walked to the line of scrimmage of standing straight up with his hands on his hips, looking around like a general scanning the battlefield before crouching down to take the snap. Scouts from south of the border who saw him play had no doubts that if he wished to do so, he could start on almost any pro team in the United States.

Jackson wasn't the only star on the Ottawa roster, however. He had magnificent running backs in Bo Scott and Ronnie Stewart and great receivers in Margene Adkins and Whit Tucker. On the other side of the ball, defensive end Billy Joe Booth and linebackers Gerry (Soupy) Campbell and Marshall Shirk were among the best. Their coach was also Frank Clair, whom the Argos had fired back in 1954. He never tired of beating his old team.

The game in Ottawa could only be described as a debacle for the Argonauts. Calling it ugly would be polite. It brought back the worst memories of Argo teams coached by Lou Agase, Nobby Wirkowski, Bob Shaw, even Hampton Pool. Both Bo Scott and Ron Stewart hit the 100-yard rushing mark in the game. The Argos' best was Joe Williams, who fought his way for 59 yards. Gabler and Wilkinson were sacked five times and combined to hit only four of 15 passes for a grand total of 27 yards with two interceptions. Jackson, on the other hand, smoothly hit on 11 of 18 passes for three touchdowns. The final score was 38-3 and the Argos departed Lansdowne Park shell-shocked. It certainly appeared that Leo and his boys were not ready to play with the league's elite yet.

Things were not going to get any easier the following week, either. They would be hosting the defending Grey Cup champion Saskatchewan Roughriders, a team loaded with talent on both sides of the ball and led by star quarterback Ron Lancaster. Lancaster, an Ohio native, had broken into the league with Ottawa, and he and Jackson had a running battle for the No. 1 job until management decided Jackson was their man and shipped Lancaster to the Prairies in 1963. Lancaster, along with bruising fullback George Reed, turned the Saskatchewan franchise around. The defence was anchored by Bill (The Undertaker) Baker, one of the most feared defensive linemen in the history of the game. Wally Gabler, reminiscing about Baker, said: "Bill was once asked how he handled my scrambling. His answer was, 'I don't chase Wally around the field, as I know he'll get cornered by our defence and head back to my area. I'll get him then.' He knocked me out cold on two different occasions in my career. He could really hit."

Toronto fans were braced for a repeat performance from the previous week. It would be fair to say that for Leo Cahill, this would be another real test for himself. His team had been utterly destroyed seven days ago. At this juncture, previous Argonaut teams would roll over and die with the airlift in full flight. Leo had promised his players that he would not panic and resort to extreme measures, but in return, he expected them to give him their greatest effort. This critical football game would determine if there really was a new Argo attitude.

Much to the surprise of Argo fans, the team did not collapse against Saskatchewan. In fact, they played with a nasty intensity. They didn't win, but gave the Green Riders all they could handle. Saskatchewan simply had better players and was able to overcome a fierce Argo effort on the basis of talent alone.

Saskatchewan won 17-15 with Lancaster being held to only 12 completions in 23 attempts and no touchdown strikes. George Reed was limited to only 67 yards on 20 carries. Gabler performed well, hitting 16 of 29 passes with one interception and a touchdown strike to Bobby Taylor. The Argos had another touchdown disallowed in the second quarter, when Taylor caught a Gabler pass deep in the end zone but the official ruled he was out of bounds. Taylor told the Globe and Mail's Rex MacLeod: "I caught the ball in bounds. My feet never did go out. When I caught the ball, I fell forward and only the upper part of my body went over the line."

If the catch had been allowed, the Argos might well have won the game. Gabler's performance was even more impressive considering he had been sacked eight times. Obviously the offensive line continued to be an ongoing concern.

The Argos would catch a break in their next contest as the Winnipeg Blue Bombers were coming to CNE Stadium. The Bombers, one of the great powers of the 1960s, were a shell of what they had been, and it appeared the Argonauts had a legitimate shot at getting back into the win column.

One player who was very eager for the game was Dick Thornton. He had been one of the biggest stars of the Winnipeg franchise, yet had been discarded to Toronto without so much as the courtesy of a phone call. "I found out about being traded to the Argos from sportswriter Al Sokol. He called me personally from T.O. to get my reaction and then filled me in on the details. I never did speak with anyone from the Blue Bomber front office or coaching staff in person or by phone. It was like I just fell off the Winnipeg planet."

On Sunday, Oct. 8, 1967, the Toronto Argonauts ensured that this version of the team would be immortalized forever in Argo lore. They did not just defeat Winnipeg, they dropped a nuclear bomb on the guys from Manitoba, leaving the shattered remnants of the Blue Bombers floating away like a cloud of radioactive fallout. The final score: Toronto 53 Winnipeg 0.

It was a day in which everything worked for the Argonauts. Gabler was brilliant, hitting on 14 of 19 passes with a touchdown pass to Joe Williams and two to Bobby Taylor. He also scored one himself on a six-yard run. Marv Luster raced into the end zone for another TD when Dick Thornton, playing like a man possessed, roared through and blocked a punt. Luster scooped up the loose ball and ran 35 yards for the score. This game was one of the greatest in Dick's career and he remembers it with great affection. "I knew I made the right choice (going to Toronto) when Winnipeg came into CNE Stadium the following season after the trade and we blew them away. I blocked a punt that went for a TD, intercepted a pass and just for laughs, Leo put me in at QB in the fourth quarter. Rolling out left, I scampered untouched for the final touchdown. I was going for 60 points on the last play of the game and tossed a perfect pass to Mel Profit in the end zone but he dropped it. In the locker room afterward, Mel said he was so shocked that it was a perfect spiral, he took his eye off the ball. We sure laughed over that one. The Winnipeg media had called me 'over the hill' after the trade but in that one single game, I proved them all wrong."

For Leo, this monstrous victory – over a team that had barely lost the Grey Cup less than two years before – was vindication of his determination to stick with his core players and not resort to change for the sake of change. "I don't think there was any question that was great for our confidence," Leo recalls. "Winnipeg had been a strong team and to score 53 points against any team is a great accomplishment."

The following Saturday, the Argos took their new sense of confidence into Molson Stadium in Montreal. They entered with a swagger and had no doubts the Alouettes would be easy pickings, but as it turned out, the Larks were a tougher opponent than anticipated. Nonetheless, the Argos beat them 20-9. Gabler returned to his hot-and-cold form, completing only four of 14 passes, with one of them a 44- yard touchdown bomb to Jim Dillard, who had gone streaking out of the backfield to make the catch and take it in for the score. Dillard had a sensational game, running for 162 yards on only 11 carries. Bill Symons looked good, too, scoring the Argos' other major on a 10-yard run. The rest of the points came from the foot of Dave Mann.

The Argonauts were now sitting with a record of 5-6 and a playoff spot well within their grasp. Nobody associated with the team realistically thought they had a shot at the Grey Cup, but getting into the playoffs would do wonders for the organization. The big question was, could they pull it off?

Ottawa was coming to town and the Argos were keen for another shot at them. Professional athletes hate to lose and, worse, get embarrassed in the process, and that is what the Rough Riders had done to the Argonauts in their first meeting. As far as the Toronto players were concerned, this was payback time in front of their hometown fans.

There was also great excitement in the stands. Sen. Robert Francis Kennedy of New York, a personal friend of team owner John Bassett, was in town on a visit and would be in attendance at the game. Bobby Kennedy, the brother of the late President John Fitzgerald Kennedy and the former United States Attorney General, was possibly the most popular political figure in the world at the time. It was rumoured that he might seek the nomination to become the Democratic candidate in the 1968 presidential election. He was also a huge football fan (having played college ball at Harvard) and was very knowledgeable about the sport. This would be his first Canadian football game and the Argos and Bassett hoped to give him a good show. It turned out to be an excellent spectacle, indeed.

The Argos jumped out to a 13-0 lead on a one-yard plunge by Dillard and two field goals by Mann. That woke up the Ottawa offence in the second quarter as Jackson fired a 56-yard home run to Whit Tucker and less than four minutes later hit Margene Adkins with a spectacular 71-yard pass-and-run play for another major just before time expired. This amazing offensive display went back and forth throughout the second half as well. Dillard scored on runs of five yards and one yard, leaving Ottawa fans wondering how the Rough Riders had let him get away. Jackson fired yet another TD pass, this one a 48-yard rocket, again to Tucker.

In the final seconds, with Ottawa leading 28-27, Dave Mann lined up for a 32-yard field-goal attempt. The Rough Riders, who were battling Hamilton for first place, had players back in the end zone to try to kick the ball out if Mann didn't connect. Sure enough, his kick was wide and the ball was immediately booted back into the field of play, but Wally Gabler scooped it up and kicked it right back into the end zone for a single point that tied the game. In the stands, Bobby Kennedy was jumping up and down with excitement. He had never seen anything like this before, of course, since there is no single point in American football. Under those rules, the miss by Mann would have ended the game with the Argos losing by a point. There was no regular-season overtime in the CFL in 1967, so this exciting game ended as a 28-28 tie.

The Argonauts were clearly disappointed not to get the win but felt they had shown Ottawa – and the rest of the league – that they would not be pushovers any longer. Gabler had given them a solid effort, completing 20 of 31 passes, and a big reason for that was a much better game by the Argonauts' offensive line. Gabler was sacked only once. On the other side of the ball, the Argo defence had got through to Jackson and put him on the ground five times.

The two teams would again wage war the following weekend back in the nation's capital, and Frank Clair and his team would not be taking the Argos as lightly as they had the week before in Toronto. Leo, on the other hand, was hoping that his young squad would be inspired by their recent shootout tie with the Red and Black and be totally pumped up for this game.

The Argonauts and their fans were also elated by the fact that they had clinched a playoff spot. Montreal had completely collapsed and could no longer catch the Argos for the final post-season slot. No matter what Toronto did the rest of the season, they were guaranteed to be in the playoffs for the first time in six years.

The second Ottawa game started off like a dream for Toronto. Ed Harrington, the ex-Toronto Rifle, scooped up a fumble and returned it 15 yards for a touchdown. Toronto then made the score 14-0 when Gabler fired a 61-yard TD strike to Al Irwin. Unfortunately, this early scoring spree simply seemed to annoy the Rough Riders, who came roaring back with Bo Scott crashing in for majors from three and seven yards and Jackson firing a TD pass to Adkins. The final score was 28-18 for Ottawa.

Gabler, despite very good pass protection (he was not sacked at all), played poorly, connecting on only seven of 21 passes with two interceptions. The rushing attack had bogged down again with Joe Williams leading the way with 53 yards on 11 carries. Jim Dillard chipped in with 18 yards on five carries.

Toronto now had a record of 5-7-1, with one game to go in the regular season, at home against their old Steel City rivals. The 24,146 fans who paid money for this sleeper would have been well within their rights to have marched on the Argonauts' executive offices and demanded refunds. Perhaps Toronto, now in third place, and Hamilton, which had first place wrapped –up, simply wanted to save themselves for the post-season. Whatever the reason, the two teams combined for only 14 points with the Ticats coming out on top 9-5. It was more like a baseball score.

Hamilton got a touchdown and two singles while the Argo offence picked up a field goal and two singles off the foot of Dave Mann. Wally Gabler was awful, completing just three of 17 passes for 51 yards and one interception. The only bright spots were Bill Symons, who had his first 100-yard rushing game as an Argo, and the defence, which kept the excellent Hamilton offence in check for 60 minutes. Jim Reynolds and Ron Arends stopped Hamilton drives with big interceptions.

Now, for the first time since 1961, the Toronto Argonauts would get to play another game at the end of the regular season. The bad news was that game would be played in Ottawa and few people, if any, gave Toronto a chance of actually winning. If they could just be competitive – that was the hope of their fans.

Leo Cahill realized his work was cut out for him in designing a game plan for the Riders. He knew his running game had evolved during the season and by this point he had two excellent running backs in Bill Symons and Jim Dillard. His passing attack, though, if anything was going downhill despite better play from the offensive line. In his final two regular-season games, Wally Gabler was good on just 10 of 38 passes with only one touchdown and three interceptions.

There were quality receivers to throw to in Bobby Taylor, Mel Profit and Al Irwin. All had shown they could catch the ball – if only Wally could get it to them. Nobody expected Gabler to be another Russ Jackson, but he simply had to play much, much better in this game for the Argos to have any chance at all.

Defensively, Toronto had progressively got stronger as the year went on. Defensive captain and safety Marv Luster and cornerback Dick Thornton had both been outstanding all season. Other strong performances were turned in by Mike Wadsworth, Pete Martin, Dick Aldridge, Ed Learn and Jim Rountree. But Ottawa had such a well-rounded offensive machine that even the finest defensive units in the league had problems stopping them. Realistically, Ottawa was likely to score at least two or three touchdowns regardless. The challenge the Argos faced would be keeping them to that and hoping that their own offence could get untracked.

Dick Thornton recalls the game plan going in. "We didn't have anything specific. With a new coach and a bunch of new players, we all just went out and played our hearts out, concentrating on the basics. Sure, we had a set of offensive plays and defensive sets but it was simply mano a mano. Ottawa didn't have any weaknesses. They were a veteran team while we were rebuilding."

The 1967 Eastern Semifinal was played on a damp field at Lansdowne Park in front of only 20,627 fans. Toronto took the opening kickoff and went to work. From the Argo 25, Gabler called two running plays to Bill Symons that netted a total of only one yard. Dave Mann then blasted a punt down to the Ottawa 26 that was returned to the 35. Ottawa tried running plays with Bo Scott and Russ Jackson that combined to lose three yards. The Riders punted the ball back, and Toronto got a drive going as Dillard and Symons began crashing through the Ottawa line. Gabler then hit Mel Profit with a 15-yard strike, but the drive stalled at the Ottawa 32 and Dave Mann came on to try a field goal. His kick was short and Argos lost a big chance to take an early lead.

Neither Ottawa nor Toronto could move the ball on their next series of plays. The Argo defence was hanging tough, giving Jackson and his huge arsenal of offensive weapons little to work with. But Ottawa got something going when Bo Scott took a Jackson pitchout and sprinted 20 yards to the Toronto 33 before being brought down by Ron Arends and Marv Luster. The Rough Riders continued to advance until a pass intended for Margene Adkins from the Toronto 17 went incomplete. Don Sutherin (who had kicked Dave Mann's punt out of the end zone in the dying seconds of the 1961 Eastern Final) was good on a 25-yard field goal, giving Ottawa a 3-0 lead.

Less than three minutes later, Ottawa was in the end zone for the first time. After Gabler failed to get anything going and Mann was forced to punt again, Jackson drove the Ottawa offence down the field and fired a 26-yard TD pass to Ronnie Stewart to take a 10-0 lead.

A sense of dread was creeping into the hearts of Toronto fans and players. Wally didn't help when on the next drive, his pass intended for Bill Symons was picked off by middle linebacker Ken Lehman at the Toronto 33 and returned to the 15-yard line. The Argo defence came up big yet again and held Ottawa to a field goal. The score was now 13-0.

Cahill had finally seen enough of Wally Gabler at this point. His starting quarterback had been terrible at the end of the regular season and showed no improvement at all in this game. Tom Wilkinson, who had seen very little regular-season action, went in at the pivot slot when the Argonauts took the ball on the next possession. Wilkie couldn't move the ball either on this drive and Mann punted to the Ottawa 41. Jackson was now red hot, moving the Rough Riders right down the field and hitting Stewart for a 33-yard TD strike. Ottawa was now up 20-0 and the rout seemed to be on.

It would have been easy at this point for the Argonauts to fold. After all, Ottawa was clearly the better team and Toronto, just by making the playoffs, had given its fans hope for the first time in six years. But Leo's players would not give up. Barking encouragement from the sideline, he kept trying to think of a strategy that would get Toronto back in the game.

Dick Thornton, who had been through many playoff battles out West, would not let his teammates give up, either, as he played his heart out on the field. Thornton kept encouraging them to play hard and tough as he had no interest in being part of an ugly defeat.

Wilkinson started moving the ball, hitting Profit for a 17-yard gain. He advanced the Argos to the Ottawa 53, where the drive stalled. Mann unloaded a booming punt into the Ottawa end zone that was conceded for a single point. Toronto was finally on the board.
Wilkinson fired an interception on the next Argo series, but the Toronto defence dug in and stopped Jackson. After another exchange of punts, Wilkinson got the offence moving and concluded the drive by hitting Bill Symons with a TD pass from the Ottawa 12. Mann converted and Toronto was now down 20-8.

At halftime, Leo tried to get his players' minds off the fact that they were trailing, emphasizing that they were on the board and still in the hunt.

Ottawa took the second-half kickoff but could not move the ball and lined up to punt from its own 37. It was here that Tricky Dick Thornton came through with a big play. Screaming in from the left side, he launched himself at the ball just as it left the punter's foot. Dick blocked it perfectly, then picked it up and ran to the Ottawa 12 where he was finally brought down. Two plays later, Wilkinson hit Profit in the end zone for a major. After the convert, the score was Ottawa 20 Toronto 15. The Argos and their fans were going wild and Ottawa was stunned. Their huge 20-point lead was almost gone.

The defences for both teams dug in and forced a series of punts. Ottawa then broke through with Jackson hitting Adkins with a 19-yard pass for a major. Sutherin was good on the convert, giving the Rough Riders some breathing room at 27-15.

Toronto came right back, though. Wilkinson hit Dillard on a beautiful 86-yard pass-and-run play that got the ball to the Rough Rider five-yard line. Then Dillard smashed through the line for a TD on the next play. The convert was good and Toronto was back within five points at 27-22.

Frank Clair constantly paced the Ottawa sidelines, cursing and screaming at his players. In the past, if a team got ahead of Toronto 20-0, the Argos would simply give up and quit. Who the hell were these new guys in double blue? They would not go away!

Before the third quarter ended, Ottawa picked up a single off the foot of Sutherin. Early in the fourth, Jackson marched the Rough Riders down the field where Sutherin was good on a 28-yard field goal to put Ottawa ahead 31-22. They were not done yet. Wilkinson threw his second interception of the game, and Ottawa turned it into a major on a 25-yard pass from Jackson to Adkins, making the score 38-22 after the convert.

The Argonauts kept on coming, not ready yet to see their season end. But forced to throw on every play, Wilkinson had another pass intercepted with only minutes left.

After an Ottawa punt, Wilkie tried to thread a pass to Profit between two defenders, but it was picked off at the Ottawa 41. It was the Argos' last gasp. Ottawa ran out the clock for a 38-22 victory.

Considering how badly Wally had played and how much better Tom had played in his place, many Monday morning quarterbacks questioned Leo's decision to start Wally in the first place. (Ignoring the fact Wally had been the No. 1 QB all year.) Al Sokol of the Toronto Telegram asked Leo about that and his response was direct and to the point: "Wilkinson did a great job for a guy who was brought back from the dead for this game. Maybe I should have started him, but Gabler was the quarterback who got us this far and I felt he deserved to start."

Looking back at that game, Leo says it was a huge step forward for the franchise. "First of all, just to make the playoffs was very important to our confidence. Second, to come back against such a great team meant so much. Coming back is an important thing in football. When you have a group of renegades like I had, that was quite the accomplishment."

The 1967 season was over. Despite their loss in the semifinal, the Argonauts and their fans felt they now had a firm foundation to build on. They had made the playoffs, put a scare into Ottawa and shown the league that the old Argos were a thing of the past. No team coached by

Leo Cahill would roll over and die. The Argos might be beaten by teams that had more talent, but they would not lose a game due to lack of effort. Nobody would outwork or outhustle them.

They were definitely going to be a force to be reckoned with – in the future.

Four

1968

In the early months of 1968, Leo Cahill could look back on the 1967 season with pride. He had accomplished what he had initially set out to do: turn the Toronto Argonauts into a tough opponent for any team to battle, and get into the playoffs for the first time in six years. He still had a lot of work to do, however.

Steve Sucic resigned from the coaching staff to move to the United States. Cahill replaced him with Jim Rountree, who was ready to retire as a player and had impressed Leo with his knowledge of the defensive side of the game. Leo knew the step from player to coach is a large one, and it's doubly difficult to go from one of the boys to an assistant coach with the same team, but he was confident Rountree could handle it.

Leo also set about adding talent to the team. He drafted a huge Canadian defensive lineman named Dave Knechtel out of Waterloo Lutheran (which later became Wilfrid Laurier University). He would go on to be named Eastern Conference rookie of the year in 1968.

Cahill hit it big with another move. Mike Eben was the first winner of the Hec Crighton Award while playing at the University of Toronto in 1967. The trophy is awarded to the best player in Canadian university football each year. Eben was an outstanding wide receiver with superb hands and shifty speed. He was utterly fearless when it came to cutting over the middle and making a catch and was just what the Argos needed to improve their passing attack. However, he had been drafted by the B.C. Lions. Eben stunned the CFL and the Lions by refusing to report to Vancouver.

It was not an issue about money. Mike was not your typical "jock." He was working on his PhD in Germanic expressionistic drama at the University of Toronto and wanted to stay in the city for that reason. His graduate work was more important to him than playing football. The Lions management flew to Toronto and "wined andined" Mike and his wife, yet Eben would not budge from his position. When Leo heard this, he went to work during training camp and swung a deal to bring Mike Eben to the Argonauts.

This was an era in which players simply did not do what Mike had done. You joined the team that drafted you and were happy about it. Eben didn't get a great reception from his new teammates when he joined them. "That was tough," he says. "I had missed most of training camp and as a rookie that is really hard. The other players were hard on me as I had missed the rookie initiations."

The signings of Eben and Knechtel would foreshadow what became one of the great strengths of Leo Cahill. He could have taken the easy route and signed Americans out of college, or players who had been cut by NFL or AFL teams, as the Argonauts had been doing for years. In fact, since the Harry Sonshine era, the Argonauts had seemed determined to build an NFL team in the CFL. Leo, however, realized that the success of any CFL team was mostly dependent on its Canadian players. On a 33-man roster, 20 players had to be "non-imports." Finding great Canadian players was hard work, but Leo knew it would be well worth it.

The reason it was harder to find good Canadian football players was simple. Canadians usually did not start playing football until they reached high school. By that age, American kids had been playing for years. In high school, Canadians were coached by volunteers and teachers. In college football, the gap became even larger. The U.S. college football system is largely geared to producing professional players. The Canadian college athletic system was set up to allow students to play sports in addition to their studies. Many college football coaches in Canada were professors who coached in their spare time, whereas in the United States, college football coaches were full-time professionals. Leo knew he had to develop Canadian players to ensure long-term success for the Argonauts.

Eben and Knechtel would be the first of a long line of superb Canadians whom Cahill would bring to Toronto. He also allowed such Canadians as Mike Wadsworth, Dick Aldridge and Peter Martin to develop and hone their skills.

Another question in everybody's mind was who would be the starting quarterback in 1968. Wally Gabler had been the No. 1 guy in 1967 but had been hot and cold all year – mostly cold – and simply terrible at the end. Tom Wilkinson had played very little, but had been sharp in the playoff game when he sparked new life into the offence and almost guided the team to an upset win. For some people, the question of whether Wally would be the starter had already been answered by his poor late-season and playoff performance. Jim Proudfoot of the *Toronto Star* declared that Wilkinson's performance in the playoff game had "stripped away Gabler's first-string status and made him only one of several candidates for the quarterbacking post in 1968."

Leo had another project to work on for the 1968 season. Always an excellent judge of talent, he saw a great deal of potential in Bill Symons. In nine games in 1967, Symons had rushed for 349 yards on 63 carries and scored a pair of touchdowns. He also caught 11 passes, and did it all on a rickety knee. Leo felt that if the doctors could do something to stabilize the knee, the Argos could have a dynamite running back. Argo trainer Mert Prophet developed a rehabilitation program that would strengthen Bill's knee. It worked and he developed into a dominant back. "The credit should go to Mert," says Leo. "He took a keen interest in Bill as he was such a classy guy and such a good team player. Sy was just a good old country boy who did everything to improve himself."

The Argonauts began 1968 training camp full of confidence. The playoff battle against Ottawa the previous year had allowed them to finish their season on a higher note than in the previous five. It was something to build on. In 1967, Leo Cahill had been a largely unknown commodity. Now the players knew him, understood his approach and felt confident he knew what he was doing.

For many fans and members of the media, the team's goal for 1968 was a .500 season. If they could win half their games, they would surely finish ahead of Montreal and make it back to the playoffs. Nobody felt they could finish ahead of Hamilton (the 1967 Grey Cup champs) or Ottawa.

The Argonauts looked sharp in camp and during the exhibition season, leading to an even greater sense of optimism among the players. Mike Eben recalls sensing that this was a team coming together. The only negative aspect of camp was the behaviour of receiver Bobby Taylor towards Wally Gabler and Eben. Bobby was a "tough piece of work." A solid receiver who played his heart out every game, he sincerely felt a team should play together and party together, too. He was crude and at times nasty.

Gabler and Eben were total opposites from Taylor: clean-cut, highly educated and well-spoken gentlemen. Gabler was a personal favorite of team owner John Bassett, who enjoyed Wally's company at formal business functions. Yet Taylor did his best to run Gabler out of town. During practices he would purposely drop many of the passes Wally threw to him. When Tom Wilkinson took over the huddle, Bobby would say, "All right, guys, here's our quarterback." He would then go out and make outstanding catches of passes thrown by Tom.

Taylor's personal relationship with Eben was even worse. Both were competing for the same wideout position. Bobby was determined to hang onto his job and tried to make life hell for Eben in the dressing room. He mocked his education, his formal language, his looks, and just about anything else he could think of.

One of Leo's philosophies was that he didn't care what his players did off the field. He would treat them like men and not subject them to bed checks or other intrusions into their private lives. In return, all he asked was that the players show up ready for every practice and be mentally prepared for every game. One of Leo's favourite expressions was: "When the band's playing, the crowd's roaring and the whistle blows, you better be ready." Taylor was always ready, so Cahill wasn't inclined to interfere with his antipathy towards Gabler and Eben.

Bobby's behaviour wasn't all bad, mind you. He had a good sense of humour, too. Dick Thornton remembers one incident in 1968 training camp. "Bobby hid a huge fuzzy fake spider that looked very real in Al Irwin's locker under his practice jersey. When this thing came flying out, Al took off running like a scared rabbit, yelling and screaming."
He and Bobby combined to pull some other stunts during camp. "During practices, Bobby Taylor and I would always scan the sidelines for good-looking girls and tell the QB to call pass plays in their direction. We would then purposely go crashing near and around them diving for the

ball, eventually helping them up and maybe setting things in motion for possible meetings later on."

Leo's attitude was perfect for the times. The year 1968 was one of the pivotal years of the 20th century. In the first six months of that year, Martin Luther King and Sen. Robert Kennedy were assassinated. The Tet Offensive in Vietnam had exploded in late January, catching the United States off guard. Millions of people around the world were glued to their television sets each night watching news reports about the siege of Khe Sanh and the bloody warfare between U.S. Marines and North Vietnamese soldiers in the streets of Hue. In Canada, Pierre Elliott Trudeau rode "Trudeaumania" to the job of prime minister. North American society was changing radically with young people growing mistrustful of politicians and authority figures, demonstrating against the war in Vietnam, experimenting with drugs, listening to new forms of rock music and wearing long hair. Leo moved right along with the times. With his attitude of "do what you want, look the way you want, as long as you're ready to play," Cahill was one of the first professional coaches not to resist the changes sweeping society. The Argonauts in 1968 were among the first teams in professional sports to allow player to sport long hair, beads and beards.

Heading into camp, Cahill knew one area that needed help was centre. Veteran Norm Stoneburgh had hung up his pads after a stellar career, leaving a huge hole to fill. But Ron Capham looked very sharp in camp and he proved to be a very solid replacement. Bob Swift was also converted from the fullback position and would also see some playing time at centre as well as offensive guard.

At the end of the exhibition season, Leo made another surprising decision: he would stick with Wally Gabler as his No. 1 quarterback. Wally had looked good in training camp, and Leo still felt he had the potential to be a star. There was a lot of pressure on Cahill for this decision. Wally had better produce . . . or else.

The 1968 season opened with a bang for the Argos on August 2 at CNE Stadium. Their opponents were the Edmonton Eskimos, who had given the Double Blue a painful whipping the year before. This year was different.

Three minutes into the first quarter, Bill Symons powered his way into the end-zone from a yard out to finish an impressive march engineered by Gabler. In the second quarter, Gabler fired a 25-yard TD strike to Mel Profit and in the second half he hit Symons and young slotback Neil Smith with TD passes. Toronto crushed the Green and Gold 34-2. Symons and Jim Dillard combined for 77 yards rushing and Gabler was good on 22 of 31 passes with the three TDs and only one interception. This was exactly the type of game Leo was hoping Wally could give the team on a regular basis. The Toronto Telegram's Al Sokol wrote: "Gone were Gabler's panic scrambles which marked his erratic play of the past. Instead Gabler looked professionally confident and capable, passing from a well-protected pocket to six different receivers."

Wilkinson saw some action late in the game, hitting on four of five passes. Meanwhile, the Argo defence was outstanding, giving up less than 200 yards in total offence, including only 71 yards through the air. The only downside for the Argos was four lost fumbles. Take those away and the score might have become ridiculously lopsided.

Next up would be Russ Jackson and the Ottawa Rough Riders at CNE Stadium. The Argonauts were hoping to build on their impressive victory over Edmonton with another big win. This game would also give them an idea of whether they were ready to compete with the league's elite.

What they learned was that they had some distance to go, at least from an offensive point of view. Ottawa slammed the Argos 38-14. Toronto took a 14-7 lead in the second quarter on TD passes from Gabler to Dillard and Taylor, but Ottawa took over in the second half, scoring 24 unanswered points. The play that really killed the Boatmen came in the third quarter with the score tied 14-14. Ken Lehman broke through and blocked a Dave Mann field-goal attempt, and Wayne Giardino scooped up the ball and raced 83 yards for a touchdown. The Argos never recovered.

Gabler wasn't bad, hitting on 18 of 28 passes, but Toronto's main problem was the complete lack of a running game. In a scene reminiscent of 1966 and '67, Gabler led the team in rushing with 29 yards as Symons and Dillard were completely ineffective. Defensively, the Argos were better than the score indicated. They sacked Jackson four times and got interceptions from Ron Arends, Ed Learn, and Dick Aldridge.

The Double Blue then flew west to battle the strong Calgary Stampeders. Calgary had split its first two games but was coming off a 41-7 defeat to the B.C. Lions. They were still led by Liske and Evanshen, and itching to repay Toronto for the embarrassing defeat the year before. Calgary also had a fine defence led by punishing middle linebacker Wayne "Thumper" Harris, who is often called the finest player in CFL history at that position.

Neither offence could get much going in this game. For the second year in a row, Toronto shut down the high-scoring Calgary passing attack. Dick Thornton intercepted two Liske passes and Ron Arends came up with another. Terry Evanshen caught seven passes but none in clutch situations. For the Argos, Wally Gabler struggled, completing 10 of 23 passes, but he did hit Mel Profit with a TD strike and scored another himself on a scramble. For the second year in a row, the Argos defeated Calgary, this time 19-7.

Toronto would next wage battle in Regina against the Grey Cup finalists from the year before. This would be the Argos' third tough game in a row. The Roughriders had been humiliated 24-1 in the 1967 Grey Cup by Hamilton and were resolute in their desire to recapture the title they had won in 1966.

Toronto got on the board first with a Dave Mann field goal. They then shocked the Roughriders and their fans with a trick play on the next series. Leo ordered a fake field goal, and Mann hit Al Irwin with a 39-yard TD strike to put the Argonauts up 10-0.

Ron Lancaster quickly went to work, though, and by half-time the Green Riders were up 19-10. They widened the gap to 26-10 before Bill Symons slammed into the end zone, but the Argos got no closer after that and went down to a 32-17 defeat.
Leo was disappointed with the entire offence. Dillard led the team in rushing with just 42 yards, and Gabler was erratic again, completing only nine of 22 with an interception.

"A Slip in the Rain"

The Argonauts were now sitting with a record of 2-2. Through four games they had shown a solid defence but an offence that was sporadic at best. Cahill expected much better production out of Dillard and Symons along the ground. Gabler was playing somewhat better than he had in previous years but was far below level of Russ Jackson, Ron Lancaster and Pete Liske. If the Argos were going to compete with the top teams, Wally was going to have to step it up a notch. Whether he was up to the challenge would dictate how the rest of the 1968 season would go.

The Argos' next opponent was Hamilton in the traditional Labour Day weekend battle. The Ticats were having an odd season and were tied with the Argos at 2-2, a source of great puzzlement for their fans. In 1967, Hamilton had finished the season in awesome form, surrendering just one touchdown in their 7 games including the playoffs and Grey Cup. The Ticats' defence had shut down both Russ Jackson in the Eastern Final and Ron Lancaster in the Grey Cup game with an ease that was almost frightening. They were odds-on favorites to roll through the CFL this year, but Ottawa had wreaked revenge upon them in the opening contest, slamming the Cats 53-13. Since then they had lost to Montreal and struggled to beat the Alouettes and Saskatchewan. Clearly something was wrong in Steeltown, which seemed to bode well for Toronto.

The game at Civic Stadium got going when Dave Mann hammered a 62-yard punt through the end zone for a single. Hamilton roared back with a single of its own and a TD strike from Zuger to Tommy-Joe Coffey. The Argos tied it in the second quarter when Gabler rolled out and hit backup tight end Paul Markle with a 21-yard touchdown pass. The Cats pulled ahead again in the third quarter on a single and touchdown but the Argos eventually broke their hearts. Gabler linked up with Symons on a spectacular 68-yard pass-and-run score to tie the game. Symons gathered in the pass and turned on the afterburners, streaking down the field for the major. In the fourth quarter Mann came through with a 39-yard field goal for the win. Final score: Toronto 18 Hamilton 15. Gabler finished the game 11 of 19 with two TD passes and one interception. Dillard led the Argos with 68 rushing yards and the defence did a fine job keeping the dangerous Hamilton attack under control. Ed Learn, who was having an excellent season, came up with another interception.

The good feelings that had been created by the big win in Hamilton evaporated before a capacity crowd at CNE Stadium the following week. The Cats came to Toronto in a nasty mood and the Argos came out horribly flat. Zuger hit Dave Fleming with a TD strike early in the first quarter and Toronto was never in the game after that. The Argos' only points came as a result of two Dave Mann field goals as they went down to defeat 20-6. The Ticats' defence, led by Angelo Mosca and John Barrow, dominated the Toronto offence. The score would probably have been much worse if the Argo defence had not battled hard to keep things close.

There was much talk in the Toronto media and among the fans about the poor showing of the offence, and pressure was being exerted on Leo to try Wilkinson at QB. Leo resisted both because he still felt Wally could do the job, and because he knew Gabler was a personal favourite of owner John Bassett. If he was going to take Wally out, he had better be sure Wilkinson could get the job done. At this point Leo wasn't sure of that, and he was not ready to jeopardize his job by making a change. With the Argos now at 3-3, Leo was running out of time. A loss in Montreal to the Alouettes, who were also struggling, would put Toronto's chances of earning a playoff spot in jeopardy. The Argos had to have a win, preferably a big one.

They got what they needed, whipping Montreal 23-8. Bill Symons was outstanding as he ran for 138 yards on 13 carries and scored two touchdowns. The Larks simply could not slow him down. Jim Dillard chipped in with 39 yards as for the first time the Argos' running attack resembled what Leo thought it could be. Gabler was also outstanding, completing 16 of 25 passes for 237 yards, and more importantly no interceptions. He also picked up a major on a two-yard run. The rumblings over his performance quieted somewhat. The Argo defence was exceptional all game, holding Montreal to less than 300 yards and intercepting three passes. Jimmy Dye picked off two and Ed Learn had the other.

The two teams would stage a rematch at CNE Stadium the following week. Could the Argos put together two good games in a row? The answer turned out to be a resounding "Yes." They looked even more impressive than the week before, rocking Montreal 37-16. Symons rushed for 80 yards and a touchdown. Dillard picked up 68 yards and a major. Gabler completed 16 of 25 passes with two touchdowns to Bobby Taylor.

The Argo defence was relentless, harassing Montreal quarterback Carroll Williams unmercifully and intercepting five of his passes. Toronto also recovered a fumble. Jimmy Dye and Ed Learn had two interceptions each and Marv Luster added another.

The outcome was still somewhat in doubt in the fourth quarter when Dick Thornton came running onto the field and into the huddle, replacing Bill Symons. Whenever that happened, the crowd knew to expect the unexpected. Gabler handed off to Tricky Dick on a sweep left. Guard Charlie Bray wiped out two linebackers and the strong safety with a terrific block, allowing Thornton to turn the corner, deke the cornerback and scamper untouched 38 yards into the end zone.

"I casually walked up to Leo on the sidelines and told him we needed to put this game away," Thornton remembers. "He gave me that puzzled look and I told him to put me in at running back and I'd score a touchdown. As a little incentive, I told him I'd even bet him $100. With that, he said, 'Get in there.' In the huddle, I just told the guys to get me around the corner because I had put my money where my mouth was. I'll never forget Charlie Bray looking me right in the eye and saying, 'Tricky, stay right on my ass and I'll spring ya!' That's exactly what I did and when I got in the open field, I knew I would score easily. When I came off the field, Leo just shook his head. He never did pay up on his debt."

The Argonauts were now sitting with a record of five wins and three losses. They had scored impressive victories over Calgary and Hamilton, two of the league's best teams, and despite some inconsistency, it looked as if the Argos were on the rise.

That opinion was solidified the following week in Winnipeg. The Argos beat the Blue Bombers 15-9 behind the powerful running of Bill Symons. He shredded the Winnipeg defence for 157 yards and two touchdowns on only 16 carries, for an average of almost 10 yards per crack. Dick Thornton, in his first game back in Winnipeg since being traded, was outstanding on defence and also got into the game at running back for a few plays. Gabler connected on 13 of 20 passes but ran into interception problems again, with three picked off. The Argo defence was brilliant. Marv Luster, Dick Aldridge, Jimmy Dye and Ron Arends intercepted passes and the Boatmen recorded three quarterback sacks.

The Argos were on a roll. Three wins in a row, a record of 6-3 and they would get a chance to show their stuff at Lansdowne Park against their hated adversary, Ottawa.

The lesson to be learned from that game was that the Rough Riders were not impressed by the new Argos. Once again they thrashed Toronto, this time 31-10. Russ Jackson hit on 10 of 18 passes for 213 yards and two touchdowns. The Argos got to him for three sacks, but more often he scrambled away from trouble. Gabler paled in comparison, completing 17 of 33 passes but throwing four interceptions with just a single touchdown pass. Linebacker Gerry Campbell was the Argo killer, picking off three Gabler passes.

The Argos' running attack, which had looked so good lately, was stopped cold. Symons picked up only 47 yards rushing and Dillard 18. Ottawa, by contrast, showed it was quite capable of running against the Toronto defence. Bo Scott picked up 91 yards along the ground and Vic Washington added 73 yards. The outcome dropped the Argos to a record of 5-4 while Ottawa improved to 6-3-1.

Figure 4-1: *"Bill Symons faces tough going during 1968 action in Ottawa."*

The Argos then began to prepare for the B.C. Lions, who were struggling in the Western Conference and looked to be a far easier opponent than that damnable Ottawa machine. That feeling was proven correct at CNE Stadium. The Argonauts tamed the Lions 43-29. Offensively it was the Wally Gabler/Bill Symons show. Gabler, hearing the boo-birds and being hounded in the media over his poor showing in Ottawa, fought back to complete 21 of 31 passes with four touchdown passes. He also tossed one interception – no Argo game of this era would be complete without Wally giving up at least one pick. Mel Profit caught two TD passes while Al Irwin and Bobby Taylor had the others. Gabler also scrambled for another major. Symons picked up 113 yards (including a brilliant 53-yard run) on 12 carries and added a touchdown of his own. The Argos rolled up 530 yards in total offence, their most impressive offensive showing since the 53-0 annihilation of Winnipeg the previous year.

With a record of 7-4, the Argos were guaranteed to finish no worse than .500, their best record since 1961. Leo had turned them into a team with a tough defence and an offence that had shown flashes of being dangerous.

They next played host to the Montreal Alouettes, who were having an odd year. They had won only three games, but two of those came against powerhouses Hamilton and Ottawa. Toronto could not afford to take the Als lightly. A surprisingly small crowd of 21,142 saw a great game. Symons broke the 100-yard mark again, picking up 129 yards on 15 carries. The highlight was a spectacular play early in the first quarter when the Argos trailed 3-0. They took the ball at their 35-yard line and Gabler handed off to Symons, who burst through the line and never stopped. He almost left a trail of smoke down the grass field of CNE Stadium on his way to a 75-yard TD run. Gabler played well for the second game in a row, completing 14 of 28 for 293 yards and two TD passes. One was a superb 63-yard bomb to Mel Profit, the other a bullet to Al Irwin.

Toronto trailed 25-22 late in the fourth quarter but in the final minutes Wally drove the Argos down field. On third and goal from the Montreal four-yard line, with less than two minutes left, Leo ordered the offence to

stay on the field and go for the win. Rex MacLeod of the *Globe and Mail* described what happened next:
"Argos advanced as far as the Montreal four. Then Wally threw a pass into the end zone, Neil Smith caught it, juggled it, and then caught the ball again in the crook of his arm. The ball never touched the ground. However, field judge Lorne Woods ruled the pass incomplete."

With the ball turned over on downs, Montreal had a chance to clinch the win by simply racking up a first down or two. Many Toronto teams of the past would have given up at this point, but the Argonaut defence dug in and forced a Montreal punt from its own end zone. With 1:10 left, Wally led the offence back onto the field with the ball on the Montreal 37. He calmly completed a pass to Bill Symons at the 30-yard line, but it was called back because of an offensive pass interference penalty. But Wally didn't panic. With the ball back on the Montreal 47, he hit Bobby Taylor with a pass to the 36. Then, with only two seconds left on the clock, he hit Irwin, who made a leaping catch in the end zone for the victory. The final score was 29-25.

The win was so very important for Wally Gabler. He had proven to Leo and his teammates that he was a leader who could be counted on to rally the team to a win in the closing minutes of a game. Wally had finally arrived as a pro quarterback.

The Argos then headed along the Queen Elizabeth Way for another battle with Hamilton. The Cats had left their fans and management completely befuddled this season. After their overpowering performance at the end of 1967, they were odds-on favorites to dominate but that simply was not happening and nobody could figure out why.

Things did not improve for Hamilton before its home fans. The Tiger-Cats could not stop Bill Symons at all. Sy shredded an outstanding defence for 160 yards on 22 carries. Gabler completed 14 of 22 passes with a TD strike to Profit, while Dave Mann contributed a field goal and two singles to the cause. For Hamilton, quarterback Joe Zuger was horrendous. He completed only nine of 33 passes and had three intercepted by Ron Arends, Pete Martin and Dick Aldridge. The Hamilton running attack was no more successful, picking up only 71 yards. Tiger-Cat players said afterwards that the Argo defence in this game was the toughest they had faced all year. The final score was 12-1 for the Argos, their second win of the year over the defending Grey Cup champions.

The Argonauts had proven to themselves and their fans that they could beat the champs, and they had also whipped western powerhouse Calgary. The only remaining obstacle was Ottawa, which came swaggering into CNE Stadium for the last regular season game. Ottawa had a record of 8-3-2 while Toronto was 9-4, meaning both teams were tied with 18 points. If Toronto won, it would finish in first place and get a bye to the Eastern Final. A loss or tie would give the Argos second place and a semi-final game at home against Hamilton the following week. This game was seen as critically important by Leo and the players: they felt determined to prove – to themselves and to the Rough Riders – that they could beat Ottawa. One way or the other, they would have to beat the Riders to get to the Grey Cup.

Unfortunately, Wally Gabler came up with perhaps the worst performance of his Argo career. He completed only 10 of 30 passes and was intercepted four times. Russ Jackson didn't have his best game, either, hitting on only eight of 17, but it was good enough. Ottawa won easily 31-9.

There was a brief period of hope when, with Toronto trailing 6-3, Allen Ray Aldridge scooped up a fumble and raced 99 yards for a touchdown. The capacity crowd at CNE Stadium was sure that big play from their defence would lead to victory, but they could not have been more wrong. The Rough Riders went to their ground game and simply wore down the Argo defence. Vic Washington rushed for 139 yards and Bo Scott added 128.

The only offensive bright spot for Toronto was once again the play of Bill Symons. He plowed his way for 116 yards on 17 carries, pushing over the 1,000-yard mark for the year. He became the first player in Argo history to hit that milestone.

Leo Cahill felt crushed by the defeat. His Argos had not only lost, they had been flattened. The offence, with the exception of Symons, was terrible and the vaunted defence had been shredded. Counting the playoff game last year, the Argos had played Ottawa seven times under Cahill. They had lost six of the games and had been whipped in all of the losses. Their only bright spot was the 28-28 tie in 1967.

A controversy came to light after the game. Earlier in the season, Ottawa wide receiver Whit Tucker had clobbered Ed Learn with a forearm smash to the back of the head. Dick Thornton got revenge in this game as he describes:

"Near the end of the (earlier) game, Russ Jackson threw up a deep floater to Tucker, whom I was covering. I easily batted it away. We're jogging back upfield and Tucker is in front of me. Our safety, Ed Learn, was walking back toward the line of scrimmage also and was just ahead of us. Tucker comes up right behind him and throws a 'forearm shiver' to the back of Ed's neck. Ed goes down hard and has to be helped from the field.

"Imagine walking down the street and someone nails you from behind when you're not expecting it. I see the whole thing happen, so I start chasing Tucker and screaming at him. But he gets to the Ottawa bench before I can reach him. I yell something like, 'You cheap shot motherfucker, somehow, you'll get what's coming to you.'

"Now it's about six weeks later and Ottawa comes to CNE Stadium in Toronto. They throw the ball deep for Tucker and I'm drifting back into that part of the field to see what's going to happen. It's badly overthrown and ironically Ed Learn makes the interception and takes off in my direction. Whit Tucker's in pursuit but he ain't trying too hard. With no second thoughts, I make a beeline for Tucker and totally forget about turning around and blocking someone in front of me to possibly clear a path for Ed."

Earlier that season, Tricky Dick had broken some ribs against Montreal. To keep playing, he covered the area with a cast made of plastic material that, when immersed in boiling water, became pliable. When cold water was applied, the cast hardened. "Being a wise old man," Thornton says, "I decided to use the same material to create a sort of cast for my right forearm, never knowing when it might come in handy. Covered it up with flesh-coloured tape and no one even knew I wore it.

"It turns out I have the perfect angle on Tucker, so I flash right past Ed Learn, cock my right arm in a clothesline position and with everything I have, lay that cast right upside Tucker's helmet with full force. He collapses, is out like a light and they carry him off. Since it was slightly away from and behind the actual play, no one sees anything. The referees, the fans and players are all watching Ed run with the ball. No flags, no nothing, but the most important thing . . . Tucker and I were square.

"That evening I'm watching the late-night news and the lead story is Violence in the CFL. I say to myself, who got caught? It seems that the isolated replay camera was being experimentally used and the guy operating it at our game decided to zero in on me, close up, on that particular play. So here I am on national TV news, big as life, paying no attention to Ed Learn's interception, taking dead aim at Tucker, cocking my arm and wham! Down he goes like a sack of potatoes.

"Of course, they show it in slow-motion about five times. Tucker's in the hospital, the whole nine yards, and now I'm classified as a dirty player. I'm getting hate mail, obscene phone calls, the works."

The furore eventually died down as the focus turned to the playoffs. The Argos were about to play host to the Hamilton Tiger-Cats in the Eastern Semi-Final, Toronto's first home playoff game since 1961. If the Boatmen could knock off the defending Grey Cup champs, they would get another crack at mighty Ottawa.

November 9, 1968, was a cloudy day with a temperature of 46 degrees Fahrenheit when the Argos kicked off. Joe Zuger immediately marched the Ticats down the field, ending the drive with a dramatic 31-yard run around right end for a touchdown. After the Argos' first drive lost 24 yards, the Cats got the ball back and went right back to work. Zuger, on the second play of the drive, fired a 51-yard TD strike to Allen Smith. With only 4:52 gone in the first quarter, the Argonauts were already trailing 14-0. The fans were stunned. It looked as if the Double Blue were going to be blown right into Lake Ontario.

When the Argos got the ball back, Gabler threw a pass for Bobby Taylor that was picked off by Hamilton's Dewey Lincoln. A sense of horror passed through the crowd. Bob Pennington of the *Toronto Telegram* writer spoke to Mel Profit after the game about this play. Mel told him: "Nobody said a word, but we all knew what the customers were saying.

'Same old Argos.' That's what they were saying. We couldn't hear them, but we all knew it and suddenly the mood changed and we got mad."

The Argo defence was able to hold and Hamilton punted to the Toronto 10-yard line. Then came one of the classic plays in Argonauts history. Gabler handed the ball to Symons on an off-tackle running play. Bill describes what happens: "I broke off tackle. Charlie Bray was the guard and I followed his block through the line. Jim Dillard cleared the inside linebacker out, Mel threw a great block on the defensive end, and it was a foot race the rest of the way. I always felt if I had a step on somebody they'd never catch me."

Nobody did. The blocks by Dillard, Profit, Bray, and another big one from Bob Swift blew holes in the Hamilton defence as sure as if a B-52 bomber had unloaded its payload on it. Symons exploded downfield, outracing Ticat linebackers Bob Krouse and Barrie Hansen for a 100-yard touchdown. It is still the longest post-season TD run in CFL history.

Hamilton looked stunned, while the Argonauts resembled a lion that has just cornered its prey. Though the Ticats were still ahead, nobody doubted that the Argos now had them on the run.

Leo, looking back at the great run by Symons, commented: "Anytime you score a tremendous touchdown like that, it picks up everyone on the team and in the stands. It is very different than if you march down the field and score on a five-yard plunge by the fullback. A play like that totally changes the complexion of the game for both teams."

The Argo defence hit the field, surging with a sense of new life. They stopped the Ticats cold on their next series, forcing a punt to the Hamilton 54. Gabler quickly moved Toronto into position for a 41-yard field goal by Dave Mann. Both defences now dug in and gave up little. The first quarter ended with the Tiger-Cats hanging on to a 14-10 lead.

The Argos erupted for another big play in the second quarter. On second down and 10 from the Toronto 24, Gabler connected with Neil Smith on an 86-yard pass-and-run score, the first TD for Smith since the first game of the year. Later on, the Argos moved in for another field goal that put them ahead 20-14.

But the Ticats were not dead yet. Late in the second quarter, Zuger showed he could also pull a big play out of the bag as he connected with Dave Fleming for a 69-yard pass play that pulled Hamilton ahead 21-20.

Gabler, playing perhaps the best game of his career, brought the Double Blue roaring back. He connected with Bobby Taylor on a 54-yard strike to the Hamilton 24. He then hit Symons with an 18-yard pass to the six-yard line. Wally then rolled out and threw to Taylor in the end zone. The ball deflected off the hands of both Taylor and Dewey Lincoln right into the hands of Neil Smith for the score. After the convert, a Ticats drive stalled and the first half ended with the Argos in front 27-21.

The first half had been one of the most exciting in CFL playoff history. This was Canadian football at its best – fast paced and unbelievably explosive.

Toronto added to its lead six minutes into the third quarter. Ed Learn picked off a Zuger pass at the Toronto 10-yard line and returned it to the Argos' 36. Gabler moved the team down field from there, the drive highlighted by a 43-yard completion to Symons to the Ticats' eight. The drive stalled and Dave Mann added a field goal to stretch the Toronto lead to 30-21.

The Argos now began to focus their offensive attention on running the ball with Symons and Dillard. Both backs were crashing through the tough Hamilton defence while chewing time off the clock. The Argo defence was also in control when it was on the field. Zuger was unable to get anything going for Hamilton. Toronto added another field goal in the fourth quarter. When time ran out, the Argos had done it! They had defeated Hamilton 33-21 for their first playoff victory in seven years.

Wally Gabler recalls meeting Joe Zuger on the field after the game: "Joe came up to me and congratulated us on the win and said, 'It was too bad somebody had to lose.' It was such a fantastic game, probably the most exciting I've ever been involved in."

CNE Stadium was bedlam and the mood in the Argo locker room was sheer jubilation. Leo remembers John Bassett coming into the locker room. "He told me they were going to tear up my contract. He'd give me a new one for five years at more than $25,000 a year, with a new car and some kind of expense account better than the one I had." (That was the last Cahill heard about that contract, however.)

All in all it was a wonderful victory for the Argonauts. Both Symons and Dillard broke the 100-yard rushing barrier: Symons picking up 153 yards on 18 carries, and Dillard 146 yards on 12 carries. Wally was good on 11 of 23 passes for 258 yards and two touchdowns. Most importantly for the Argos and Wally, he had finally shown he could rise to the occasion in a big game.

Argo fans were thinking that maybe the good times had returned, that the cloud of misfortune hovering over the team since 1953 might finally have lifted. The 100-yard run by Symons, aided by devastating blocks, was something right out of the days of Joe Krol. The touchdown pass tipped right into the hands of Neil Smith was the type of play that over the past 15 years had always gone against the Boatmen. This seemed like a return to the days when the Argos always got a break in a big game.

The Argos savored the victory briefly and then got ready for a monumental battle. Russ Jackson would be leading the Ottawa Rough Riders into CNE Stadium for the first game of the Eastern Final the following weekend. It would be a two-game, total-points war.

As they prepared for the first game, the Argonauts were obviously underdogs. In the two seasons under Leo Cahill, they were 0-6-1 against Ottawa. Leo was determined to end that losing streak starting with that first game. The game plan he decided on was simple. If given time, Russ Jackson would pick apart any defence; therefore he should not be given the opportunity to throw. The Argo defence would have to go after him like a pack of sharks after a bleeding swimmer. He could not throw if he was on his butt all game.

To assist his defence, Leo decided to take responsibility for calling most of the blitzes that would be launched at Jackson. Marv Luster, the defensive captain and all-star safety, usually called the defensive alignments. For this game, Cahill would handle that chore, leaving Marv to simply worry about executing the calls.

On the offensive side, the Argo ground attack had been devastating against Hamilton. Leo decided he would run the ball right down the Rough Riders' throats with Symons and Dillard, until Ottawa proved it could stop them. Wally Gabler remembers: "We were so full of confidence going into the final. We knew Ottawa was a great team, but we had proven to ourselves with that win over Hamilton that we had a very good team."

The city of Toronto was gripped by Double Blue fever. Talk about the Grey Cup was rampant. The championship game was scheduled for CNE Stadium that year, so if Toronto could beat Ottawa, it would play for the Grey Cup at home. What an opportunity awaited.

The first game of the Eastern Final was played on Sunday, November 17, on a muddy field at a sold-out CNE Stadium. Disaster struck Toronto early in the first quarter. On the Argos' second possession, Gabler fired a pass to Al Irwin that was intercepted by Bill Van Burkleo at the Toronto 18-yard line. Van Burkleo took it in for the touchdown. Ottawa made the score 10-0 early in the second quarter on a 32-yard Don Sutherin field goal. Late in the second, Gabler marched Toronto down the field, only to see Billy Cooper step in front of a pass intended for Bill Symons deep in the Ottawa end zone. Argo fans were getting increasingly angry at Gabler, who despite his improved play this season seemed incapable of playing well against Ottawa.

The Argo defence dug in, and Marv Luster roared in on a safety blitz, plastering Jackson and knocking the ball up in the air. Linebacker Mike Blum, who was also charging Jackson, grabbed the ball in mid-air and ran untouched into the end zone for the score. The crowd exploded in joy and Ottawa looked stunned. Dave Mann missed the convert, making the score 10-6 in favor of the Rough Riders. Late in the second quarter, Mann drove a punt deep into the Ottawa end zone for a single point and the Argos trailed 10-7 at the half.

Toronto's defence came up with another huge play early in the third quarter. Peter Martin blocked a punt and Luster recovered the ball at the Ottawa 12. Gabler could not convert the turnover, though. A pass to Bobby Taylor was incomplete and another to Mel Profit netted only six yards. Mann missed an easy field goal when the snap went awry, instead trying a desperate pass to Al Irwin that went incomplete.

Russ Jackson could not get a drive going against the fierce Toronto defence. After a Van Burkleo punt, Symons and Jim Dillard smashed through the Ottawa defence with punishing runs. Mann capped the drive with a game-tying 13-yard field goal.

The Argos picked up another Mann field goal late in the quarter to take the lead 13-10. By the fourth quarter, the Toronto offence was sticking mainly to the ground with Symons and Dillard grinding through the Ottawa defenders and winding down the clock. Jackson was under savage pressure and was having no luck moving his offence.

Late in the fourth, Ottawa caught a break when Dillard fumbled at the Toronto 26 yard-line. Ottawa recovered, but the Argo defence stopped the Rough Riders dead in their tracks and Don Sutherin missed an easy field goal, managing only a single point. That was as close as Ottawa would get as the Argos pulled out a 13-11 victory.

Leo's game plan had worked. His running backs had been almost unstoppable, with Dillard picking up 100 yards on 19 carries, and Symons 95 yards on 19 carries. Even more impressive was how ineffective Russ Jackson was against the Argo defence. The all-star quarterback was held to only four completions in 16 attempts for 56 yards, sacked three times and had numerous throws rushed while under heavy pressure. Wally, by comparison, was not great – nine of 18 for 103 yards and two interceptions – but he settled down in the second half and didn't make any fateful mistakes. It was not a performance to remind one of Sam Etcheverry, but considering all the problems Wally had previously against Ottawa, it was a big step forward.
Leo and his players had shown themselves and football fans across Canada that they could beat the Rough Riders. Now, with a two-point lead in the series heading to Ottawa, all they had to do was win again, tie or lose by one point and they'd face the Western Conference champs at home in the Grey Cup in two weeks time.

Ottawa had probably come into the first game somewhat overconfident, and with good reason. The Riders had handled the Argonauts with relative ease over the past couple of seasons and there was no reason to think this would change. But now it seemed like a new and very different story. Ottawa had been manhandled by the Argos in the first game. The Rough Riders' defence had done a decent job handling the Argonauts' offence, but their own offence had been completely ineffective. If they were going to go to the Grey Cup, they would have to find a way to overcome the fired-up Toronto defence.

The Rough Riders were also facing another challenge. They were developing a reputation as a team that couldn't win the big game. The previous year, Hamilton had annihilated them in the Eastern Final. Saskatchewan had thumped them in the 1966 Grey Cup. They had lost to Hamilton in the playoffs each year from 1962 to '64, and lost to Toronto in the 1961 Eastern Semi-Final. Russ Jackson, the finest quarterback in the CFL through the 1960s, had won only one Grey Cup, and that was back in 1960. A loss to the Argonauts in the next game would cement Ottawa's reputation for choking when the pressure was on.

Looking back on the first game, Leo attributed the Argonauts' success to a good attitude and an effective game plan: "I think Ottawa came into the ball game thinking it was going to be simply another sunny afternoon for them, considering how they had handled us in the past. We went in with a positive attitude and some good things happened and we beat them. We put in some different blitzes for that game and Jackson didn't adapt."

Gabler recalls that the field conditions were also a factor. "Ottawa's offence really struggled on the muddy field. Those conditions really slowed them down, and that along with the great play by our defence stopped them. Danny Nykoluk and Charlie Bray also did an outstanding job controlling Billy Joe Booth and Marshall Shirk, which gave me time to do what I had to do."

The final game of the 1968 Eastern Final was played on November 23. The field at Lansdowne Park was decent and the temperature was just below freezing under an overcast sky.

Ottawa kicked off to start the game. Determined to stick with the same plan they had used to beat Hamilton and win the first game, the Argos started running. Dillard took a handoff from Gabler and was stuffed by linebacker Gerry "Soupy" Campbell for a two-yard loss. A pass from Gabler to Bobby Taylor picked up 18 yards and a first down. Another pass, this time to Mel Profit, was good for eight yards. Bill Symons was stopped for no gain on the next play, and Dave Mann punted to the Ottawa 40-yard line.

Toronto then caught a break. Russ Jackson rolled out to pass and was clobbered by Peter Martin, who was charging in from his linebacker's position. Jackson fumbled and Ed Harrington recovered for Toronto on the Ottawa 53. Symons was buried by Ken Lehman, Billy Joe Booth and Marshall Shirk for a four-yard loss. Gabler was then sacked for a nine-yard loss and Dave Mann punted again.

Jackson got a drive going for Ottawa but it ended in a missed Don Sutherin field goal. Gabler hit Taylor with a bullet pass that was good for 34 yards, but on the next play Dillard fumbled at the Argo 51 with Ottawa recovering. Now Jackson would not be denied. He swiftly moved the Rough Riders downfield and hit Margene Adkins with a 32-yard pass for a touchdown. Ottawa was up 7-0 after the convert, and had pulled ahead on total points 18-13.

The Riders added to their lead early in the second quarter on a Sutherin field goal and shortly afterwards picked up a safety when Mann, back to punt, had a snap sail over his head into the Argonauts end zone. Mann fell on the ball there and gave up two points. The cumulative score was 23-13.

Ottawa was not yet finished. After another Argo punt, Jackson, getting plenty of time to throw and playing like a man possessed, moved the Rough Riders deep into Toronto territory. He rolled out and hit Bo Scott with a 20-yard pass that added another touchdown to the Ottawa total. After the convert Ottawa was up in the game 19-0 and 30-13 on total points.

This was the worst possible scenario for Toronto. Jackson was getting time to throw and was being devastatingly effective. Now down by 17 points, the Argos would have to abandon their running game (such as it was on this day) and go to the air. With Wally's history against Ottawa, this was not a comforting thought.

Figure 4-2: *"Wally Gabler gets off a pass under heavy pressure in the 2nd game of the 1968 Eastern Final."*

Before the first half ended, Ottawa struck again. After another Toronto drive stalled, Dave Mann was forced to punt once more. The Rough Riders took over on their 46. Bo Scott slammed his way for four yards. On second down, Ronnie Stewart exploded through the Toronto line and picked up 19 yards before a desperate Dick Thornton and Ron Arends brought him down, saving a sure touchdown. Three plays later, a pass interference call gave Ottawa first down at the Toronto 10. A Jackson pass to Adkins was broken up by Thornton. Another pass to Whit Tucker was incomplete and Ottawa was forced to settle for another Sutherin field goal. At half-time, Ottawa was up 22-0 in the game and 33-13 in total points.

The Argonauts left the field shell-shocked. They had come into this game with such high hopes, and their worst possible nightmare had become a reality.

To add to their woes, Mike Wadsworth had injured a knee and Mike Blum suffered a concussion. Wadsworth was gone for the day while Blum would stagger in and out of the lineup…., huge blows to the defence. Leo still had hope, however. The game may have been out of reach but they were down by only 20 on total points. They still had hope, however faint, and Cahill focused on that in the locker room.

The picture didn't get any prettier at the beginning of the third quarter. Unlike the playoff game between these teams the year before, Ottawa seemed determined not to allow the Argos back into it. Jackson took the opening kickoff and marched the Rough Riders down field, finishing the drive off with a seven-yard run for a touchdown. At 29-0, the score was beginning to get ridiculously lopsided.

The Argos finally showed some life offensively when they got the ball back. Gabler connected with Taylor for a 46-yard gain. But the drive died and Dave Mann missed a field goal that went instead for a single point. On Toronto's next possession, Gabler directed a drive that finished with a 34-yard TD strike to Taylor. Slotback Neil Smith made a key block on Ottawa defensive back Gene Gaines, allowing Taylor to run unimpeded into the end zone. After the convert, Ottawa was ahead 29-8 in the game and 40-21 in the series.

The Argo defence was now fired up and stopped Ottawa again. Gabler drove the Argo offence down the field once more, this time throwing a 37-yard touchdown pass to Symons. Symons was sprung free by a devastating block from Danny Nykoluk. Ottawa blocked the convert but the Argos appeared to be back in the series, if not the game, down by just 13. Their vital signs might have been faint, but their hearts were still beating and a sense of concern was setting in on the Ottawa sideline.

It was now time for the Ottawa defenders to step it up, and they rose to the occasion. Forced to throw on every down, Gabler was under constant pressure. The Ottawa secondary was all over his receivers, and Wally could not find anyone open. Mike Eben went into the game for a couple of plays and was knocked unconscious by Billy Joe Booth. Looking back Mike comments;

"I lined up, the ball was snapped and Billy Joe just levelled me with a forearm smash to the head. I never knew what hit me. I went down like I was killed. The guys really let me have it later when we watched the films of the game. They replayed that a few times!"

The hit on Eben seemed to remove all remaining life from the offence. They got nowhere in their efforts to further narrow the gap.

The end came midway through the fourth quarter when Jackson hit Whit Tucker with a 13-yard pass for a major. The score was 36-14 for Ottawa in the game, 47-27 overall. Coming back from a 20-point deficit was next to impossible.

Nonetheless, Toronto was not quite ready to quit. With less than two minutes to go, Jackson moved the Rough Riders into field goal range. The Argo defence, as if to say, "We will not go quietly into the night," stormed through to block the kick. It was a final act of defiance.

When the final gun sounded, the Argonauts left the field, battered and disappointed, but with their heads held high. A better team had beaten them – again – but they had given it their all.

The final statistics were telling. Toronto had managed one yard rushing in the game. For a team with backs the quality of Symons and Dillard, that was unbelievable. Symons lost four yards on four carries, Dillard carried five times for no yards and Gabler led the team with five yards on two carries. Gabler was also good on 14 of 29 passes for 236 yards, two touchdowns and one interception. For once, it seemed Wally could not be blamed for a loss to Ottawa.

The Argonauts flew back that night to Toronto to be met by a huge crowd at the airport. It seemed to be the fans' way of saying, "Thanks for a wonderful year." The feelings of the fans were summed up in a column by *Telegram* columnist Al Sokol titled "Losers, yes; but beaten, no!"

"Head coach Leo Cahill has turned Toronto Argonauts' motto of Wait Until Next Year into a promise of fulfillment. Respect and admiration has replaced the cynicism and bitterness that conditioned followers to expect the worst from the Argos and to receive it with callous disinterest. When every other Argo team in these young fans' memories would have surrendered to the inevitable, Cahill's club collected its pride and began clawing its way up hill starting from scratch. . . . It's no wonder the Toronto fans are proud to relate to the renegades of the Canadian Football League."

Although their season was over, there was one final event for Argo fans to look forward to. During Grey Cup week, running back Bill Symons was presented with the Schenley Award as Most Outstanding Player in the Canadian Football League for 1968. Symons, who finished the season with 1,107 yards rushing, 44 receptions and 11 touchdowns, was the first Argonaut in history to win the award.

"Nobody ever worked harder than Sy or deserved the Schenley more," said Gabler. "He used to put me on his back and run the steps of CNE Stadium to strengthen his legs. He was the best team player, and he never quit. Our offensive line would have died for him."

Five

1969

Leo Cahill could be proud of the steps he and the Argonauts had taken in his two seasons at the helm. The joke of the league before Leo arrived, the team was now considered a well-coached squad that presented a tough challenge to any opponent. Leo's next task was to improve the Toronto Argonauts enough that they could beat Ottawa, the top team in the East.

The job was not made any easier when Jim Dillard announced he had signed with the NFL's Minnesota Vikings. Vikings coach Bud Grant had seen Dillard play in the CFL and felt he would be a welcome addition to his offence. With Dillard gone, the Argos had lost not only an outstanding running back but also a superb blocker. Opposing defences would now be able to focus on stopping Bill Symons, the Argos' lone running threat.

Along with Dillard, another hero of the 1968 post-season left in 1969. Neil Smith had been called up for active duty in the U.S. Army and would be with the military for the next two years. Leo hoped that Canadian Jim Henderson would be a capable replacement.

A new addition to the squad was Jim Tomlin, who became known to his teammates as Jiminy Cricket. A product of Stephen F. Austin College in Texas, Tomlin had spent the 1968 season with the New Orleans Saints. Unhappy at his lack of playing time, he asked to be released by the NFL club and immediately called Leo to seek an opportunity in Toronto.

Tomlin had blazing speed, running the 40-yard dash – the standard evaluative tool for football speed – in 4.2 seconds. To take advantage, the Saints had converted him from cornerback to flanker. "I ran a 4.2 40 and those coaches had never seen a 4.2 40," recalls Tomlin. Tom Fears (the Saints' head coach) decided I was too fast to be a cornerback, so he said I would be a wide receiver. No problem, or so I thought. We had Billy Kilmer as QB, who loved to throw option passes. The option of throwing it end over end! He could get never get the ball to me on a fly pattern because after four seconds, I was 40 yards down the field. I spent a miserable year as a backup to Danny Abramowitz and finally picked up the phone, called the Toronto office and they signed me."

Leo was not going to follow the Saints' lead and use Tomlin as a flanker. Jiminy Cricket would be staking out the right cornerback position in the 1969 Argo defence.

Mel Profit made headlines off the field when he opened his own clothing store, The First Asylum, on Wellesley Street near Yonge Street in downtown Toronto. Mel, always marching to the beat of his own drummer, sold clothes that he designed himself. He was among the few professional athletes who made headlines in the fashion pages.

Profit seemed to live an ascetic lifestyle. "Mel had this apartment that had all of two pieces of furniture in it," remembers Gabler. "There was a futon on which he slept, and a barber's chair in the middle of the room. When you went to visit him you'd have to sit on the floor, while he'd sit in the barber's chair and look down on you. Very different."

The opening of training camp was delayed in 1969 due to a players strike. The issue was pay during training camp and the exhibition season. Pete Martin describes the situation. "Back then we didn't receive any money from the team before the regular season. We were not paid for expenses such as gas to get to camp, nor were we paid for the entire period of two-a-days or for any of the exhibition games. You didn't receive a cheque from the team until you had made the team and played in a league game. We wanted something like $100 a week to cover this period of time."

Since pro sports salaries were not out of control back then, most Canadian players and imports who lived in Canada year-round had full-time jobs outside of football. To attend training camp, they had to take vacation or an unpaid leave of absence from those jobs, so not being paid for training camp caused a huge financial burden for many players. Mind you, the Argos did pay some players for attending camp. Bill Symons was paid $150 per exhibition game.

"I think we were all getting $50 a week from the beginning of training camp and didn't begin getting real paycheques 'til the beginning of the season," recalls Dick Thornton. "Some of the veterans began to talk about how shitty this was, so we decided to test the waters by naming a figure like 500 bucks per exhibition game and promptly went on strike. Leo went ballistic. I think we missed two or three days of practice."

The players held their own training camp at the high school where Peter Martin taught. Leo went to the school and appealed to them to come back to camp, saying he would see what he could do for them. Mel Profit, the players' designated spokesman, politely asked him to leave. This was a battle they were determined to win.

Leo was considering finding replacement players when John Bassett, Sr., intervened directly. Bassett got the Argos back into camp by using old-fashioned, tough business talk.

"I can't understand for the life of me why mature men would ignore valid contracts," he told Rex MacLeod of the *Globe and Mail*. "This is a threat to try and compel us to do certain things. We can't operate a football team or anything else under those circumstances. These chaps have signed a valid contract. It covers practices, exhibition games, league games and playoffs. That's what they're paid for."

Thornton recalls the end of the strike. "One afternoon John Bassett, Sr., walks into the locker room all decked out in his camel-hair coat, three-piece suit and cane, looking very mad. He was there about three minutes and said he would look into the matter but if we weren't back on the field that day for practice, he would cut every one of us and personally make sure none of us would ever play pro football again. He then promptly walked out. A very powerful man and very believable, and that was the end of the strike. I believe there was some improvement in preseason pay, though."

If anything, the strike brought a tightly knit team even closer together. "I had never seen a team so close," says Randy Beatty, the ball boy from 1967 to '73. "These guys were all friends on and off the field. After practice they'd always go for a beer together. Tuesday nights they'd all gather at the Domed Stadium (a bar owned by Bobby Taylor and Bill Symons) and on

Thursday nights, they'd all be at the Jarvis House. There was no racial split on the team. White and black players would mix and socialize with each other."

Even with the stress caused by the strike, there was time for some laughs at the Argo camp. Tricky Dick recalls a rookie sneaking out of the dorm in Aurora to meet up with a girl one night. "They needed somewhere to go and found an unlocked car in the car park. They used it all night to make love, and needless to say, it was a wreck in the morning. Turned out the car was Leo's. I think he got cut the next day."

Heading into camp, it appeared the quarterbacking position was Gabler's again. While clearly not up to the standards of Russ Jackson or Ron Lancaster, he was rounding into a solid, professional who seemed to be able to get the job done even when circumstances were tough. To add some depth at QB, Leo shipped dependable Canadian flanker Al Irwin to the Eskimos for a solid Canadian quarterback, veteran Frank Cosentino.

During camp and the exhibition season, an interesting battle for the No. 1 quarterback position developed. Gabler, who had led the East in passing yards in 1968, was trying to hold off Tom Wilkinson and Cosentino, both of whom were looking sharp.

Before the regular season started, Leo was approached by a group of veterans who said they would prefer to see Wilkie as the starter. It wasn't just that Tom had looked better in the preseason. The players simply had more confidence in his abilities. Mike Eben describes the situation: "Wally was a very nice, clean-cut fellow, however I didn't think he had a strong enough throwing arm. Wilkinson was short, pudgy – we called him "Groceries" – and he didn't have a great arm. However, he knew where to place the ball."

Wilkie was also a tough, no-nonsense field general and the players believed in him. Wally was personable and well-liked, and the players respected how hard he tried. But, says Thornton, "Wilkie had those unexplainable leadership qualities. All of the receivers preferred him behind centre. He didn't look like an athlete, but he sure could throw it on the money and was very cool in ball games."

Looking back, Wally seems frustrated at losing the confidence of his teammates. "Leo let the players take charge here. I felt both Wilkie and I could work together. Hell, we did for two seasons before. I didn't understand what happened. I led the Eastern Conference in passing the prior year and Bobby (Taylor) was the leading receiver."

Leo, who always tried to stay in tune with a core group of veterans, respected the opinions of the players who spoke to him about this sticky situation. He was also of the opinion that while Wally was a good quarterback, he might not be the best one for the Argonauts. With such players as Bobby Taylor, Dick Thornton and Mel Profit, the Argos were developing the image of a group of long- haired mavericks and renegades. Wally, with his soft-spoken speaking style and clean-cut good looks, didn't fit the mold. The slightly dishevelled, tobacco-chewing Wilkinson did.

"Wilkie was a great team favourite," Leo says now. "There was a feeling with him in there that you could always come from behind. I don't think there was that feeling with Wally in there. Wally was a good athlete but he lacked something insofar as getting something done out there on the field."

Leo decided to give the starting role to Tom Wilkinson.

The other challenge facing Leo was getting Bill Symons signed to a new contract. After his superb 1968 season, Symons was a hot commodity on both sides of the border. He actually had a deal struck with the AFL's Denver Broncos to play out his option in 1969 and join the Broncos in 1970. But Argos assistant coach Blackie Johnston, who had coached Bill at the University of Colorado and in B.C., helped convince him to stay in Toronto. Bill felt great loyalty to Blackie, who had convinced Bob Shaw in 1967 to bring Symons to Toronto and in doing so saved his career.

Symons also considered the fact that he had a good full-time job with Canadian Admiral TV that offered him long-term financial security. If he accepted the Denver offer, he would lose that job. Pro football in the U.S. was a full-time job whereas in Canada the time commitment was less and players could hold down outside jobs. Leo matched the Broncos' offer, meaning Bill would be paid the same amount to play football part-time for Toronto as he would full-time with Denver. "Sy" re-signed with the Argonauts, creating great sighs of relief across Toronto.

<u>"A Slip in the Rain"</u>

The Argos had one bizarre experience in the preseason. In those days it was customary for players to take "bennies" or "uppers" before games. These were pills designed to pump players up. The team got a new doctor who didn't know about this practice.

"We went to Ottawa for an exhibition game and at the pre-game meal, Marv Luster, who was in charge of handing them out to the guys, went to Doc and asked for them," recalls Thornton. "He didn't know anything about it. There was almost a riot when we found out there wasn't any 'candy' available. The doctor wrote a prescription for something like 500 pills and handed it to (an Argo official who asked to remain unnamed). He goes to the local drug store and hands in the prescription. The pharmacist goes crazy and calls the Mounties, who arrest the official. They thought he was trafficking."

The Argo team official involved recalls: "I handed in the prescription, the pharmacist took one look at it and said, 'Wait here.' He makes a call and suddenly there are two huge Mounties beside me. They ask me who I am, etc. I tell them I am with the Argos and finally they drive me back to the team hotel and check my story out. They released me there, but the guys never did get the pills."

Dick laughs about it now. "I think we lost like 60-0 in that exhibition game. Everyone was psyched out."

The Argos opened the 1969 season before a capacity crowd of 33,135 at CNE Stadium. Their opponents would be their hated rivals, the Hamilton Tiger-Cats, itching to repay the Double Blue for their loss in the playoffs the year before.

The Ticats struck first on a 17-yard TD run by Willie Bethea. The Argos tied it on a one-yard plunge by Bill Symons and pulled ahead on a 16-yard TD pass from Wilkinson to Mike Eben. That was the first pro touchdown in Eben's career.

The lead went back and forth throughout the game. Wilkinson, looking very sharp, hit Bobby Taylor and new slotback Jim Thorpe with TD strikes in the fourth quarter, but when the final gun sounded Hamilton had come out on top 34-28. Wilkinson ended the game completing 23 of

35 passes with three touchdowns, two interceptions and 438 yards in the air. Symons was kept under control by the Hamilton defence, rushing for only 50 yards on 13 carries. Bob Morgan, who had replaced Jim Dillard, added 47 yards on nine carries.

Toronto had not won the game, but there was great excitement over the play of Tom Wilkinson. There had not been a game like that by an Argo quarterback since the days of Tobin Rote.

Next up for Toronto were the Alouettes in Montreal. This would be a good opportunity for the Double Blue to even their record against a supposedly poor team.

The Argos did exactly that. For the second game in a row, the offence was firing on all cylinders. They jumped into the lead early in the first quarter when Wilkinson hit Symons with a 13-yard TD pass. Minutes later, the Alouettes' Larry Fairholm (whose son Jeff would become a star receiver for Saskatchewan in the 1980s) scooped up a fumble and returned it 82 yards for the major, tying the score. Wilkinson didn't panic, responding with a big play of his own: an 87-yard pass-and-run play to Jim Thorpe that sent the Argos into a 14-7 lead. In the second half, Wilkie hit two 75-yard passes for touchdowns, the first to Bob Morgan and the second to Thorpe.

The Toronto defence also came up big with Dick Thornton intercepting a pair of Sonny Wade passes. His partner on the other side, Jim Tomlin, also had a pick, as did linebacker Allen Ray Aldridge. The final score was 33-26 for Toronto. Wilkinson was outstanding again, throwing for 368 yards and four touchdowns.

Next came the Winnipeg Blue Bombers, who were looking to show that they could play with one of the powers of the Eastern Conference. The Bombers were a faint shadow of the powerhouse coached by Bud Grant that dominated the CFL from 1957 to 1965. The one remaining star of their Grey Cup days was running back Dave Raimey, and he wanted out of Winnipeg, partly because he could not get along with Grant's replacement at head coach: "Joe Zaleski took over and he was terrible. This guy was the bottom of the barrel. He didn't have a clue. He wasn't very smart at all. He and I were constantly at odds."

The game started off great for Toronto. The Argonauts took the opening kickoff, moved quickly downfield and finished things off with a Wilkinson-to-Thorpe pass for a major. After a single made the score 8-0, Winnipeg responded with a field goal before Mel Profit hauled in a 35-yard pass from Wilkinson to extend the Toronto lead to 15-3. The Argos struck again before the half was over, this time with a long Wilkinson TD pass to Taylor.

The Argo offence stalled in the second half. For the first time all season, Wilkie ran into problems. He threw three interceptions and was replaced when Gabler entered the game for his first appearance of the season. Midway through the fourth quarter, Wally dived into the Blue Bomber end zone for a touchdown, making the score 29-3, which was how the game ended.

The Argos had received an excellent effort from their defence. Winnipeg was held to only 214 total yards and rarely threatened. Offensively, Toronto played well enough to win although Leo was concerned over Tom's three interceptions and the fact that Symons, for the third straight game, failed to rush for 100 yards. Bill was getting the ball regularly, but it seemed that without Jim Dillard in the backfield, opposing defences were concentrating all their attention on him.

Leo now swung perhaps the biggest trade of his career. Since arriving at the helm of the Argonauts, he had tried to get Dave Raimey, the star running back of the Winnipeg Blue Bombers. Raimey had been an outstanding two-way player at the University of Michigan and was a member of the 1964 NFL champion Cleveland Browns before joining Winnipeg in 1965.

"I always thought Raimey was one of the best running backs of all time," says Leo. "Indescribable. He didn't run, he floated. He was like a ghost. He would seem to be just tippy-toeing, didn't look physically strong but he had great strength in his legs for breaking tackles."

During the Winnipeg game, Raimey recalls, "I was running a sweep and Marv Luster raced up from his safety spot and drove me out of bounds at the Argo bench. As I got up, Leo grabbed me and said, 'Be careful because you are coming here.' I said, 'You mean it?' Leo nodded and I had tears in my eyes I was so happy when I ran back to the Bombers huddle."

The price Winnipeg would demand in previous seasons for this perennial 1,000-yard rusher was always too high, but things had changed somewhat in the 'Peg. The Bombers were struggling and in desperate need of a quarterback, and Raimey was unhappy and wanted out. Leo felt confident that he was set at quarterback with Tom Wilkinson, and that Frank Cosentino was a capable backup. That left Gabler available for the right trade opportunity.

Leo knew it would be a tough sell with John Bassett, a big Gabler supporter, but he pursued the deal anyway. It was going to be Gabler for Raimey and defensive back Chip Barrett, whom Leo had sent to Winnipeg in the Dick Thornton trade. Bassett was not happy but allowed Leo to complete the trade, implying that the Argonauts had better win.

Wally was horrified at the trade news. "I was absolutely devastated. I heard the news while driving to practice on the Queen Elizabeth Way. I got into CNE Stadium, my locker was cleaned out and Mert Prophet handed me my plane tickets to Winnipeg. I had a home in Toronto and a job outside of football. John Bassett called me a day or so later to wish me well and tell me the trade was not his decision, but he had to back his coach."

The news rocked the CFL, as it was the biggest trade in years. People were stunned that Raimey had been made available. The Argonaut players, to a man, felt Dave could be the missing piece of the puzzle and couldn't believe that Leo had been able to get him. Mike Eben is still amazed more than three decades later. "I really felt this was it. When I watched Raimey at university, I always though he was a wonderful running back. He almost looked like he was floating. We were elated that we got him as everyone figured he was untouchable."

Dave made his Toronto debut against the British Columbia Lions at Empire Stadium in Vancouver and was an instant hit. In his first game in Double Blue, he carried the ball 13 times for 98 yards and a touchdown. Bill Symons, with defences no longer able to key on him, added 104 yards on 10 carries and also scored a touchdown. Wilkinson got into the act, running nine yards for a major, and the Toronto defence got on the scoreboard twice itself. Thornton returned an interception off Paul Brothers 52 yards for a score and Allen Ray Aldridge took an interception back 32 yards for another TD. The final score was 42-20 for Toronto, boosting the Argos to a record of 3-1.

Staying out west, the good ship Argonaut rolled into Edmonton next to do battle with the Eskimos at Clarke Stadium. The Eskimos had no more success handling the Argos then the Lions had. Raimey, playing inspired football, picked up 106 yards on 14 carries and Symons added 68 on 13 carries. Sy also scored a touchdown on a 31-yard pass from Tom Wilkinson. Wilkie added a major on a one-yard plunge, and "Tricky Dick" did it again, returning another interception 30 yards for a touchdown.

It was an impressive 24-12 victory for Toronto, which was starting to be viewed around the league as a powerhouse. Leo, in less than three seasons, had turned the Argonauts completely around. This was a team that had a rock-solid, at times vicious defence and an explosive offence featuring the finest backfield duo in the CFL. Cahill wanted to build a team that could beat Ottawa and win the Grey Cup, and this team looked as if could do just that.

But first the Argos faced another obstacle in Ron Lancaster, George Reed and the rest of the Saskatchewan Roughriders. Since taking over the Argonauts Leo had never beaten the Green Riders. But he seemed to have the team to do it at this point, although the Roughriders were considered by many to be the best team in the Western Conference. This would be the first real test of the 1969 Toronto Argonauts.

That being the case, the Argos passed with flying colours. They took the lead on an early Dave Mann field goal after a drive stalled inside the Roughriders 10-yard line. Less then 90 seconds later the Riders were in the lead when Lancaster linked up with his favourite receiver, Hugh Campbell, on a 50-yard pass and run for a touchdown.

The Argos seemed to relish the challenge of battling a great opponent this night. With a capacity crowd at CNE Stadium putting up a deafening roar, the Double Blue came fighting back. First, Wilkinson fired a 12-

yard TD strike to Raimey. In the second quarter, Raimey capped off a drive by diving into the Saskatchewan end zone from two yards out. Dave was back in the third quarter, this time stunning the superb Roughriders defence by exploding through the line and outrunning the rest of the defenders on a 48-yard TD run. In the fourth quarter, Frank Cosentino made his regular-season Toronto debut and threw a 17-yard pass to Mel Profit for another major. The final score was 34-15 for the Argonauts. Raimey had been simply out of this world, scoring three touchdowns and rushing for 165 yards.

Wilkinson was good on 15 of 24 passes for 209 yards, a touchdown and an interception. Toronto's defence was even better than the offence, holding George Reed, perhaps the finest runner in CFL history, to 21 yards on nine carries. The Argos came up with four sacks and Jim Tomlin picked off two Rider passes. The Roughriders had been thrashed and many felt this had been the finest overall performance by the Argonauts in years.

With a record of 5-1 and coming off a simply dominating performance over Saskatchewan, many were calling Toronto the class of the league. Next stop was Ottawa and a long-awaited crack at Russ Jackson and his squad. If Saskatchewan had been a tough test, Ottawa would be the mid-term exam. Defeat Ottawa and there would be no doubts among the players or fans that the Argos were capable of beating anyone, and a definite contender for the 1969 Grey Cup.

The eyes of football fans across Canada were glued to Lansdowne Park on September 13 for this anxiously awaited duel. Toronto got on the board first with a single off a 64-yard rocket of a punt by Dave Mann. The Argos added to the lead when Bill Symons, who had been somewhat in the background since the arrival of Raimey, broke off tackle and sprinted 30 yards for a major. Ottawa roared back before the first quarter was over with Jackson hitting Margene Adkins for a 20-yard TD pass. In the second quarter, Jackson threw a 42-yard TD pass to Vic Washington and Sutherin added an 80-yard single. The Argos came right back with Wilkinson engineering a drive that finished with Symons crashing into the Ottawa end zone from one yard out.

Figure 5-1: *"Pete Martin #77 fails to prevent Russ Jackson # 12 from getting off a pass during action in Ottawa in 1969."*

In the second half, Sutherin added two field goals and two more singles while Toronto picked up a single from Mann. With less than two minutes to go and trailing 22-16, Wilkinson shocked the crowd with an 85-yard pass-and-run play to Jim Thorpe for a touchdown. The convert put Toronto ahead 23-22 and Argo fans figured they could sit back and watch their great defence protect the lead.

But Jackson drove Ottawa down the field. On the last play of the game, Sutherin lined up for a 34-yard field-goal attempt. The crowd roared as Leo sent Dave Mann into the end zone to kick out a possible wide attempt. The snap went back and Sutherin hammered the ball. Allen Ray Aldridge launched himself over the line and got a hand on the kick! Unfortunately, he didn't block it but deflected the ball up and over the crossbar, through the posts for three points. The Toronto players and fans were stunned; even the Rough Riders were amazed. Nobody had ever seen anything like that before. The "Jackson Jinx" seemed to be in place as Ottawa came out on top 25-23.

"We had them that game and then Allen Ray Aldridge deflected the ball through the goal posts," remembers Symons. "I had never seen that happen before . . . none of us had. When you get your hand on a ball like that, 99 per cent of the time the kick is blocked."

Despite the loss, there were many positives for Toronto in the game. Symons had been outstanding, picking up 114 yards on 13 carries and Raimey added 46 yards on 11 carries. With both Symons and Raimey in the same backfield, the Argo running game seemed almost unstoppable. Stop one and the other took over.

Raimey was asked by the author if there was ever any conflict between him and Symons over who should get the ball. "Never. There were times in the huddle that Bill would say, 'Give the ball to Dave,' and then he would go out and block his tail off for me.

"It's funny, when I was in Winnipeg and saw Bill play I would think, 'This guy can't be a running back with that hunched-over running style of his.' But he was great. He was strong and as a defender he was on you so fast you had no time to prepare. In fact, a lot of people don't know this but he was faster than me. I remember once fumbling around the other team's goal line. A defender grabbed the ball and took off. I couldn't catch him, but Bill ran him down and made the tackle."

Wilkinson struggled in the game, completing only six of 21 passes for 164 yards, but Toronto had been solid defensively, holding the superb Ottawa running attack to only 83 yards. The Argos could not stop Jackson, however, as he passed for 382 yards and two touchdowns.

Toronto would get another shot at Ottawa the following week at home. Players and fans were convinced that the previous game had been lost on a fluky play, and that revenge was at hand.

There was another capacity crowd at CNE Stadium for the rematch. Once again Toronto jumped out in front early as Bobby Taylor took a 36-yard pass from Tom Wilkinson for the score. Ottawa tied it on a two-yard run by Vic Washington in the second quarter. Wilkinson restored Toronto's lead later on an 11-yard TD run.

The exciting play went back and forth in the second half as well. Wilkie ran into interception trouble and had to leave the game after suffering a banged-up shoulder. His backup, Frank Cosentino, engineered two drives that both ended in TD passes to Jim Thorpe. Russ Jackson, however, was red-hot again. He threw two touchdown passes to Margene Adkins and scored another himself on a one-yard plunge.

The final score was 34-27 for Ottawa, leaving Toronto fans and players almost shaking in frustration. There was something infuriating about Ottawa's dominance over Toronto. It seemed that no matter what the Argonauts tried, they couldn't beat the Rough Riders. Offensively they were scoring points, but their otherwise outstanding defence could not shut the Ottawa offence down. Russ Jackson always found a way to beat them.

Since Leo became head coach in Toronto, counting regular season and playoff games, the Argos had a record of 1-10-1 against Ottawa. The talk about going to the Grey Cup became subdued. Dave Raimey and Tom Wilkinson were supposed to be the answers, and while both had played well, it hadn't helped the Argos break the jinx against Ottawa.

Their record now at 5-3, Toronto headed to Montreal for a game that would become infamous. Before the game, they found out they would be without the services of veteran kicker Dave Mann, who had injured a leg. Tom Johanson was brought in to handle the place-kicking duties and the ever-versatile Dick Thornton would take over punting while continuing to play defensive back.

Cosentino would also be making his first start for Toronto in place of Wilkinson, who was nursing a bad shoulder. Coming off two crushing losses and without Mann and Wilkinson, an upset by Montreal certainly seemed possible. But Toronto was too good to let that happen. Cosentino had an excellent game, throwing touchdown passes to Profit, Raimey and Thorpe. Symons churned out 89 yards along the ground while Raimey, although held to just 55 yards, scored two rushing touchdowns. Thornton and Jim Tomlin came up with two interceptions each. Punting full-time for the first time since 1963, Tricky Dick did a solid job, averaging 35 yards with one 51-yard kick.

The Argos won 36-33, but the game was marred by two ugly incidents. After one Tomlin interception, Montreal quarterback Sonny Wade almost started a riot by stepping on Tomlin's head. Later, frustrated after being sacked by Ed Harrington, Wade allegedly screamed a terrible racial slur at the Argo defensive end, further enraging the Argos. Leo Cahill called this perhaps the dirtiest game he had ever been involved in. Jim Tomlin remembers this game well:

"Wade threw three interceptions in the second half, two to me. The last one killed their final drive to take the lead with two minutes left. I ran the interception back about 60 yards to their 30-yard line. Wade and a couple more tackled me out of bounds. As I was lying there sucking air, Wade stomps on the back of my neck in frustration. Chaos erupted on both benches and a lot of the fans started fights. Ron Arends got hit in the helmet with a spark plug! They were throwing beer bottles, rocks, spark plugs at us on the sidelines."

Toronto was outraged over these incidents. Wade apologized to Tomlin but not to Harrington. CFL commissioner Jake Gaudaur, never one for confrontation, used all his political savvy to smooth things over and keep it from blowing up into a huge scandal. Nonetheless, while Wade would go on to lead Montreal to three Grey Cup victories in the 1970s, many fans would always remember him for these two unfortunate lapses in judgment.

The savage hitting of the game is reflected in another memory for Jim Tomlin, this one relating to perhaps the hardest hitter of that era, Marv Luster: "A lot of times if a running back is hurting you, you do extra work trying to slow him down. It was common practice to gang-tackle, put a lot of hits on the ball carrier. You had to be careful with Marv, though. If you had someone stood up waiting for Marv to 'clean up,' you stood a good chance of taking a hard hit yourself.

"This particular day, Pete Martin and I had Dickie Smith stood up at the line of scrimmage. He had already put up some huge numbers that day running and catching the ball. This was the infamous Wade stomping incident game and there was not a lot of goodwill being exchanged that day. Anyway, (Smith) twisted away from me just as Marv arrived at 100 miles per hour. I got most of the hit, and my left arm was numb the rest of the game. Luster was the hardest hitter I ever played with. He went after a ball carrier like a heat-seeking missile."

With their two-game losing streak behind them, the Argos now turned their attention to the powerful Calgary Stampeders. Calgary had lost Pete Liske to the AFL's Denver Broncos but was still a very powerful team. Liske, the league's MVP in 1967, was replaced by Jerry Keeling, who was a star defensive back and a very capable quarterback himself. Keeling also had an outstanding group of receivers to throw to, led by the incomparable Terry Evanshen, and the Stamps' defence was its usual tough self.

The Argo running attack was the story of this game at CNE Stadium. Raimey picked up 115 yards and a touchdown on 11 carries, while Symons smashed for 89 yards and a TD on 18 carries. Wilkinson and Cosentino combined for only eight pass completions, but two went for touchdowns as the Argos pulled out a 31-25 victory.

Toronto next moved into Civic Stadium in Hamilton. This game would feature outstanding defence by both teams as neither could get much going on the offensive side of the ball. Tom Wilkinson saw the bulk of playing time at quarterback and did a capable job although it certainly would not go down as one of his best games. He was good on five of 11 passes for 76 yards, including a 40-yard scoring strike to Dave Raimey, who came out of the backfield, seemed to vanish, then reappeared deep down the field to softly gather in Wilkinson's pass and take it in for the score. Bill Symons actually led the team in passing courtesy of a 79-yard pass to Bobby Taylor off a halfback option.

Hamilton kept the Toronto running attack largely in check, holding Symons to 51 yards on 13 carries and Raimey to 72 yards on 16 carries, but Dave did slip into the end zone on an eight-yard run in the opening quarter. The final score was 17-7 in favor of the Argonauts, boosting their record to 8-3.

The two teams resumed their rivalry the following week at CNE Stadium before a sold-out audience, the fifth sellout in six home games. Leo had not only turned the team around on the field, but at the box office as well. To go along with that, the colourful Argos were also the best road draw in the league. Toronto was and forever will be the city the rest of Canada loves to hate, and fans across the country love to see the Argonauts get hammered. Combine that with the exciting, outspoken renegades Leo had brought to the Argos and you had the team everyone across Canada wanted to see.

In the rematch, Hamilton jumped in front on a touchdown by Tommy Joe Coffey. Toronto tied it when Ed Harrington returned a fumble 26 yards for a score. Shortly after that, Profit and Wilkinson combined on a 10-yard passing play for a major followed by, of all things, a touchdown pass thrown to Tom Wilkinson by Dick Thornton, who had lined up at running back. Dick took a pitchout from Wilkie and, while the Ticats converged on him, lobbed the ball back across the field to a wide-open Wilkinson, who scored easily.

That play seemed to leave the Ticats stunned and they collapsed in the second half to an extent never seen before against Toronto. Tom Johansen kicked a field goal, and then Ed Learn scored the second touchdown of the day by the defence on a 35-yard interception return. The onslaught continued in the fourth quarter with Frank Cosentino scoring on a 25-yard run. On the resulting Hamilton possession, Ron

Arends picked off a John Eckman pass and took it back 30 yards for a touchdown although he was injured on the play. *Globe and Mail* writer Rex MacLeod described what happened" "Tiger-Cat tackle Doug Mitchell threw him to the ground with such force that Arends' face mask was ripped off his helmet. He was knocked unconscious."

Late in the game, with the CNE crowd chanting, "We want 50, we want 50," Dick Thornton came in at running back and scored on a five-yard run. The convert made the final score 51-8. The Tiger-Cats left the field taunted by the jubilant Toronto fans, who had just seen a simply overpowering performance by the home team. The defence had intercepted six John Eckman passes, with Ed Learn getting three of them. Arends, Peter Martin and Jim Dye had the others. Eckman also suffered four sacks. The offence had looked good as well. Wilkie had completed eight of 13 for 131 yards and a touchdown. Symons led the team in rushing with 79 yards on 10 carries.

The game was not without a very dark moment, however, as Dave Raimey suffered torn knee ligaments that would put him out for the remainder of the regular season and playoffs. The injury occurred late in the second quarter on a routine run. Angelo Mosca and Mike Strofolino jumped on Raimey and the two Hamilton behemoths, with a combined weight of more than 500 pounds, crushed Raimey. "My knee was bothering me before that play," he remembers. "I was coming off the field regularly in a lot of pain. Something was torn in it before. When they hit me, everything else just went." It was a clean tackle . . . with devastating results. The great one-two punch of Symons and Raimey was gone for this season.

Dave Raimey was simply too great a player to be adequately replaced. For the rest of the year, Bill Symons would carry the brunt of the load, with Dick Thornton doing double duty at running back and defensive back. To assist with the running game, Leo signed Dickie Moore, who became known to his teammates as "The Head" due to his huge cranium. "I don't know where Leo found this guy," says Symons. "You have never seen a person with such an incredibly sized noggin before. It was unbelievable."

Without Raimey, but with the addition of "The Head," Toronto went into Ottawa for yet another battle with the powerful Rough Riders. Once again the Argos were facing their nemesis late in the year with first place on the line. If they could win, they would have first place practically wrapped up.

The only thing that was even somewhat close about this game was the score. The Argos came up horribly flat on offence and were whipped 20-9. The score flattered them and was a reflection of their tough defence. Toronto was down 14-0 at the half as Jackson fired TD passes to Whit Tucker and Margene Adkins. Symons blasted into the end zone from one yard out early in the fourth quarter, but the Rough Riders added two late field goals by Don Sutherin to clinch the game. Both Wilkinson (who unknown to the press and fans was battling two shoulder separations and was being injected with painkillers before games) and Cosentino struggled to get any offence going. Symons was kept pretty well in check, picking up only 55 yards on 11 carries. He was also battling a dislocated big toe that required extensive freezing before each game and was hurting his running ability.

The media in Toronto were now full of stories regarding the "Jackson Jinx." It made for good press but the players didn't believe in it. "I never really thought of it as a Jackson Jinx but more Ottawa itself," says Mike Eben. "They were so loaded with great players at all positions." Bill Symons agreed: "They had an awful good team. We were confident enough to know we could beat them, we just had some bad breaks. The media made the story of the jinx up."

Montreal headed into Toronto for the final game of the regular season. Desperate to avoid any more key injuries, Leo kept Symons out of the lineup and decided to split the quarterbacking duties between Wilkinson and Cosentino, with Frank getting the start.

The Alouettes, playing with nothing to lose as they were out of the playoffs, jumped in front on a first-quarter touchdown. In the second quarter, after a single off a Thornton punt, Cosentino threw a 32-yard TD strike to Bobby Taylor. The Argos pulled ahead in the third quarter on a five-yard lob from Wilkinson to Mike Eben and padded the lead in the fourth when Cosentino hit Mel Profit for a touchdown.

Sonny Wade suffered a dose of revenge for his appalling actions earlier in the year, courtesy of Argo defensive linemen Ed Harrington and Vernon Vanoy. In the third quarter, Vanoy charged in from his defensive tackle position and plastered Wade, who staggered off the field, blood streaming down his face. Vanoy's hit had rammed four or five teeth down into his lower jaw. Wade came back into the game after treatment and then Harrington took over. He roared in from the blind side as Wade was setting up to throw, knocking the QB out of the game and almost out of the stadium.

There were other nasty incidents. Ron Arends was kicked in the face by offensive lineman Pierre Desjardins while lying helpless on the field. Desjardins was thrown out of the game. Linebacker Mike Blum, meanwhile, was kicked in the crotch by Montreal flanker Tom Cassese.

The final score was 22-18 in favour of Toronto, allowing the Argonauts to finish the regular season at 10-4 and in second place behind – who else? – Ottawa. Dickie Moore carried the bulk of the rushing game, picking up 99 yards on 15 carries. Leo, always willing to try new things, had Jim Thorpe, normally a slotback, in at running back. He carried eight times for 18 yards.

Thornton also had seven carries, including one 62-yard run, and picked up his seventh interception of the year, capping a remarkable season. It's doubtful anyone ever had as versatile a season as Tricky Dick had in 1969. On defence he intercepted seven passes, returning two for touchdowns, and recovered a fumble. His interception total is significant when one considers that quarterbacks wary of his veteran savvy generally stayed away from passes to his side of the field. His tackling was always ferocious and he seldom missed bringing down hard-charging running backs or fleet wide receivers. On offence, while still playing his regular role at defensive back, he replaced the injured Dave Raimey at running back and carried the ball 14 times for 106 yards and a touchdown. He threw one pass that went for a touchdown. He replaced the injured Dave Mann at punter and kicked 52 times for a total of 2,012 yards and two singles. A strong case can be made that Dick Thornton was the finest all-around athlete to grace the playing fields of Canada.

Hamilton moved into CNE Stadium seven days later for the Eastern Semi-final, and there was great concern among the Argo players and management. This was a very battered team on offence. Raimey was out for the year. Symons' toe was so bad he could hardly walk. Wilkinson had both shoulders separated, and although he could play with them frozen, his passing was still adversely affected. On the upside, Dave Mann was back and would handle the punting duties while Tom Johansen would continue place-kicking.

Hamilton was relieved that its No. 1 quarterback, Joe Zuger, was back in action. The Ticats had no desire to throw John Eckman back out against Toronto after his nightmare three weeks before.

On Hamilton's first play from scrimmage, Zuger fumbled, but offensive lineman Ellison Kelly recovered. The Ticats punted and Mike Eben returned it to the Toronto 51. On the Argos' first play, Wilkinson completed a pass to Taylor for a quick 10 yards. From there Dick Thornton lost four yards on a run and Wilkinson missed Taylor on a pass. That was the pattern for most of the first quarter, with neither offence showing much life. Ed Learn continued to be a Cat killer, picking off a Zuger pass at the Toronto 35 to stop a Hamilton drive.

Hamilton broke through in the second quarter on a 40-yard field goal by Tommy-Joe Coffey. Midway through the quarter, in an attempt to get something going, Leo ordered a fake punt. However, Dave Mann's pass intended for Mel Profit fell incomplete. That turned the ball over to Hamilton at the Toronto 45. Hamilton was then stopped cold by the Argo defence, and Coffey missed a 49-yard field goal attempt.

Late in the quarter, Cosentino replaced Wilkinson but had no more success, missing on all four of his pass attempts. At the half, Hamilton led 3-0 in a game that was close due to the outstanding play of the Toronto defence and the erratic play of Joe Zuger. He had been good on only six of 17 passes and had thrown interceptions to Allen Ray Aldridge as well as Ed Learn. For Toronto's offence, neither Wilkinson nor Cosentino had been able to move the ball through the air, and Bill Symons and Dick Thornton were having no success running the ball, either.

The Argos caught a break early in the third quarter when they recovered a fumbled punt at the Hamilton 46. Cosentino quickly threw two incompletions, but the drive stayed alive because of a pass interference call against the Ticats. Symons carried the ball to the Hamilton 28 before the Argos stalled again. Johansen then tied the score with a 35-yard field goal.

Zuger got another drive going, highlighted by a 30-yard pass to Dave Fleming, but Ron Arends stopped the drive with an interception at the Toronto 14. On second and eight, Cosentino attempted to throw deep to Jim Thorpe at the Ticat 39. Garney Henley stepped in front of Thorpe and picked off the pass. Zuger then began to move the Hamilton offence, climaxing the drive with John Manel smashing through the Toronto defence from 11 yards out for the first TD of the game. Coffey missed the convert, making the score 9-3 in favor of Hamilton.

The score came at a price for Hamilton, though, as Zuger left the field lurching from a huge hit that left him dazed and disoriented. He was finished for the day and the quarterbacking duties would now fall to young John Eckman, who had been battered by these same Argonauts only three weeks earlier.

An excellent kickoff return by Jim Tomlin started the Argos on their own 46-yard line. From there, Cosentino ran for 12 yards and Thornton ran for 10. A couple more runs moved them in closer and at the beginning of the fourth quarter, Tom Johansen kicked a 44- yard field goal to narrow the gap to 9-6.

After an exchange of punts, Cosentino threw his second interception of the game into the hands of Henley at the Hamilton 23. The boo-birds at CNE Stadium were really letting Frank have it as he jogged off the field, his head down in shame. That should have been it for the Argos, but the defence refused to collapse and in fact came up huge. At the Hamilton 36-yard line, Ed Buchanan made a costly error at a critical time. It was shades of the 1967 Grey Cup, when, as a member of the Saskatchewan Roughriders, Buchanan slipped into the open behind the Hamilton defensive coverage, only to drop a pass that Ron Lancaster put right into his hands. This time, Buchanan took a handoff from Eckman and

fumbled. Ed Harrington punched the ball out of his hands and recovered at the Ticats 41.
Leo now sent Tom Wilkinson back into the game. After Bill Symons lost two yards on a run, Wilkie hit Thornton with a slant pass for a gain of 28 yards. He moved it down to the three-yard line with a completion to Profit. Two plays later, Wilkie dived in for the score. The convert made it 13-9 and the Argos held the lead for the first time.

The Argos were now in the position they wanted to be. They had the lead with less then 10 minutes to go and could rely on their outstanding defence to preserve the victory. Dave Mann hammered two punts through the Hamilton end zone in the last couple of minutes for singles, bumping the score to 15-9. With less than thirty seconds to go, Eckman faded back from his own 25-yard line and threw deep to Garney Henley, who made a breathtaking grab at the Toronto 45. With time for one more play, Eckman threw deep once more but Learn picked it off at the Argo one-yard line to clinch the victory.

Despite a horrific game by the offence, the Argos had pulled the victory out and would now battle – who else? – Ottawa, for the chance to advance to their first Grey Cup in 17 years.

Despite the happiness over the victory, there was deep concern in Toronto about the lack of offensive punch. Jim Proudfoot, writing in the *Toronto Star,* made it clear he didn't think the Argos could beat Ottawa. "Riders, who took three straight from Argos during the EFC schedule, will be making that trip (to the Grey Cup) unless things change dramatically in Toronto. What's happening to the Boatmen is that their attack has gone pfftt. The defence has been carrying the load, as it did in yesterday's semi-final before 33,125 CNE spectators. Against Ottawa's Grey Cup titlists, winning 11 of 14 games this fall, that won't be good enough."

The Argos had not informed the media about the injuries to Wilkinson or Symons, as they didn't want opposing defenders to take extra cheap shots at either player. Linked to the concerns over the physical well-being of Wilkie was more anxiety over the play of Frank Cosentino. In the semi-final, Frank had played very poorly. The last time Frank completed at least 50 per cent of his passes had been late September

against Montreal. If he had to take over from Wilkinson, the Argos looked like they would be in deep trouble.
On the positive side, Bill Symons had bounced back from a poor first half to play well in the second and finish with 82 well-earned yards on 18 carries.

Going into the Eastern Final, the Argonauts were the unequivocal underdog. Few people gave them any chance of beating the Rough Riders, based on their regular-season record and tough struggle against Hamilton.

Leo was never one for elaborate, complicated game plans and he didn't change for this game. He felt the only way the Argonauts would beat Ottawa was by playing tough, aggressive football on defence and wearing down the Rough Riders physically. The one change he made was to go with six defensive backs to try to shut down the Ottawa air attack. If the Toronto offence could just get a couple of touchdowns, Leo and the rest of the Argo coaching staff felt the team would be in good shape.

November 16, 1969, was a cloudy day in Toronto with temperatures sitting at an unseasonable high of 42 degrees F. CNE Stadium was packed with Argo fans who were hopeful, yet clearly nervous.

The game started off badly for the Argonauts. Bill Symons returned the opening kickoff to the Toronto 29. Dickie Moore picked up a yard off tackle and Wilkinson then missed Jim Thorpe on a pass. A Dave Mann punt pushed Ottawa back to its own 39-yard line. On Ottawa's first play from scrimmage, the Argos were penalized 15 yards for unnecessary roughness and Leo winced. You simply could not take penalties like that against the Rough Riders. You had to be aggressive, but not dumb.

Russ Jackson took full advantage, moving his offence down the field and at the Toronto three-yard line, Jackson ran a bootleg around right end for an easy touchdown.

Things got worse right afterwards. After an exchange of punts, the Argos were backed up inside their own 10-yard line. Mann punted from deep in his own end zone to the Toronto 32. A couple of running plays and another unnecessary roughness call against the Toronto defence moved the ball to the eight. But the proud Toronto defence dug in; the players were determined not to allow a touchdown here.

An Ottawa running play netted three yards. Then Marv Luster, the magnificent safety and defensive captain, figuring Jackson would be passing, called a blitz. Jackson dropped back to throw and Mike Blum exploded in from his linebacker spot to bury him back at the 14-yard line. Don Sutherin came in and kicked a field goal to make the score 10-0, but the aggressive play of Blum had saved a potential touchdown and kept Toronto close early.

The Argo offence continued to sputter and go nowhere. Jackson moved the Rough Riders back into Toronto territory and they had a first down at the Argo five. Yet once again the defence slammed the door. Dave Knechtel, who missed much of the regular season with a broken leg, charged in from his tackle position to plaster Wayne Giardino for a four-yard loss. A Jackson pass then went incomplete in the end zone due to the tight coverage by Dick Thornton and Jim Tomlin. Sutherin came on again but missed a 22-yard field-goal attempt, instead picking up a single point to make it 11-0.

Even though the offence was not moving the ball, the defence was keeping Toronto in the game. By all rights, the Argos should be down 21-0 but instead they were trailing by only 11.

In the second quarter, the defence took matters further into its own hands. With Ottawa backed up to its own four, Wayne Giardino was stopped dead in his tracks by Luster. Then Jackson dropped back to throw. Knechtel and Walt Balasiuk smashed through the Rough Rider protection, slamming Jackson to the turf in the end zone for a two-point safety touch. The sack was aided once again by air-tight Toronto pass coverage that left no Ottawa receiver uncovered.

Toronto then got another break. On the next offensive possession, a Wilkinson pass intended for Bobby Taylor was intercepted by Bill Van Burkleo at the Argonaut 43-yard line. After an incomplete pass, Jackson linked up with Whit Tucker, who broke away from the coverage and was sprinting for the end zone when he lost control of the ball and fumbled it away at the Toronto 15-yard line. Marv Luster, who was in hot pursuit, hurled himself on top of the ball. The Rough Riders seemed stunned at this bizarre, unforced fumble. To make matters worse for the Riders, they got hit with an unnecessary-roughness penalty on the same play, moving the ball up to the Toronto 31-yard line.

Bill Symons took a handoff and blasted his way through the defence for 14 yards. Wilkinson then hit his old reliable receiver, Bobby Taylor, for a gain of 19. Taylor took a brutal hit on the play, which *Toronto Telegram* reporter Jim Coleman described well: "Taylor caught a pass from Wilkinson for a 19-yard gain and as he caught the ball, Taylor was rammed squarely on the sternum by Gerry Campbell. It was a rocket shot! Taylor was hit so hard that the air from his chest squirted through the ear holes of his helmet."

CNE Stadium grew very quiet after the hit as Bobby stood up, took a couple of steps and collapsed. Argos trainer Stan Wilson and the team doctor bolted onto the field to aid Taylor. After some tense moments, the veteran receiver got up and was able to walk off the field on his own.

A bomb into the end zone went incomplete, but Ottawa got nailed for pass interference, giving Toronto a first down on the Rough Rider 10-yard line. From there, Wilkie coolly dropped back and hit Taylor – who had quickly recovered and was back in the game – in the end zone for a major. The convert made the score 11-9 in favour of Ottawa at the end of the first half.

At halftime the Argos felt a strong sense of confidence. They had weathered the storm early on and had given up only 11 points to the mighty Ottawa offence. The Tucker fumble was something that used to happen to the Boatmen when they played Ottawa. Now the luck seemed to have reversed. In the minds of the Argos, they were destined to win.

On Toronto's second possession of the second half, they got rolling. Wilkinson hit Mel Profit with a quick strike and as Mel was going down he lateralled to Taylor. Bobby was nailed after a 23-yard gain to the Ottawa 44. From there, Symons exploded up the middle for 40 yards to set the Argos up at the Ottawa four. Dickie Moore picked up a hard two yards and then Wilkinson hit Taylor with a flip pass for the score. Tom Johansen missed the convert and the score was now 15-11 for Toronto. The Toronto defence took control and put Jackson under constant pressure from the front four of Knechtel, Harrington, Balasiuk and Wadsworth. The quarterback had no time to set up and throw, and the pass defenders were giving him no open targets and hammering Ottawa receivers any time they ventured into coverage. In the third quarter, both Jim Tomlin and Ed Learn intercepted Jackson passes, and for the first time in memory Russ Jackson looked somewhat rattled.

The Argos added a single early in the fourth quarter on a missed 45-yard field-goal attempt by Johansen to make the score 16-11. Ottawa managed a field goal to make it close, but then seemed to lose all heart on the ensuing possession. Jackson was buried by an Argo blitz and staggered off the field with blood streaming from his face. The sellout crowd stood and roared as Jackson left the field, battered and defeated. As the clock wound down, Wilkinson marched the Argos from their own 28 down to the Ottawa eight where he scampered around right end for the score. Johansen again missed the convert and the score was now 22-14 in favour of the Double Blue. That was it for the scoring. Ottawa left the field physically beaten up and losers in all facets of the game.

Bill Symons led all rushers with 100 punishing yards on 13 carries. Wilkie completed 10 of 21 for 168 yards, two touchdowns and two interceptions. Not great stats on paper, but he got the job done – bad shoulders and all. For Ottawa, Wayne Giardino picked up 93 yards rushing but took a ferocious beating. The passing game was also a nightmare for the Rough Riders. Jackson was good on only six of 22 attempts for 100 yards, no touchdowns and two interceptions. Even more shocking, he did not complete a single pass to an Ottawa receiver in the entire second half.

The Argonauts appeared to have done it. The Toronto media declared the "Jackson Jinx" dead. Ottawa had been so physically mauled by Leo's rampaging Argos that there was doubt all over the CFL whether the Rough Riders would even be able to field a complete lineup for the second game the following Saturday.

"A Slip in the Rain"

It was a confident Argonauts squad that went through practice that week. Destiny was in their own hands and they had no doubts that they would be heading to Montreal to play for the Grey Cup.
In mid-week, Leo spoke to the Argo Playback Club. His comments appeared in sports pages across Canada and have since become the stuff of legend. "It will take an act of God to beat us on Saturday," he declared.
Leo later explained that he meant the Argos would only be stopped by a major storm or some other calamity beyond the control of mere mortals. Still, the words weren't entirely innocent. Cahill had the utmost respect for the Rough Riders, but he also supreme confidence in his own squad.

Argo players had mixed reactions. "That was just Leo," says Mike Eben. "He never knew when to shut up." Bill Symons, however, was disturbed. "I always believe you should let sleeping dogs lie," he says.

Near the end of the week, as the Argos headed to a very cold Ottawa, the papers were still full of stories about Leo's "act of God" statement. Would it fire up the opponent? That was the question on the minds of football fans across the country.

The temperatures for the first game in Toronto had been very moderate, but that would not be the case for the second. A cold snap had hit the national capital and the temperature was well below freezing. During their workout the day before the game, Argo players became horrified at the shape of the field at Lansdowne Park. They had no traction and were sliding all over the frozen, pitted turf. After practice Dick Thornton spoke to both Leo and the equipment managers and emphasized the need to ensure that players had the right shoes for the game.

But there were no magical shoes waiting for the Argonauts when they got to the stadium on game day. The Argos headed out on the field for the pre-game warmup and their spirits dropped. The field was mostly frozen, with patches of snow and mud. "God, it was awful," remembers Pete Martin. "Leo made us sit on the field for our stretches, and the cold, wet field just froze your balls." Jim Tomlin added: "It was colder than a mummy's nuts out there that day."

Russ Jackson had announced late in the season that 1969 would be his final year, so this would be his final appearance as a player at Lansdowne Park. The club held a ceremony honouring him before the game. As players on both sides watched the festivities, the cold seeped ever deeper into their bones.

The Argos were freezing, but more importantly they were increasingly frantic over the lack of traction on the field. Some of them tried long cleats, hoping they would dig into the frozen turf. Others such as Mel Profit put on canvas gym shoes, figuring the flat sole would give them the most surface contact and better footing.

Ottawa, meanwhile, gave up entirely on the idea of cleats. The Riders went with broomball shoes. Broomball is played on ice and the shoes have tiny suction cups on the soles. These shoes were designed to give the best possible traction on ice and would more than likely be the best possible choice on this type of field.

The game started with Ottawa kicking off. Jim Tomlin scrambled to the Toronto 28 with the return. Tom Wilkinson handed off to Bill Symons, who slipped and slid for three yards. On the next play, Symons was thrown for a four-yard loss.

On Toronto's second possession with the game still scoreless, Wilkinson had a pass intercepted and Ottawa took over at the Argos' 48-yard line. Any hope Toronto had of winning seemed to end on this possession. Ottawa moved with stunning ease as their broomball shoes gripped the icy tundra. It took them just four plays to move down field. Jackson handed off to Wayne Giardino, who roared around the right side and into the end zone for the touchdown. The convert pulled Ottawa to within a point on the two-game, total-points scoreboard.

On the sidelines, Leo felt sick. "I could see their running backs going wide on sweeps and our linebackers pursuing them. When the runners cut back inside, our linebackers just kept going towards the sidelines. They couldn't stop."

The Argos went two and out on their next possession, a sense of horror creeping into their hearts and minds. They had no traction on the field and without it, they simply could not perform on either offence or defence. The Rough Riders were having no such problems. After the punt, Ottawa was on the move again. It took over on the Toronto 43 and Jackson promptly hit Whit Tucker with a laser beam of a pass. Tucker was open as the Argo pass defender had slipped on the icy field. Tucker was tackled by Mike Blum and Jim Tomlin at the Argo three. On first down, Jackson tried to run it in himself but was nailed by Pete Martin for a loss of four yards. A Jackson pass for Margene Adkins went incomplete and Don Sutherin came in and kicked a field goal. Ottawa was now ahead 10-0 in the game and 24-22 in total points.

The next Toronto drive went nowhere and Mann punted it away again. This time, Jackson marched Ottawa down field before a Sutherin field goal fell short. It was only a short reprieve for the Argonauts, however. Early in the second quarter, Ottawa was back and it was Giardino crashing his way into the Toronto end zone from a yard out.

Frustration was mounting on the Argo sidelines and in the huddle. The great Ottawa receivers were just blowing by the slipping and sliding defensive backs. The linemen and linebackers were no better off. They could not dig in and get any sort of pass rush going or pursue a runner. Offensively, the situation was nothing short of hopeless. Bill Symons could not get enough traction to run the ball. The offensive linemen were being blasted off their feet by the sure-footed Ottawa defensive line, which poured in on Tom Wilkinson, giving him no chance to throw.

Ottawa picked up a single at the end of the half when a Sutherin field goal from 28 yards out sailed wide. Mike Eben made a desperate attempt to run the ball out of the end zone, but was easily run down and tackled. At halftime, Ottawa was ahead 18-0 in the game and 32-22 on total points.

In the dressing room, Leo did his best to calm the players. He emphasized that while they were getting their asses handed to them in this game, on total points they were trailing by just 10. They still had a real shot at winning.

The second half opened with Toronto kicking off. After a two-yard gain on the first play, Jackson dropped back to pass. Dave Knechtel stormed in from his defensive tackle position and knocked the pass down at the line, forcing a punt to the Toronto 51-yard line. From there, Wilkinson put together a short drive that ended in a 43-yard field goal by Tom Johansen. It cut the Ottawa lead to 18-3 and 32-25 on total points.

A feeling of hope passed over the Argo bench. Even though they had been playing terribly and were struggling against the elements, they were down by only a touchdown in the series. They were back in the game!

The optimism didn't last long. After an exchange of punts, Ottawa moved the ball again; the big play a 19-yard pass-and-run from Jackson to Adkins. The drive finished off with Giardino leaping over centre and into the end zone for a touchdown, moving Ottawa ahead on points 39-25.

At the end of the third quarter, Ottawa capped off another drive with Ronnie Stewart busting his way in to score from six yards out. It was now 31-3 and 46-25 on total points. Though there was still a quarter to go, the Argos were long gone.

They showed a brief spark of life midway through the final quarter when Mel Profit recovered a fumbled punt at the Toronto 40-yard line. Wilkinson dropped back to pass, then tucked the ball under his arm and scrambled up the middle for 17 yards. He then hit Profit with a seven-yard pass but another incompletion and a loss of 11 yards on a sack turned the ball back over to the Rough Riders. Ottawa ended this drive with a single as Bill Van Burkleo punted into the Argo end zone.

The scoring for the day was over. Just before the end, Leo sent Frank Cosentino into the game at quarterback. Frank had no more success than Wilkinson did, and the clock ran out on the 1969 season for the Toronto Argonauts. The final score was 32-3 in the game and 46-25 in the two-game, total-points series.

Ottawa would now move on to Montreal where the following week in the Grey Cup, the Rough Riders thumped the Saskatchewan Roughriders 29-11 in the final game of Russ Jackson's magnificent career.

The Argos headed home shattered, angry and embarrassed. Dick Thornton is still upset more than 30 years later when he looks back on that game. "That 'act of God' statement was just another in a long line of Cahill classics. But it actually was sort of an act of God – plus the tightwad management of the Argos who wouldn't spend the money to get us the proper footwear." Mike Eben concurs. "The team didn't feel the investment of around $1,000 in shoes would pay off."

Leo indignantly denies that the Argos were too cheap to buy proper footwear. "Absolutely not. I had the freedom to spend whatever I thought was necessary in order to help the team win. If John Bassett thought it would have won the game, he would have bought high-top boots or whatever for the entire team. It was probably our not looking into the weather reports that hurt us more than anything. In fact, I think we tried to get broomball shoes once we got to Ottawa and there were none available. The Rough Riders had bought the entire supply.

"And as far as the 'act of God' statement goes, I'm from Illinois and we used that comment to mean something like a snowstorm or tornado. It was a tragedy that happened as we were good enough to beat them that year."

In the *Toronto Star*, Leo's response to the debacle was to blame the team, not the elements or the shoes: "We bumbled. We waited until the last game of the year to play our worst game of the year. We didn't belong on the field with them, and we're going to have to live with that all winter."

From a statistical point of view, the game was as ugly as the final score. Symons carried six times for seven yards. Moore rushed for six yards on five carries. Wayne Giardino led all Ottawa ball carriers with 62 yards on 19 carries, with three touchdowns. Through the air, Wilkinson completed 10 of 19 for 62 yards and two interceptions and was sacked seven times. Jackson was good on 14 of 23 for 260 yards. The most telling statistic was this. The Argonauts, the CFL's highest-scoring team in 1969, had a grand total of 32 yards in offence and only six first downs.

At the team's end-of-season party, while the booze flowed, Leo and Pete Martin had a heart-to-heart chat. They agreed that while the year had

ended on a dismal note, overall it had been a positive season and the team had made great strides towards getting to the Grey Cup. Pete looks back and laughs at Leo's reaction to one comment he made.
"I said to Leo, 'Do you know when we really became a team? It was when we held out at camp for a week and nobody broke ranks' Leo's eyes nearly bugged out when I said that. However, that is when we all knew we would stick together and stand up for each other. Leo smiled at that and simply said, 'You are right.' "

Older Argo fans found something other than just the end result very disturbing. Nineteen years before, during the "Mud Bowl" Grey Cup of 1950, it was the Argonauts who had come up with the right footwear that allowed them to overcome the elements and win. Now the opposite had occurred.

Since Leo Cahill had taken over the team in 1967, he had built a truly outstanding squad that had managed to stay ahead of the black cloud that had been chasing the franchise since 1953. But now it seemed to have descended on the team with a vengeance. It remained to be seen whether Leo and his team could bounce back from this most frustrating of seasons.

Six

1970

Planning for the 1970 season, Leo and the Argos could take comfort in knowing that they would never have to face Russ Jackson again. That fact alone seemed to make them conference favourites for the upcoming season.

Leo received some unexpected surprises in the early winter months of 1970. Defensive back Jimmy Dye retired to take a position as an assistant coach with the University of Miami, and veteran Ed Learn hung up his cleats at the age of 35. Frank Cosentino also announced his retirement from football after being offered the head-coaching job along with a position on the teaching faculty at the University of Western Ontario. It was an opportunity he could not turn down. Leo would have to find another quarterback to back up Tom Wilkinson.

He dipped into his bag of tricks and signed Don Jonas, the No. 1-ranked quarterback in the Continental Football League. Jonas had been an outstanding college pivot at Penn State but was considered too small for the NFL so had been relegated to the semi-pro Continental League, which he had shredded. He could also handle place-kicking duties. Dave Mann was a fine punter but had always been erratic at place-kicking, while Tom Johansen had not shown himself to be the answer.

Leo also had his eye on one of the biggest names in U.S. college football. Jim Corrigall was an enormous linebacker at Kent State University in Ohio (which would become infamous due to the National Guard shootings on campus there in May 1970) and was considered one of the finest players in the history of that school. He could also play defensive end and had even played some fullback.

More important to Toronto was the fact that Corrigall was a Canadian citizen. He had been born and raised in Barrie, Ontario, north of Toronto, before heading to Kent State on a scholarship. The thought of adding a Canadian with such incredible credentials made

Cahill almost salivate. Leo faced a challenge, though. The St. Louis Cardinals had picked Corrigall in the second round of the NFL draft, making him the highest-drafted Canadian ever to that point. They were looking at Jim to be the future kingpin of their defence. The Argos also knew they could build their defence for the next decade or so around Corrigall, so negotiated hard to persuade him to come home. Finally, as Leo describes it, Jim was taken over to the *Toronto Telegram* corporate offices where team owner John Bassett stepped in to clinch the deal.

"Bassett got up and proceeded to stride back and forth with his thumbs in his belt. All the time he was talking. 'Now, Mr. Corrigall,' he began. 'This is what we have to offer you.' In his special way, you know. Forceful. Splendid. This big kid from Barrie was sitting on a chair. 'I'm not going to have you say anything,' Bassett told him. 'You just listen to what I have to say.' He stopped at the Bobby Kennedy picture from time to time. He talked for half an hour. I could tell he thought he was just overwhelming the guy. At the end he said, 'Now, Mr. Corrigall, what do you have to say?'

"Corrigall stretched out his legs with those size 13s so that his neck was just about resting on the back of the chair, his heels on the floor, and said, 'Well, Mr. Bassett, I'm not too impressed.' The look Bassett gave back! He didn't know whether to go to the bathroom or wind his watch."

The surprisingly tough negotiator went back to Kent State, and the talk around town was that he was going to sign with St. Louis. But he agreed to come back to Toronto for one more negotiation session. At that meeting, the Argonauts offered him a much better deal, one that would make him the highest-paid Canadian in CFL history. When Corrigall expressed concern over the CFL players' pension, Bassett designed a deal where Jim would begin receiving retirement funds from the Argonauts starting at age 42, above and beyond any pension funds from the CFL. This clinched the pact and Jim "Country" Corrigall became a Toronto Argonaut.

Leo had another deal up his sleeve, and this was a beauty. He was concerned that Mike Eben had seen little playing time at flanker since joining the team in 1968. He had simply been unable to push Bobby Taylor out of his role. Mike was not going to develop if he didn't play and yet Taylor at this point was a more valuable receiver. Leo, never one to simply look at traditional solutions, glanced around the league for someone to help him out. He knew the Edmonton Eskimos were short in the receiving area. He called general manager Norm Kimball and offered Eben in exchange for "future considerations." Those considerations were that he would return to the Argonauts for the 1971 season after getting a full year of playing time in Alberta.

Kimball, trying to shore up his receiving corps for the 1970 season, accepted the unconventional deal. The fact that Eben would return to Toronto the following season was not announced to the public, though, for fear the league might veto the deal.

Training camp was its normal drudgery for the players, but there was one funny moment – at least it was funny if you were not the player involved. Dick Thornton recounts it: "Bobby Taylor chased Larry Watkins with a rubber snake and Larry ran through a plate-glass window on the fire escape door and put 70 stitches in his arm. He was out for a month. It was a funny moment but turned out not so funny in the end."

Randy Beatty adds: "It was well known that Larry was terrified of snakes. He was really badly hurt."

The Argos came out of training camp and the exhibition season looking and feeling like the team to beat in the Eastern Conference, but first Leo had to resolve another quarterbacking dilemma. Both Tom Wilkinson and Don Jonas had looked very sharp in preseason. Who should be No. 1?

Leo initially planned to use Jonas as the starter, but then he came up with the bold – and entirely unconventional – idea of using them both regularly.

The Argos opened the 1970 season in Montreal. The Alouettes had made big news around the league when they had signed free-agent wide receiver Terry Evanshen away from the Calgary Stampeders. The Denver Broncos of the NFL (the AFL and NFL by this time had merged) offered Terry a huge contract in an effort to reunite him with Peter Liske, but Montreal came up with more loot and Evanshen jumped at the chance to play in his home town. He would give quarterback Sonny Wade a great target to throw to and the Als also had a new head coach: Sam "The Rifle" Etcheverry, the pre-eminent passer of the 1950s. Fans were hoping he would help restore the Alouettes to their days of glory.

Toronto jumped in front on a 39-yard field goal by Jonas. In the second quarter, Montreal picked up two quick touchdowns, one on a Wade-to-Evanshen pass play. Trailing 14-3, Wilkinson hit Bobby Taylor with a nine-yard TD strike to close the gap and before the first half ended, Wade scored on a one-yard plunge to make it 21-10.

The scoring continued through the second half. Wade picked up his third touchdown of the game and threw another scoring strike to Evanshen. Don Jonas, who entered the game in the second half at quarterback for Toronto, threw TD strikes to rookie tight end Tony Moro and Bobby Taylor, but it was not enough. The Alouettes won the game 34-27.

Bill Symons led all rushers with 57 yards on eight carries while Dave Raimey added 44 yards on nine carries. Wilkinson was good on seven of 10 for 77 yards and a touchdown. Jonas completed 10 of 20 for two touchdowns but had two interceptions. On the defensive side of the ball, Dick Thornton picked up where he left off in 1969, intercepting a Sonny Wade pass when Wade made the mistake of throwing into "Tricky Dick's" defensive zone of coverage.

The loss to Montreal was completely unexpected, as the Alouettes had been pushovers since Leo took over the Argos in 1967. This made the following game against Hamilton very important. A loss to the Tiger-Cats would drop Toronto to 0-2 and make the rest of the season an uphill battle.

CNE Stadium was packed for the home opener against Hamilton. With Don Jonas starting at QB, the Argos jumped out 2-0 on two singles off booming Dave Mann punts. They then stretched the lead when Dave Raimey went streaking out of the backfield and gathered in a 60-yard bomb from Jonas and took it all the way. Jonas then hit newcomer Tommy Bland (who had been a teammate of Jonas in the Continental League) with an 11-yard strike for a major to increase the lead to 15-0.

The Ticats fought back with a single and safety before Toronto struck again. Despite the early success, Leo put Tom Wilkinson in at quarterback and he linked up with Tony Moro on a 62-yard passing play for a touchdown. In the fourth quarter, with Jonas back in under centre and Thornton in at wide receiver, the Argos put the final nail in Hamilton's coffin. Jonas hit Thornton with a 44-yard bullet for a touchdown. That made the final score 29-3 for the Argonauts.

The only way to describe Toronto in this game was devastatingly effective, as they dismantled a strong Hamilton squad. Jonas was outstanding, completing 10 of 18 for three touchdowns and two interceptions. Wilkinson was also solid, completing six of eight for 138 yards, a touchdown and an interception. Bill Symons again led the way along the ground with 88 yards on 19 carries. The Argo defence was also brilliant. Joe Zuger was held to 138 yards passing on 11 completions. Both Marv Luster and Mike Blum picked off Zuger passes. Dick Aldridge recovered a Ticat fumble and Hamilton's running attack was stopped dead, gaining only 69 yards on 24 carries.

Next on the schedule were the Edmonton Eskimos, who would be invading CNE Stadium and bringing Mike Eben with them. Before yet another sellout crowd, the Argos struck first when Tom Bland took a 12-yard pass from Don Jonas in for the score. In the second quarter, Tom Wilkinson fired a 10-yard strike to Jim Thorpe for a major to send the Argos into halftime with a 15-7 lead. In the second half, neither QB could generate any offence aside from a single off a missed 39-yard field-goal attempt by Jonas. Edmonton quarterback Don Trull made things close with a one-yard plunge for a touchdown late in the game but the Argo defence held for a 16-14 Toronto victory.

Neither Wilkinson nor Jonas looked sharp in this one. Wilkie was good on six of 11 for 64 yards, with a touchdown and an interception. Jonas went six for 12 for 110 yards and one touchdown. Bill Symons carried the load on the ground, picking up 73 tough yards on 15 carries. The Toronto defence was again outstanding, holding the Esks to only 55 yards along the ground although Mike Eben, facing his old teammates for the first time, caught four passes for 68 yards.

The next game prompted interest all around the league. The Argos would be heading to Winnipeg to face Wally Gabler for the first time since the Gabler/Raimey deal the previous season. How would Wally and Dave play against their former teammates? Looking back, Wally remembers: "Before a game Leo would always go through the opposition, player by player, and would make a comment about each of them. One year Hamilton had a new DB named Teddy Page who was rather short. Leo, when he came to him said, 'This guy is so short he would have to stand on two bricks to kick a duck in the ass.' The dressing room was in hysterics. Anyway, Mel Profit told me that when Leo was going over the Blue Bomber team before this game, when he came to me he stopped. He didn't say anything. The room was silent. Leo then says, 'Well, what can you say about a guy who wears pyjamas to bed on a road trip?' (My wife always packed my pyjamas before I left on road trips.) The room just cracked up."

The Argos got on the scoreboard first when Don Jonas missed a 35-yard field goal that went for a single, but the Bombers came right back with two quick majors on runs by Bob Houmard after long drives engineered by Wally to open a 14-1 lead. Bill Symons closed the gap with an eight-yard run for a touchdown and in the third quarter Symons smashed his way into the end zone from a yard out to put the Argos ahead 15-14. Early in the fourth quarter, Jonas hit Mel Profit with a 15-yard touchdown strike to increase the Toronto lead to 22-14, but Winnipeg came right back with Houmard scoring his third TD of the game on a two-yard plunge. Then, as all-star receiver Ken Neilsen and Dick Thornton were running downfield side by side, Thornton suddenly fell. Gabler hit Neilsen with a 40-yard bomb with less then a minute to go for the winning touchdown. The final score was 28-22 for the Blue Bombers.

Jack Matheson, sports editor of the *Winnipeg Tribune,* wrote an article on the Argos for the game program. It read in part: "Don't let it get around, but I hear the Argonauts are going to win the Grey Cup. I keep reading it in all the Toronto papers. If you don't believe the great communicators, ask the Argos themselves. They're supposed to be the team of the century. Some say they will place 24 men on the all-Canadian team this year. Well, they have quite a few good football players, but they have no tradition. Most of their players were banished by other teams though their long-suffering fans find something romantic in this stormy band of football misfits, but romance isn't enough."

Wally finally got his revenge against the Argos. He completed 10 of 15 passes for 180 yards and the touchdown bomb to Neilsen. Jonas was good on nine of 17 for 118 yards, one touchdown and a pick. Wilkinson looked sharper, hitting nine of 10 passes for 130 yards and an interception. Along the ground, Raimey carried the ball only four times but picked up 36 yards. Symons added 71 yards on 14 carries and Thornton went in for a play at running back and picked up 19 yards.

Unfortunately for Toronto, Tricky Dick was lost to injury in this game. While covering Neilsen on the final touchdown play, his right knee simply went out. Dick would be out of the lineup while his knee was surgically repaired.

The Argo team doctors, with Thornton's consent, decided on a revolutionary new procedure called arthroscopic surgery. Instead of opening the entire knee and thereby costing Dick the entire season, they would make a small incision in the kneecap, go in with a camera, or "scope," and repair the damage that way. If the surgery proved to be successful, Dick would in all likelihood be back in the lineup before the season was over.

The Argos continued their journey west with a stop in Regina and a date against the always tough Saskatchewan Roughriders. The Roughriders were Grey Cup finalists the previous year and most observers felt they would be representing the Western Conference in the title game in 1970.

The game was not one Toronto would like to remember. Ron Lancaster was unstoppable, completing 11 of 19 passes for 234 yards and three touchdowns. The Green Riders blasted the Toronto defence for 195 yards along the ground as well. In comparison, Jonas hit Jim Thorpe with a 56-yard TD pass but was only good on nine of 20 passes and threw three interceptions. Wilkie was also erratic, completing six of 13. Neither Dave Raimey nor Bill Symons had any success along the ground as Regina blew the Argos out of Taylor Field 36-14.

"A Slip in the Rain"

Leo Cahill was livid over the results of the last two games. His defence, which was supposed to be among the top two in the CFL, had been hammered for 64 points, and although the offence had looked sharp in Winnipeg, it had been ghastly in Regina. Going into the season, Cahill had not expected to be sitting at 2-3 five games into the season.

The players could see several reasons for the Argos' lack of success. Bobby Taylor had been hurt in the first game and was in and out of the lineup. Others like Mel Profit were battling nagging injuries that were cutting down their effectiveness. Thornton was out with a bum knee. The players also had some concerns over Leo's coaching. They were frustrated over his constant switching between Jonas and Wilkinson, which meant neither quarterback was able to get into a rhythm. Most of the players felt both Jonas and Wilkinson were capable quarterbacks. "Just give one of them the job and leave him in there" was the prevailing attitude.

Another source of friction was Leo's use of Jim Corrigall. "Country" was most comfortable at middle linebacker but Leo was happy with Pete Martin in that role. The coach was using Jim at defensive end and he was struggling, although trying constantly to improve.

The Argos now went staggering into Lansdowne Park for their first battle with Ottawa since Russ Jackson retired. Leo, trying to get the Boatmen back on an even keel, decided Don Jonas would start and finish the game. The game was notable for a couple of reasons. One was the play of both Symons and Raimey. Sy scored four touchdowns, three on the ground (while grinding out 83 yards on 14 carries) and one on a five-yard pass from Jonas. Raimey, meanwhile, rushed for an incredible 175 yards on 18 carries. Jonas also looked sharp, completing 17 of 32 passes for 288 yards, two TDs and two interceptions.

Ed Harrington was the other big story of the game. Early in the game, Gary Wood, who had replaced Russ Jackson at quarterback, ran a pitchout to the right. Harrington charged in and levelled him with a forearm smash to the head. Wood went down as if he had been shot (he was, in fact, knocked unconscious by the blow) and Harrington was ejected. League commissioner Jake Gaudaur suspended Harrington for the following game as well.

Amidst all the anger and angst over the Harrington hit, the Argos won the game 37-21 to even their record at 3-3. The two teams would resume their rivalry at CNE Stadium the following week.

The Argonauts came up with another big effort in the rematch and knocked off Ottawa once again, this time 30-25. Jonas was the main man at QB once again, completing 12 of 19 passes for 157 yards, a TD to Jim Thorpe and two interceptions. (Jonas, like Wally Gabler before him, really struggled with interceptions.) Tom Wilkinson made a brief appearance late in the game. Bill Symons turned in another strong game, rushing for 116 yards on 18 carries. Dave Raimey added 86 yards on 15 carries and scored a touchdown. Don Sutherin, whom Leo had picked up from Ottawa, showed he was not washed up when he intercepted a Gary Wood pass and returned it 11 yards for a major. Wood had a terrible game, throwing five interceptions in total, with Sutherin and Dick Aldridge each snatching two and Ron Arends adding another.

Even though the Argo had won to raise their record to 4-3, the big news was not the score. When the game was over, the Argos held a brief ceremony on the field. Ed Harrington, who did not play due to his suspension, was called out of the stands by Leo and awarded the game ball. Some of the Argonauts players were stunned by this move. More than 30 years later, Pete Martin still cannot believe what Leo did.

"Ed was a real Jekyll and Hyde character. Off the field he was kind and quite gentle. On the field he was as mean as could be. That hit on Wood was an incredible cheap shot. The following week, we play Ottawa again, without Ed, and play our asses off to beat them. When the game is over, Leo calls him out of the stands and gives him the game ball, while we – the guys who played and won the game – stand there looking like idiots. In eight years of playing pro ball, I won three game balls, which shows you how hard it is to get one. I don't know what Leo was trying to prove there, when he did that."

The Argos then played host to the Montreal Alouettes, hoping to build on their two-game winning streak. Montreal quickly jumped out front with a field goal five minutes into the game. The Argos then took the lead on a spectacular play 22 seconds later. Don Jonas took the snap and flipped the ball to Mel Profit, who was behind the line of scrimmage. Profit unloaded a bomb that sailed into the arms of Jim Thorpe streaking down field. Thorpe hauled the pass in and scored on a play that covered 75 yards.

The Argo offence then stalled, and by the fourth quarter Montreal was ahead 16-7. Jonas kicked a field goal to close the gap to 16-10 before Montreal scored another major. With less then three minutes to go, Jonas hit Thorpe with a 19-yard touchdown pass, but that was as close as the Double Blue would get. The final score was 24-17 for Montreal. Jonas struggled in this outing, completing only 14 of 30 passes for 199 yards, and throwing three interceptions. Sonny Wade, in comparison, blew apart the Toronto secondary by throwing for 307 yards on 17 completions. The Toronto running attack was cold as well, with Raimey leading the way with 64 yards on six carries.

Figure 6-1: *"Mel Profit hauls in a pass against Montreal in 1970."*

"A Slip in the Rain"

So the Argos, the team picked by all the experts to go to the 1970 Grey Cup, were back at .500 with a record of 4-4. They now headed into Calgary to battle the Stampeders, who were also struggling, much to the surprise of many observers.

Calgary found playing Toronto might be a good way to turn their fortunes around. In what may have been the worst performance to date by an Argonauts team coached by Leo Cahill, Calgary thumped Toronto 27-12, and the score flattered the Argos. Calgary got on the board early in the second quarter on a yard run by Hugh McKinnis to open up a 7-0 lead. Shortly after, quarterback Jerry Keeling, hit slotback Dave Cranmer with a 13-yard scoring strike and before the half ended, Larry Robinson added a 33-yard field goal for a 17-0 lead. It increased when Jerry Keeling dived into the Argonaut end zone from a yard out in the third quarter. Halfway through the fourth, Calgary was up 27-0. The Argos looked confused and uncertain on the field until Jonas, who was playing poorly, finally got a drive going and scored a touchdown on a three-yard run. With five seconds left in the game, Jonas hit Dave Raimey with a 26-yard TD strike to make the final more respectable.

Jonas had now played two poor games in a row. Against Calgary, he had completed 13 of 29 passes and thrown three interceptions. The running attack was once again a failure, with Raimey picking up 36 yards on nine carries and Symons adding only 11 yards to his totals. The one bright spot for Toronto was that Dick Thornton was back in the lineup and Tricky Dick picked off a Keeling pass to mark his return. The revolutionary arthroscopic surgery had been a success, and although heavily taped, Thornton was back at cornerback after missing only four games.

When the Argos got back to Toronto, Leo was summoned to appear before the Argonauts board of directors. There was talk around the city that the debacle in Calgary would result in Cahill being fired. Leo was in a tight spot here. For his first three seasons, he could argue with credibility that the team was improving and that they had lost in the playoffs to better teams. But that explanation wouldn't hold up to scrutiny this year. The 1970 Argos seemed to be a very talented group of under-achievers.

It was at least partly Leo's fault. His switching back and forth between Don Jonas and Tom Wilkinson had clearly hurt the offence at the beginning of the season. Now, even though he seemed to be sticking with Jonas at pivot, people were still questioning his judgment due to Don's erratic play.

There were other factors as well. The retirements of Ed Learn and Jimmy Dye had cost the team two solid, well-respected veterans. Injuries also had not helped. Losing Bobby Taylor and Dick Thornton had hurt the Argos badly. Thornton was back now but Taylor, after making a brief attempt to return, was out for the year.

The meeting with the board did not go well for Leo. In particular John Bassett, Sr., and Len Lumbers, Sr., tore a strip off Leo's hide for the play of the team. They demanded that Jonas and Wilkinson be released. Leo listened and then responded, "Well, evidently you want to run the football team and make the decisions on this football team. If you do, then fire me. But if I'm going to run the football team, I'll tell you what we are going to do – we're not going to make any changes at all. Because that is not my style and that's not what I've done in the past and we're not going to panic." The board listened to Leo and gave him a reprieve. His job was safe for now, but he had better start winning and fast.

The Hamilton Tiger-Cats, who were sitting on top of the Eastern Conference, came into CNE Stadium next, brimming with confidence. Making things even more interesting, the Ticats had traded for Wally Gabler and he would be making his first appearance in Toronto since his trade to Winnipeg. Knowing he was going into what was perhaps the most important game of his coaching career, Leo whipped his team into a frenzy.

He figured Don Jonas had had a fair chance to see what he could do, so he went back to old reliable Tom Wilkinson as the starting quarterback. Wilkie got the team moving quickly. He marched the offence down the field and then ran three yards into the end zone. Before the half ended, he led Toronto to another seven points on two field goals by Jonas and a single on a 64-yard punt by Dave Mann.

In the second half, Bill Symons electrified the home crowd. Wilkinson had been shaken up and replaced at QB by Jonas again. He handed off to Bill at the Toronto 12-yard line and, in a play reminiscent of his magnificent 100-yard run in the 1968 Semi-Final against Hamilton, Symons exploded through a gaping hole opened by his offensive line and raced untouched 98 yards for a touchdown. The crowd noise was so loud, CNE Stadium was almost shaking. Less than two minutes later, Jonas hit Tom Bland with a 17-yard scoring strike to increase the lead to 26-0. Hamilton showed some life early in the fourth quarter, scoring a major. But Toronto came back with a 68-yard pass-and-run play from Jonas to Jim Henderson, a solid Canadian wide receiver, for another touchdown. The final score was an impressive 33-14 victory for Toronto.

Figure 6-2: *"Bill Symons heads up field during 1970 action at C.N.E. Stadium."*

Both Wilkinson and Jonas had looked solid. Wilkie was five of nine for 86 yards and Jonas five of nine for 108 yards and two touchdowns. In Wally's first game back in Toronto as a Ticat, he completed 11 of 20 for a touchdown and had passes intercepted by Dick Thornton and Chip Barrett. Symons plowed for 152 yards on 10 carries.

Leo had got his reprieve. The Argos would now host the struggling British Columbia Lions in a game that was considered to be an easy two points. With Wilkinson still not feeling well, the starting job went back to Jonas. Leo also decided to finally move Jim Corrigall to the middle linebacker position. He was coming along at defensive end but had been pressuring the coach to make the move, and Leo finally relented.

The Lions gave the Argos a scare when quarterback Paul Brothers scrambled into the end zone seven minutes into the first quarter to give B.C. a 7-0 lead, but the Argos came back before the end of the quarter to tie things up on a three-yard gallop by Raimey. Toronto pulled away in the second quarter, starting with a 75-yard pass-and-run play between Wilkinson (back in the lineup) and Symons.

The second half was a nightmare for B.C. When it ended, the Argos had won 50-7. Wilkinson finished the game 13 of 21 with three touchdowns and an interception, while Jonas was five of 12 with two touchdowns and one interception. Tommy Bland scored two majors and Tony Moro, Mel Profit and Bill Symons also scored TDs. Profit in particular was outstanding, with seven catches. Symons pounded out 80 yards along the ground while Raimey added 89 yards. A key factor in an outstanding defensive effort was that Corrigall, now at middle linebacker, came up with a strong game.

With their record now 6-5, the Argos got ready again to face the Montreal Alouettes. The Larks had beaten them twice this year and this was a game the Double Blue needed badly. There was a good chance the two teams would face each other in the playoffs and Toronto didn't want to go into such a match having lost all of its games to the opponent.

Overshadowing the game was the ongoing terrorist crisis in Quebec. Members of the Front de Liberation du Quebec (FLQ) had for years been involved in low-level terrorist actions such as bombings of mailboxes.

Now they had moved onto kidnapping. British Trade Commissioner James Cross and Quebec Labour Minister Pierre Laporte had been taken hostage by the FLQ. With politicians gripped by panic, Prime Minister Pierre Trudeau invoked the War Measures Act, putting the Quebec under martial law. Canadian paratroopers surrounded Parliament Hill in Ottawa and the streets of Montreal were filled with troops. Police across Quebec rounded up FLQ suspects (along with hippies, American draft dodgers, political opponents of the government and others). Montreal was usually a favourite road trip for the Argonauts with its bars, nightclubs and attractive women. But with soldiers on the streets and police on a rampage, the players were very happy to take on the Alouettes at home.

The end result was a 16-13 Toronto victory, improving their record to 7-5. Tom Wilkinson started but was not outstanding. He completed 11 of 19 passes for 176 yards, no TDs and two interceptions. The offence under him was unable to get the ball into the end zone. Leo switched to Jonas in the fourth quarter with the Argos ahead 9-7 on two field goals, a safety and a single point. Jonas came out hot and quickly took the offence on a drive he finished with a three-yard touchdown run.

The main story, however, was the Toronto defence. It was simply tremendous. Montreal did not get on the scoreboard until the third quarter when running back Dennis Duncan scored on a spectacular 85-yard run. Sonny Wade had one of the worst games of his career, completing 10 of 25 passes for 121 yards, one touchdown and an unbelievable six interceptions. The Argo pass defence simply killed him that day. Luster and Aldridge picked off a pair each and Jim Corrigall and Dick Thornton had the other interceptions. Terry Evanshen was held to only three receptions in the game, taking away Montreal's main offensive weapon. The Argonauts front four also came up with three sacks to aid the cause.

The Argos seemed to have shaken off the malaise that had affected them through the first half of the year and looked like they were peaking at exactly the right time. Gearing up for the playoffs, they headed into Civic Stadium to battle the Ticats, who were also at 7-5. The winner of this game would in all likelihood finish in first place and get an important bye into the Eastern Final.

Perhaps someone, somewhere, has an explanation for why the Argos came out as flat as they did in such an important game. If that person exists, have him or call Leo Cahill, who would still love to know what happened. In a game reminiscent of the calamity in Calgary, the Argos had their asses handed to them on a silver platter.

Hamilton jumped in front in the first quarter when Wally Gabler hit Tommy-Joe Coffey with a 15-yard touchdown pass. The Cats increased their lead to 14-0 in the second quarter on a three-yard run by Garney Henley. In the third quarter, Coffey kicked a field goal and Gabler fired a five-yard pass to Dave Fleming for another major, pushing the lead to 24-0.

Toronto finally got on the board when Don Jonas ran four yards into the end zone, but Hamilton came right back with another field goal to make the final score 27-7. Offensively, nothing worked for the Argonauts that day. Jonas was only 11 for 30 for no touchdowns and was intercepted three times. Wilkinson was equally ineffective, completing one of five for eight yards. The leading rusher was Dave Raimey with only 36 yards on eight carries. Wally Gabler was outstanding against his old teammates, throwing for 175 yards and two touchdowns.

Toronto had one game left in the regular season to get itself righted in time for the playoffs. The Argos would be playing host to Ottawa, which in its first season without Russ Jackson was destined to finish out of the playoffs. Nonetheless, the Riders would love nothing better then to finish off with a victory against the Argos.

Toronto's offence again came up erratic. They took a lead in the first quarter when Dave Mann drove a 61-yard punt into the Ottawa end zone. Early in the second, the Argos front four sacked Gary Wood in the end zone for a safety, making the score 3-0. After yet another Mann single, the Toronto defence, weary of waiting for the offence to get something going, took matters into its own hands. Chip Barrett stepped in front of a Wood pass and returned it 34 yards for a touchdown.

The offence continued to sputter for Toronto and the Rough Riders picked up a safety and a touchdown from flanker Hugh Oldham in the third quarter to narrow the gap. Ottawa took the lead in the fourth quarter when Bill Van Burkleo returned an interception 57 yards for a major, making the score 17-15 for the Rough Riders. Mann added a single and then in the final minutes, Wilkinson drove the Toronto offence down the field and into field-goal range. With six seconds left on the clock, Don Jonas kicked an 18-yard field goal to give the Double Blue a 19-17 victory.

Toronto had won but it was an ugly victory. Both quarterbacks struggled again – Wilkinson completed 12 of 23 for 191 yards and threw two interceptions, but in fairness he did show a real coolness under fire, moving the team into position at the end for the winning field goal. The running attack contributed little to the victory, with Symons racking up only 39 yards. Even the return of Bobby Taylor to the lineup didn't seem to help. The Toronto defence was the saving grace. It was outstanding in holding Ottawa to only 20 yards along the ground and 147 yards through the air. The Argo defenders also came up with four interceptions: two by defensive back Gerry Sternberg and one each by Chip Barrett and linebacker Dick Aldridge.

So the 1970 regular season was over. Toronto had finished with a disappointing record of 8-6, good for second place behind Hamilton, and was clearly no longer the favourite to represent the East in the Grey Cup. The offence was seemingly in shambles and played terribly down the stretch. Any success in the post season would have to be as a result of an outstanding defence. If the offence, which had not played well since the destruction of B.C., could do anything, it would almost ensure a win. But was that too much to ask at this point?

The Eastern Semi-final was played at CNE Stadium on November 7, 1970. The Argos would once again do battle with the Montreal Alouettes, who had finished one point behind at 7-6-1. Toronto was in the rather unusual situation of finishing ahead of its opponent and the home team, yet clearly the underdog. Days before, coach Sam Etcheverry of the Alouettes had stunned the football world by announcing that running back Dennis Duncan and slotback Bob McCarthy were suspended for breach of club rules. Duncan was Montreal's best runner and a move such as this was simply unheard of. Would the loss of these two players give Toronto a badly needed edge or would the Alouettes rally in the face of this adversity?

As the Argos gathered to prepare, Leo made a bombshell announcement. Bill Symons describes it: "We got together for the pre-game meal and Leo announces that the blocking schemes we had used on offence for the entire season were going to be changed. Can you believe that?"

Luckily the Argo veterans that Leo was always wise enough to keep on the team were able to convince him that making such a fundamental change at this late stage was not such a wise idea. It does go to show, however, the extreme pressure Leo was under to win this game.

Don Jonas pulled a muscle in his kicking leg during practice so Tom Wilkinson would be starting at QB for Toronto. There was no concern with the news about Wilkie starting, but could Jonas kick? That was one of the worried for Argo fans heading into the game.

Just before the opening kickoff, Toronto got a boost when Jim Corrigall received the Gruen Award as the Eastern Conference's most outstanding rookie, and Bill Symons received the Jeff Russell Award as outstanding player in the East. Considering Corrigall had struggled moving from linebacker to defensive end, this award was really a reflection of his superb talent.

Montreal broke out in front less than five minutes into the first quarter. On second and long and penned deep in Argo territory, Wilkinson dropped back to pass. With good pass protection, he fired for Mel Profit. Wilkie's pass sailed over Profit's head and right into the arms of all-star defensive back Gene Gaines, who returned the ball to the Toronto 17-yard line. The Argo defence dug in and Montreal had to settle for a 26-yard George Springate field goal.

Minutes later, the Argos pulled ahead when Wilkinson, throwing from his own 22-yard line, hit Jim Thorpe who had burst between Alouettes defenders Bobby Lee Thompson and Larry Fairholm. With Thorpe's blinding speed, nobody on the Montreal side had a chance of catching him and suddenly it was 7-3 in favor of Toronto.
Montreal came back with another Springate field goal in the second quarter to narrow the gap to 7-6. The game by this time was clearly settling into a defensive battle. Montreal was moving the ball well along the ground. Both Moses Denson and fullback Bruce Van Ness were

churning out the yards consistently, but the Toronto defence was stopping them when they really had to. Mike Blum, Dick Aldridge and Jim Corrigall were doing an outstanding job at the linebacker spots. Sonny Wade, under constant pressure from Ed Harrington in particular, was having little success moving the ball through the air.

The Montreal defence was also in total control when it was on the field. Neither Symons nor Raimey had any success running the ball against linebackers Steve Smear, Mark Kosmos and rookie Mike Widger.

Desperate to move the ball, Leo called for a halfback option pass midway through the second quarter. Wilkinson flipped the ball to Symons who rolled out to pass. Widger, having a career game, blew through the Toronto offensive line and smothered Symons for a huge loss before he could get a pass off.

Later Leo called for a quick kick to catch Montreal off guard. Centre Bob Swift made a terrible snap to Wilkinson who had to make a spectacular one-handed grab to pull the ball in. Wilkie just got the kick away as the Alouettes defenders poured in on him. The kick sailed downfield to Gene Gaines, who watched in horror as the ball glanced off his foot and was recovered by the Argonauts. Toronto was jubilant over the break, as it had picked up a huge first down in Montreal territory. Jubilation turned to fury, however, when the officials ruled Gaines had not touched the ball and called a no-yards penalty against the Argos. Leo was outraged on the sidelines and the CNE Stadium crowd booed lustily. On the field, Argo players could only shake their heads in frustration and anger.

In the second half, Toronto got burned by another poor call by the officials. Midway through the third quarter, Wilkinson finally got a sustained drive going. Just past midfield, the Argos faced third down and less than a yard to go. Not wanting to lose the offensive momentum, Leo ordered the offence to go for it. A fraction of a second before the snap, Montreal defensive end Steve Booras shot through the line. He grabbed Wilkinson, who was just stepping back with the ball. Tom frantically tried to flip the ball to Jim Thorpe only to see the ball sail behind the slotback and hit the turf. It was clear to everyone in the stadium and watching the telecast that Booras had been offside. Clear to everyone, that is, except the officials. No penalty was called and the Alouettes took over the ball.

On the sidelines, Leo was almost beside himself with rage. That was the second horrendous call by the officials that had hurt the Argonauts that day. Making matters worse, Jim Corrigall left the game with an injury late in the third quarter. Pete Martin, the reliable, wily veteran, ran in to replace him.

Wilkinson shook off the bad call and began another drive before the quarter ended, only to see Bobby-Lee Thompson pick off a pass intended for Bobby Taylor at the Montreal 20-yard line.

Moving into the fourth quarter, the score remained 7-6 in favor of Toronto. Disaster then struck the Double Blue. Montreal, with the hard running of Denson and Van Ness, had moved the ball across midfield. Wade dropped back to throw under a fierce pass rush from the Toronto front four. Just before being imbedded into the soft CNE Stadium grass, he fired deep for tight end Peter Dalla Riva, who was being tightly covered by Chip Barrett. Despite excellent coverage from Barrett, the huge Dalla Riva stretched out and hauled in the pass, finishing off by slamming stomach first into the turf. It was a breathtakingly spectacular catch that seemed to stun the Argos. From there, Wade rolled out and hit slotback Tom Pullen, who had Ron Arends all over him, in the end zone for a major. Leo and the Argos could only curse their luck. Sonny Wade was far from the CFL's most accurate passer, and yet on both plays he had thrown pin-point passes and his receivers had made great catches, foiling almost air-tight pass coverage from Barrett and Arends.

The convert made the score 13-7 for Montreal, but with most of the fourth quarter to go, the Argos still had plenty of time to score and win the game. After the kickoff, Wilkinson went to work and began driving the offence down the field. He dropped back and fired a screen pass to Symons, who made a brilliant grab to give Toronto a badly needed first down in Montreal territory. However, just as Wilkie released the ball, Montreal lineman Wally Highsmith stormed in and crushed him with a devastating hit. Tom lay unmoving on the field, knocked out cold. He finally staggered off the field with help, but was clearly gone for the day.

Now it was up to the hot and cold Don Jonas to generate any offensive comeback. Aided by a 15-yard roughing-the-passer penalty called on Highsmith for the hit on Wilkinson, which moved the ball to the Alouettes' 32-yard line, Jonas went to work. A sweep by Symons picked up four yards. Jonas then hit Thorpe for a first down at the 17. Two plays later, Toronto faced third down at the Montreal 11. Leo had a tough decision to make now. He could try a field goal and hope to close the gap to three points. However, with Jonas's bad leg there was no guarantee he could make even an 18-yard chip shot. Leo ordered the offence to go for the first down. He wanted to tie the game right now.

Jonas dropped back to pass and missed Thorpe by a fraction of an inch at the five-yard line. Argo fans could feel the game slipping away. Faced with the injuries to Corrigall and Wilkinson, terrible officiating and now a golden opportunity wasted, it seemed like a win on this day was not meant to be.

The Argo defence, however, would not give up. It dug in and forced a punt. Wade got a booming kick away to Gerry Sternberg. Desperate to get the offence closer, Sternberg tried to twist away from a Montreal tackler and in the process lost the ball, giving Montreal possession deep in Toronto territory. Wade drove Montreal to the Toronto 18, where George Springate kicked his third field goal of the game to make the score 16-7.

Jonas tried to rally the Argos, moving the offence into Montreal territory but missing Tommy Bland in the end zone with a desperate bomb. That was Toronto's last gasp. Montreal took over and killed most of the remaining time. With only seconds left and the game out of reach, Jonas started one last drive. With one second left he fired for Bill Symons. The heart and soul of the offence, the fierce warrior who never, ever gave up, Symons made the catch and headed for the end zone. Inside the Montreal 25-yard line he broke one tackle before being corralled by three Alouettes at the Montreal 19. With legs pumping and driving, Sy went down and a strange, confusing 1970 came to an end.

The statistics from the game were not overly impressive for either team. Sonny Wade completed 14 of 33 passes for 147 yards and one touchdown. Unlike the six-interception nightmare of a couple of weeks earlier, he avoided throwing any this game. Moses Denson had a solid game taking over for Dennis Duncan. He picked up 90 yards on 15 carries. For the Argos, Wilkinson completed 13 of 19 for 158 yards, one touchdown and two interceptions. Jonas was good on eight of 16 for 100 yards. Symons led the Argo rushers with 34 yards on nine carries but Bill had a strong receiving effort, catching the ball eight times to lead the team in that category.

The Toronto defence had not let the team down. It had played more than well enough to allow the team to win. The offence once again just could not get the job done. Dave Raimey has an explanation for the offensive failure. “We had an excellent team with veterans who knew what we had to do. During the week we would practice well and the timing would be great. We would be ready to play and very confident. And then on game day Leo would panic and come up with some brand-new plays and want us to use them. The plays were ingenious and well-thought-out, but it was the wrong time to do that. Leo was an excellent coach and he knew more about football then almost anyone I ever met. But things like this hurt us. That was when guys like Mel Profit, Mike Blum and such lost some confidence in Leo.”

In the deathly quiet Toronto dressing room, both Dave Mann and Danny Nykoluk announced their retirements, ending long and glorious careers. They would be followed in the next few months by Mike Wadsworth and Ron Arends, who were both leaving to devote more attention to their off-field careers. (Wadsworth was an outstanding lawyer who years later would be named Canadian ambassador to Ireland by Prime Minister Brian Mulroney. He also served a stint as athletic director at Notre Dame University and was more than once rumoured to be a top candidate for CFL commissioner.)

John Bassett quickly ended any speculation regarding the status of Leo Cahill. He was quoted in the *Toronto Star* as saying that Leo “has a very good record and nobody can be more disappointed than coach Cahill. It is up to him now to make certain readjustments on which I won’t comment but it must be perfectly obvious to anybody.” It was easy to figure out that the biggest change the Boss wanted to see was at quarterback. After the game, Bassett made it very clear to Leo that he did not believe Toronto could win the Grey Cup with Tom Wilkinson or Don Jonas at quarterback.

Was it fair to blame the quarterbacks? On one hand, neither had a particularly good year in 1970 although both had shown flashes of excellence. Pete Martin has an interesting opinion: "Sometimes I think we simply were not well coached on offence. Leo tried to change too many things too fast. He was not patient enough." Case in point, the constant switching of Wilkinson and Jonas.

In Leo's first three seasons of coaching, the Toronto Argonauts had shown steady improvement every year. In his fourth year, they had clearly taken a step backwards. The following year would be a real test both for him and for the team he had built.

Seven

1971

In the early winter months of 1971, Leo and his coaching staff knew their team was close to being a championship-calibre squad. The defence, which Jay Teitel described as "tough, even violent," was among the finest in Canadian football. During the bizarre, up-and-down season of 1970, it had rarely let the team down. The offence, while clearly possessing some outstanding players, was at best erratic and inconsistent. The biggest improvement would have to come on that side of the ball.

Under pressure from John Bassett, Leo set out to find a new starting quarterback. He first spoke to Gary Beban, the 1967 Heisman Trophy winner from UCLA. Beban had been a huge disappointment with the Washington Redskins of the NFL and had been released. The CFL would be a chance for him to restart his career. However, the talks went nowhere as Beban decided to explore other options. Cahill then spoke to Russ Jackson and tried to persuade the legendary ex-Rough Rider – and Argo killer – to come out of retirement. Jackson had a few talks with Cahill before declining.

Leo was not about to give up in his quest for a new quarterback, so he turned his sights on two other candidates: Joe Theismann, the runner-up in voting for the 1970 Heisman Trophy from Notre Dame University, and Greg Barton, the third-string quarterback of the Detroit Lions.

Joe Theismann was a legend in U.S. college football. He had led Notre Dame to a huge upset of the University of Texas in the 1970 Cotton Bowl with a sensational performance. Other than his slight size, Theismann seemed to be the "complete package" as a quarterback. He had a good throwing arm, could run as well as most running backs, and had a wild, devil-may-care attitude on the field. Joe had no qualms about throwing into heavy coverage to try to make good things happen.

Greg Barton was a different breed altogether from Theismann. He was not at all mobile but had a cannon for an arm. Some observers even said

Barton had the best arm in football. Unlike Theismann, he didn't try to force things to happen. He was patient and liked to see what the opposing defences were doing before he began to attack them. Barton was drafted by the Detroit Lions but had been riding the bench behind Greg Landry and Bill Munson, who were both outstanding young quarterbacks, too. It was no knock against Greg that he wasn't playing in Detroit. He was simply in a situation in which he had little chance to play. Barton played out his option during the 1970 season and would be a free agent in the spring of 1971.

Many NFL observers felt he was among the finest young quarterbacks in the league; the Philadelphia Eagles, in fact, traded three high draft choices to the Lions for his playing rights. They were looking at Greg as being their No. 1 quarterback. But the Argos had other ideas. Assistant coach Blackie Johnston had been tipped off by a friend on the Detroit coaching staff that Greg was a hell of a player and was available. So Leo went after both Barton and Theismann.

Theismann was selected in the fourth round by the Miami Dolphins, who appeared to be one of the up-and-coming powers in the NFL. Coached by the legendary Don Shula, the Dolphins had an excellent young quarterback of their own in Bob Griese. Theismann would have gone higher in the draft if he was taller, but at just six feet and with a slim body, there was some concern about his ability to see over the huge linemen and to handle the physical punishment they would deliver. His mobility and daring nature, however, made him an ideal candidate for the CFL, where size was not such a factor.

Both the Argonauts and Dolphins tried to sell Theismann on what they had to offer. Leo emphasized that in Toronto he would play right away. That was highly unlikely in Miami, where Bob Griese would clearly be ahead of him. John Bassett personally delivered Toronto's offer to Joe, but impressive as it was, the Argonauts could not persuade him to sign. On March 18, 1971, the Dolphins held a press conference to announce Joe Theismann was theirs.

Leo then made his move on Greg Barton. Greg would not become a free agent until May 1 so he could not sign a contract until then, but that didn't stop the Argos. To avoid any publicity over their skirting of the rules, they met Barton and his agent in Indianapolis on March 26. A deal was hammered out, and Barton signed. The team could not announce it until May, and Greg, being honourable, would not take any Toronto money until then. But most importantly, the Argos had their new quarterback.

It was huge contract: four one-year contracts worth $30,000, $35,000, $40,000and $45,000 per year along with a $30,000 signing bonus. (To put it in perspective, veteran star Dick Thornton made $27,000 in 1971.) The deal also included a no-cut clause, meaning Barton was guaranteed to be paid even if he didn't make the team. Leo was planning on using Greg as the starting quarterback, with either Tom Wilkinson or Don Jonas backing him up.

Days after signing Barton, Cahill got a shock. Jack Carmichael, the owner of City Buick/Pontiac in Toronto and a huge Argo fan, phoned him. Carmichael had been speaking to a fellow car dealer in South Bend, Ind.,, home of Notre Dame University, who told Carmichael that Joe Theismann was in his office having a drink. Carmichael asked to speak to him to wish him luck in Miami. But when Joe got on the phone, Carmichael came away with the distinct impression the quarterback was not sure he had made the right decision in opting for the Dolphins. Carmichael hung up, called Leo and told him his impressions.

Leo describes the rest: "I called Joe, and learned he had signed the Miami contract all right, but hadn't mailed it because he didn't have a stamp. He asked if I could send our contract from Toronto to him so that he could compare one more time."

Sensing a chance to steal Theismann away from the Dolphins, Leo declined to send him the Toronto contract. Instead, he invited Joe and his wife back to Toronto for one more visit. When they arrived, a meeting was held at the home of Herb Solway, a prominent Toronto attorney and close friend of John Bassett. Leo went back over the contract with the Theismanns, then told Joe: "If it was only you and I was in your position, I'd definitely go to Miami and take my best shot. But if you want to think about future security, the kind of outside career you can build here, and the overall picture for your family, our offer is much better." Leo also emphasized that in Toronto, Joe would have a real shot at being the No. 1 quarterback, and regardless he would get lots of playing time. With Bob

Griese already in Miami, the opportunity would not be the same with the Dolphins.

Joe and his wife, Sherri, spoke alone in Solway's study for about 30 minutes. They then came out, and Sherri broke the news that they were coming to Toronto! The contract would pay Joe in the area of $50,000 per season, making him the highest-paid player in the CFL and among the highest in professional football. When the news came out that Theismann had signed with the Argos, the Dolphins were simply floored – and furious. But the deal was done, and Toronto and Leo were the winners.

Leo then turned his attention to a young running back at the University of Tampa by the name of Leon McQuay. Both Bill Symons and Dave Raimey were getting up there in age, and Leo figured he had better start looking for a younger back to take over the reins. This feeling was not shared by everyone, mind you. Bill had rushed for 908 yards and been the all-Canadian running back in 1970. Dave, despite being bothered by his knee, chipped in 839 yards. The statistics didn't show any reason to be concerned about either running back.

Nonetheless, Leon McQuay was the man Leo wanted. Known as X-Ray, McQuay was an unbelievable player; perhaps the finest running back in the NCAA and a player any team would want, based on his pure physical ability. He had churned out 3,039 yards along the ground and added 37 touchdowns in three seasons, but the statistics didn't reflect his electrifying style. Leon had the acceleration of a Mach 1 Mustang and the remarkable ability to make a cut without losing speed. He was the type of player a coach might see once in his career – if he's lucky. He was also not yet eligible to go to the NFL because he was still in his junior year. NFL rules did not allow teams to draft a player until his class had graduated, which for Leon would be 1972. The CFL had no such rule, and Leo was determined to sign him.

Cahill began talking to McQuay in the spring. Leon, eager to leave school and turn pro, signed on May 13, 1971. His contract was huge by CFL standards, paying him more than such Argonaut stalwarts as Dick Thornton, Dave Raimey and Bill Symons – without having played a single down of pro football. Ominously, though, while fans of the

University of Tampa were outraged at the Argos for stealing a player before he had graduated, there didn't seem to be much anger coming from Leon's teammates. Was it because they were thrilled for him, or that they were not sorry to see him go?

After all, there was a dark side to Leon McQuay. Aside from being a great running back, he also had a reputation for being moody, immature and at times lazy. It was known among opposing players that Leon did not like to get hit. One good lick early in the game could render him ineffective for the rest of the contest.

But Leo wasn't worried about that. An already strong team now had two outstanding new quarterbacks and a potentially great running back. Cahill wasn't done, however. His next target was perhaps the finest defensive lineman in the history of the NCAA: Ohio State University's Jim Stillwagon.

Stillwagon was a legend at OSU. As a sophomore, he had anchored the Buckeyes' defence on the way to their 1968 national championship season. In 1970, his final year of college ball, he was awarded the Outland Trophy as the finest lineman in college football, along with the Vince Lombardi Trophy for being the best defensive player in college football.

Most opponents found Stillwagon simply impossible to block. He came off the line with lightning speed and thunderous power. Unlike McQuay, there was no dark side to Jim Stillwagon. He was a quiet, thoughtful man who was well liked and respected by teammates, coaches and opponents alike.

Despite all of his credentials, Stillwagon was not taken until the fourth round of the NFL draft, by Green Bay. He may have terrorized the NCAA, but at only six feet, he was considered too small to play defensive tackle in the NFL. When Stillwagon went to Green Bay to talk contract, he got a rude surprise. The Packers teams of Vince Lombardi were just a memory. The current Packers were made up of a lot of unproven kids and tired, battered veterans. Stillwagon felt there was also little cohesion in the front office. He heard someone in the organization refer to Ray Nitschke, the renowned middle linebacker who had been the heart and soul of the great Green Bay defensive squads of the 1960s, as a "washed up old fart." Stillwagon, who had idolized Nitschke, was simply horrified and wondered, "If they talk about Ray like that, how will they treat me?" The Packers then told him he was too small to play defensive tackle and they were going to shift him to linebacker, and increased his discomfort by making a very low initial contract offer.

Leo made his move. He had Jim flown up to Toronto for a visit and arranged for ex-Argos such as Rod Smylie, one of the heroes of the Grey Cup victory in 1952, to meet with Stillwagon and give him a sense of the history of the team. When the contract talks began, Leo came in with a better offer than Green Bay had made, and told Jim he would immediately become a starting defensive tackle for the Argonauts.

Stillwagon really liked the city, felt the Argos respected his ability far more than Green Bay did, and the money was significantly higher as well. He went back to Columbus, Ohio, to think it over. Leo was pushing for a response as he knew Stillwagon was a player around whom he could design his defence. He sent assistant coach Gord Ackerman to Columbus to try to increase the pressure. Ackerman, though, could not find Stillwagon, who just happened to be on the phone to Cahill listening to Toronto's final offer.

Leo outlined the offer, then said; "There is one other contingency here. Pat Peppler, the assistant general manager at Green Bay, is a personal friend of mine. This is our final offer. This is as far as we go. I want Stillwagon to tell me right now, Yes or No. If you say no, I've got Pat Peppler's number right here and I'm picking up the phone and telling him we're out of it. We've got Stillwagon on our negotiation list and nobody else in Canada can touch him. But if he doesn't want to go along with the contract we're offering, we're out of it and you can settle with Green Bay for whatever they want to offer you."

Leo was playing hardball here, and Jim was in a tough spot. If he refused to sign with Toronto now and Leo followed through with his threat, he'd be stuck taking whatever Green Bay would give him. He'd also be playing for an organization he didn't respect, at a position he didn't know. Jim made the decision – he would sign with Toronto. An already great Argo defence had just become considerably better.

Yet Leo was still not finished rebuilding for 1971. He picked up Canadian slotback Dave Cranmer, an all-star who had requested a trade to be closer to his Toronto home. Calgary wanted defensive back Ron Arends in return. Arends had privately indicated to Leo that he was retiring, but the Argonauts had not announced it yet. When Leo informed the Stampeders that Arends was retiring, they accused him of lying and insisted they had to have Arends in any deal for Cranmer. What the hell, figured Leo. He traded Arends, who had no intention of playing again (and didn't), and got Cranmer. He didn't win any friends out west with that deal.

Cahill then made a couple of trades with Winnipeg. Quarterback Don Jonas, centre Bob Swift and receiver Jim Thorpe were shipped to the Blue Bombers in return for all-star centre Paul Desjardins and offensive lineman Joe Vijuk. Desjardins, nicknamed "Doc" due to his PhD in biochemistry, was considered perhaps the finest centre in the CFL. Vijuk was a capable lineman who could play both sides of the ball.

With two new quarterbacks coming in, Leo also didn't need Tom Wilkinson. He was shipped to the British Columbia Lions for basically nothing in return. To replace Danny Nykoluk's veteran influence on the offensive line, Leo picked up offensive tackle Ellison Kelly from Hamilton in return for linebacker Mike Blum. Kelly, a former all-star, had been a key member of Hamilton's Grey Cup winning teams in the 1960s but was getting a bit old. Ralph Sazio, the Ticats general manager, felt Kelly was finished but Leo was willing to gamble that he wasn't.

Leo also signed a couple more highly touted rookies. From the University of Texas at El Paso he signed a tough, hard-hitting outside linebacker named Gene Mack. Mack had been a seventh-round pick of the Minnesota Vikings but Leo convinced him his future would be better in Toronto. Cahill also signed kicker Zenon Andrusyshyn, a native of nearby Oakville, out of UCLA.

Stepping back for a moment, one can appreciate the brilliance of Leo's moves before the 1971 season. He had added some great talent in Theismann, Stillwagon and McQuay, among others. However, he had also shown his great understanding of the need for top Canadian talent by getting players such as Cranmer and Desjardins. With a roster limit of 15 Americans or "imports," teams needed good Canadians. By adding

Canadians of the calibre of Cranmer and Desjardins, Cahill had no problem finding room for the great Americans he was signing. By signing Andrusyshyn, he also had a Canadian to take over the kicking chores. The previous season the job had been split between two Americans, Don Jonas and Dave Mann.

The passing game would be further bolstered by the return of Mike Eben. He had shown himself to be a superb receiver in his one year on loan to Edmonton. To make room for Mike, Leo decided to release Bobby Taylor, a very difficult decision. Bobby wore his heart on his sleeve and was one of the most aggressive players on the team. But he had missed most of 1970 due to injuries, and Leo also felt he could not afford to have Taylor's confrontational, abrasive personality on the team. If he was not going to play regularly, he would make life miserable for whoever was. Leo felt Eben had more pure ability and he did not want to rekindle the nasty Taylor/Eben battles of 1968 and 1969.

Also departing was Tommy Bland, the veteran receiver from the Continental League who had played solidly for the Argos in 1970. Leo was looking to mainly count on Eben and Jim Henderson as his wide receivers. If this worked out – having two Canadians in those roles – it would free up room for some of the new American stars Cahill had signed.

There would be still one more high-profile signing but it did not take place until after the season started. Leo spent much of the spring talking to Jim Stillwagon's Ohio State teammate, safety Tim Anderson., who was a first-round draft pick of the San Francisco 49ers. When the CFL season started, Anderson was still talking to Toronto and San Francisco. By early August, Leo got his name on a Toronto contract and Tim Anderson became the highest NFL draft pick ever to sign with a CFL team.

There were two other major issues to be worked through before the 1971 season began. The first was Dick Thornton's first attempt to become an author. (A few years later "Tricky" did have a book of his poetry published.) Thornton was approached to write a book that would allow readers to really experience life as a professional football star. It was to be a no-holds-barred, tell-all book, as Tricky Dick recounts:

"Being somewhat of a journalist, I often freelanced as a writer, primarily for the *Globe and Mail,* and also did lots of work on radio and TV. One day, the publisher Longman's of Canada called and asked if I could write a book about the life of a CFL pro. They would advance me a decent sum of money to do it. I said, 'Sure, why not?'

"You have to remember the life and times of that era. We all wore weird clothes and had long hair. Women were always surrounding us night and day and we did a lot of crazy things back then.

"I wrote about one week leading up to a particular game during the 1970 season and incorporated lots of humourous anecdotes and stories. Looking back, it wasn't too well-written but it was pure me, my vivid perspectives of football life and personal views at that point in time.

"Dick Beddoes was going to write the foreword and once said, 'Richard Quincy Thornton is the biggest flake this side of a box of cereal.' I thought that was a great one-liner.

"After completing a couple of chapters, I would send them to the editor at Longman's for review and corrections. The guy kept coming back, saying, 'Great stuff – more, more.' Finally, upon completion, the editor and I spent an entire day at my house, going over it page by page. All I remember is he left with a big smile on his face and the manuscript under his arm. I figure if he's happy, I'm happy, so I begin to promote it.

"I'm getting all kinds of ink now as sportswriters are speculating what's in the contents. I'm doing interviews and there is great anticipation by everyone for its release, which I think was scheduled for near the beginning of the 1971 season. Great title, too: *Get It While You're Hot, 'Cause Baby, You're Going To Be Cold For A Long, Long Time*.

"Beddoes, I think, hit the nail on the head in one of his later columns. Longman's sent the galleys to the *Telegram* for possible excerpts in the Sunday magazine. The *Telegram* was of course, owned by John Bassett, Sr., who also owned the Argonauts. Leo got hold of the manuscript, read parts of it and went nuts. Bassett must have put pressure on Longman's to cancel, which they did. The editor was quoted in the papers all across Canada as saying the book was too subjective. 'Dick tried to out-Namath

Namath without being Joe Namath and it made him look like a terrible ass.' He said a lot of people would have been hurt by the book. The sexual exploits were too vivid and there was a total attack on the football Establishment.

"Longman's never even had the courtesy to call and give me an explanation – no nothing. I read all this shit in the paper. The next day, I get calls from three other publishers who immediately wanted the rights and would have loved to publish it. I confront Leo with the latest development. His exact words were, 'Tricky, if that book hits the streets, your professional football career is over and even if it doesn't hit the bookstores, your chances of making my football team are slim and none, and slim's out for lunch.' "

Needless to say, the book died on the spot and was never published. Thornton was smart enough to figure out that one can write a book any time, but you only have so many chances to play pro football. The second development hit the Argos players and coaches like an earthquake. John Bassett decided that the team needed to become tougher, so he moved Lew Hayman out of his role of general manager and hired ex-Hamilton lineman John Barrow to replace him. Leo, in particular, was aghast at this move. Barrow had always been one of the most hated Ticats and had no experience at all in the front office of a professional football team. Leo, who had been handling all recruiting and contract negotiations since 1967, was terribly hurt that he was not even interviewed for the job. When he complained to Hayman, who was moved into an executive position, Cahill was told, "You are not the general manager type." Leo could only respond, "What the hell does that mean?" This was perhaps the first inkling Leo had that his future with the Argonauts might be in doubt. He knew he had better win in 1971.

The new-look Toronto Argonauts hit training camp at St. Andrews College in Aurora with a tremendous amount of publicity. Leo was always excellent at generating publicity for himself, the team, the sport and the city, and had outdone himself with the many big-name signings he made in the off-season. That, along with the controversy over Thornton's book and the hiring of John Barrow, had the eyes of the Canadian football world on the Argos as camp opened.

On the first day the entire team was together at training camp, Barrow came in to speak to the players. He had so far kept a very low profile; none of the players had even met him in his new capacity as GM. Pete Martin still shudders when he things back to the meeting.

"John came into the dining room and asked Leo to leave. Leo looked shocked. He finally did leave but definitely wasn't happy. John then told us that we were too soft and when he played in Hamilton he always knew that we made too much money and our hair was too long. He wanted all of us to get haircuts! At that point we just tuned him out. He lost us. Leo eventually came to us and asked us what John had said. When we told him, he exploded. 'He fucking said what?' he yelled. God, Leo was so mad."

Mel Profit wrote about this ill-fated meeting in his book, *For Love, Money and Future Considerations*:

"In keeping with Argonaut tradition, John Barrow opened his tenure as general manager in 1971 with an absurd welcoming address to the veterans. It is impossible to duplicate the emotional changes I went through as I sat there with 28 other men – some the age or nearly the age of John Barrow – and listen to him address the people he had been hired to deal with, reportedly because of his leadership qualities. John opened by stating he felt he was in a position to bridge the gap that existed between management and the players, which in fact he was, having just come from a 14-year career as a player. In the next breath he told us that, inasmuch as we represented the city of Toronto, we had an obligation to present a 'respectable appearance' and since he didn't feel long hair was respectable, those present would have to get haircuts. He quickly assured us, though, the fact he wore a crew-cut had nothing to do with his decision.

"I sat there thinking: 'This is 1971, this is a group of relatively intelligent people and this really isn't happening.' It was. A few minutes later he categorized everyone as a bunch of 'overpaid losers.' After that I kind of lost interest in our new leader."

It was a disastrous start for Barrow in his new job. In his first meeting he had alienated the entire team, including the head coach. Leo would be hard pressed to keep things on an even keel from this point onwards.

The Argo players shook off their shock over the meeting with Barrow and hit the field. Along with all the high-profile new faces, there were some position changes affecting veterans. To make room for McQuay, Dave Raimey was moved to defensive back. Raimey had played DB at the University of Michigan and with the Cleveland Browns in 1964, so this position was not at all alien to him. Dave, in fact, was very happy to make the move. "With Leon joining the team I figured I would battle for my job, but then Jim Rountree came to me and said, 'Dave, I'd love to have you play DB for me.' I was thrilled, as Cleveland had taught me to love playing defence.

"During training camp I worked against Mike Eben. He was a great receiver. He had the most incredible concentration and could catch anything. We had some great battles during that camp. I also made a deal with Joe Theismann that he couldn't complete a pass against me. If he did I bought him a milkshake and if I stopped him he owed me a beer."

The other change affected Dick Thornton. Leo, still furious over Thornton's aborted book, decided Dick would have to make the team at wide receiver instead of his regular position at defensive back. "I thought the best way to put him in his place and let him know I didn't want any more of this book kind of jazz was to put on a little pressure. So we put him on offence in camp and told him he had to make the team at wide receiver."

The move made no sense. Dick was an all-star-calibre DB. Why would you move him when you were already going to have a new face, Raimey, in the secondary?

Thornton had played some wide receiver before as an emergency replacement, but there is a big difference filling in for an injured player on a temporary basis and becoming a regular at that position. In essence Leo was weakening the defence and possibly weakening the offence as well, all to make a point to Thornton.

Leo also decided that Jim Corrigall belonged back on the defensive line. Jim had looked stronger at middle linebacker the year before, but Leo felt his defence was tougher overall with Corrigall playing end and Pete Martin at middle linebacker.

When the preseason games started, the Argos came out flying. They looked awesome and the new additions looked great. Thornton worked relentlessly at his new position and, much to Leo's amazement, quickly became Toronto's best receiver. Dick looks back at this time with fond memories. "I owe a lot to Joe Theismann. I told him, 'Joe, my career is on the line and in a way yours is too – being new in the league, having to prove yourself and with you and Barton fighting for the starting job. Let's team up and show 'em all how to play this game.

Joe and I stayed after practice every day working on our timing, and in the exhibition games he threw to me every chance he could. Must have caught about 30 balls, but the one I remember most was in the last exhibition game against Montreal, when I made a leaping, over-the-shoulder, one-handed catch for a TD in the end zone. That solidified my spot on the team and at the starting position of wide receiver."

Jim Stillwagon, at his first pro camp, was making it clear to all that he was going to be worth every cent of the big contract Leo had given him. Leo described the newcomer to *CFL Illustrated*: "That Stillwagon is an animal. I've never seen such a determined player. He has that low centre of gravity, so that when he gets hit he just keeps grinding ahead."

Leon McQuay was also awing teammates and opponents alike with his running ability. Based on his early performance in training camp, some players were saying he was the finest running back they had ever seen. "He could run faster sideways then most people could run forwards," remembers Leo. But McQuay was already causing a lot of problems as well. He was sullen and argumentative, and his teammates were already questioning his heart and courage. Dick Thornton, while seeing McQuay's brilliant talents, was wary nonetheless. "Leo really built him up in that first training camp meeting and he was truly a fine physical specimen. He had all the physical attributes of becoming a great athlete but it didn't take long for the veterans to realize he was cocky, arrogant, spoiled, immature, had no communication skills and faked a lot of injuries to avoid many of the drills. Mel and I were talking those first few days of camp and saying this guy is trouble with a capital T."

The veterans on the team were also livid that Bill Symons, who had played his heart out for the team for years, was seemingly cast aside as the feature back in favour of Leon. They could not understand (nor could Bill) how Leo could cast aside a player who had rushed for more than 900 yards the year before, was an all-Canadian and team captain for an untried rookie with a bad attitude and questionable work ethic.

Amidst all of this chaos created by Leon, Leo and Barrow (who had not mellowed in his approach to the players) the Argos were to opened the 1971 season at home against the Winnipeg Blue Bombers before a sellout crowd.

Leo had not been able to pick a starting quarterback between Greg Barton and Joe Theismann, so he decided on the unusual tactic of alternating quarterbacks every series of downs. This would not add to the stability of the offence, if previous attempts to rotate Wilkinson and Jonas were any indication.

Toronto would face a tough challenge getting to and winning the Grey Cup this year. Montreal was the defending Grey Cup champion. After beating the Argos in the 1970 Eastern Semifinal, the Als upset Hamilton in the Eastern Final and then defeated Calgary 23-10 in the championship game. Hamilton, as always, looked strong and Ottawa was expected to be much improved over the previous year. In the Western Conference, Saskatchewan with Ron Lancaster and George Reed was always a Grey Cup threat. Winnipeg, with the addition of Jonas at quarterback, looked solid. Calgary, which always had a tough, relentless defence, was looking to fight back into the Grey Cup. Edmonton and British Columbia were not considered threats but had enough talent that no one saw them as pushovers.

CNE Stadium was rocking with a loud, boisterous crowd for the season opener. Toronto jumped on the score board first when Leon McQuay burst into the Blue Bombers end zone from five yards out, but Winnipeg moved ahead 10-7 in the second quarter on a one-yard dive and a 25-yard field goal by Jonas. Before the half ended, Toronto came back with a seven-yard strike into the end zone from Theismann to Mel Profit. Zenon Andrusyshyn, who was punting great but struggling with his place-kicking due to a leg injury, missed the convert.

After Winnipeg tied the score at 13-13 in the third quarter, Toronto roared back with a huge play. McQuay took a handoff at the Argo 40-yard line, blew through the Winnipeg defensive line like a vapour and was gone. Seconds later he spiked the ball in the Blue Bombers end zone after a 70-yard touchdown run. The run was simply awe-inspiring. "Leon had the quickest feet I ever saw," says Bill Symons. No Bomber even had a shot at catching him.

But Don Jonas was determined to show the Argos they had made a mistake in letting him go. He responded by driving Winnipeg down the field and firing a 24-yard touchdown pass to Bob Larose. Winnipeg failed to tie it when Jonas missed the convert, but in the fourth quarter, a missed field-goal attempt went for a single point and the game was tied. With less than two minutes to go and the game looking as if it would end in a tie, "Big Z" blasted a 50-yard punt through the Blue Bombers end zone for a single point, giving Toronto a 21-20 victory in the season opener.

McQuay had been the star of the game, rushing for 152 yards on 16 carries and scoring two touchdowns. Symons chipped in with 63 yards on eight carries and did a tremendous job blocking for McQuay. The Argos' air attack was another story, however. Calling it disappointing would be charitable. Neither Theismann nor Barton looked sharp in their CFL debuts. Joe completed five of 15 passes for only 38 yards, with a touchdown and an interception. Greg was good on one of four for nine yards and an interception. The running game obviously looked great but the passing game needed lots of work.

Don Jonas, in his return to Toronto, was fabulous for Winnipeg. He was good on 22 of 40 passes for 301 yards and a touchdown, and scored a major himself. His only major error was a pass that Pete Martin picked off in the middle and returned 22 yards.

Aside from McQuay, the Argos' other new additions looked good. Andrusyshyn's punting was excellent although he was having problems place-kicking. Jim Stillwagon and Gene Mack both looked good in their pro debuts. Stillwagon was a thorn in Jonas's side, storming in from his defensive tackle position to pressure him constantly, while Mack did a credible job at outside linebacker.

In the days following the game, Leo went to work finding a place-kicker. He settled on Ivan MacMillan, a young man who had handled place-kicking for Ottawa the year before. He would make his Toronto debut against Saskatchewan the following week

Ron Lancaster and the Saskatchewan Roughriders came into CNE Stadium on August 6 and would be the first real test of the Argo team Leo had so carefully assembled. Toronto again scored first, with McQuay grabbing a pass from Theismann and taking it in for the major. The Green Riders and Argos then exchanged field goals to put the score at 10-3 late in the second quarter. Greg Barton, in at quarterback, faded back to throw under heavy pressure and unloaded a bomb deep down field. It sailed threw the air right into the hands of X-Ray McQuay, who had gone streaking out of the backfield and down the sidelines. Leon had slipped behind the pass coverage. Another seven points pushed the Argo lead to 17-3.

The lead was increased to 21-3 in the third quarter when the Argos' defensive line of Stillwagon, Corrigall, Knechtel and Harrington came up with two safeties by dropping Lancaster and Alan Ford in the end zone. The Roughriders scored a couple of late touchdowns but the final score was Toronto 22 Saskatchewan 17.

Leon McQuay was held to 70 yards rushing on 12 carries, but he was Toronto's leading receiver with five catches for 104 yards and two touchdowns. Mel Profit also caught five passes as the aerial attack was definitely better than in Week 1. Barton looked very sharp, completing five of seven for 102 yards and the TD bomb to McQuay. Theismann was good on nine of 17 for 158 yards with one touchdown and two interceptions.

Toronto was in a Double Blue frenzy. Keep in mind that this was six years before the Blue Jays came along. The Argos ruled the sports scene in Toronto from June until Grey Cup time. The entire city was talking about the Argos, and Leon McQuay was being called the most exciting athlete in the history of Toronto sports by some excited fans. Leo was being hailed as a genius for building this apparent juggernaut.

The Argonauts then rolled into the Autostade in Montreal to do battle with the defending Grey Cup champion Alouettes. After moving ahead 3-0 on an Ivan MacMillan field goal, the Argos erupted with another huge play. McQuay took a hand-off at the Toronto 29, darted through a hole and was off again, pulling up 81 yards later in the Montreal end zone. Even his teammates, many of whom thoroughly disliked McQuay, were amazed at the sheer beauty of the run.

Early in the third quarter, with Toronto leading 10-3, Joe Theismann dropped back to pass from his 26-yard line and received a complete shock. The Montreal defence had gotten completely confused and Steve Smear, their brilliant middle linebacker, was on the sidelines. The middle of the field was wide open so Theismann tucked the ball under his arm and roared down the seam. The Argo receivers cleared the Alouette defenders from his path and Joe took it 84 yards for the major. Montreal fought back with a field goal, but then Toronto hit yet another big play. Theismann dropped back in the pocket to throw from his own 18-yard line and fired deep to Dave Cranmer, who broke away from a desperate Alouette defender and went all the way, 94 yards for the touchdown. When it was all over the final score was 26-14 for Toronto.

Figure -7-1: *"Mike Eben makes a big gain against Montreal in 1971."*

Leon McQuay broke the 100-yard barrier again with 141 yards on 14 carries. Theismann rushed for 104 yards on six carries and completed seven of 16 passes for 215 yards, one touchdown and two interceptions. Greg Barton passed for 38 yards while completing four passes in nine attempts. Defensively, both Marv Luster and Dick Aldridge picked off Sonny Wade passes. Aldridge and Chip Barrett also made fumble recoveries to stop key Montreal drives.

The Argos was rolling with a record of 3-0, and including exhibition games were 7-0 in 1971. While the media and fans in Toronto were already talking Grey Cup, there was concern on the team. Bill Symons was worried. “I didn’t think we were playing that well offensively. We were not a ball-control team and were winning with big plays and fluky plays. I mean, Steve Smear forgot to come on the field and Joe runs up the middle for a touchdown. How often does that happen? We were not a disciplined offensive team; we were winning on talent alone.”

Next up for Toronto was a home game against Ottawa. CNE Stadium was jammed for the battle with the Rough Riders, and – as was the case in every game so far this year – Toronto got on the board first. Joe Theismann sprinted out and fired a 45-yard bullet to Dave Cranmer for a touchdown. By the early part of the second quarter, Toronto had stretched its lead to 13-0 on two Ivan MacMillan field goals.

Ottawa then came fighting back. Quarterback Rick Cassata hit all-star flanker Hugh Oldham with a short swing pass from the Ottawa 10-yard line. Oldham spun away from a Toronto defender and exploded up field. Ottawa’s receivers knocked defensive backs Jim Tomlin and Dave Raimey out of Oldham’s path, and a simple, short swing pass became a 100-yard touchdown play. CNE Stadium became dead silent.

The fireworks continued in the third quarter. Toronto picked up another field goal from MacMillan and added a touchdown on a four-yard run by Bill Symons that stretched the Toronto lead to 23-7. But Ottawa roared back early in the fourth on a 17-yard touchdown pass from Gary Wood to Billy Cooper. Trying to hammer the final nail into Ottawa’s coffin, Leon McQuay erupted for a 52-yard touchdown run that increased the Toronto lead to 30-14, but Ottawa again refused to roll over and play dead. In the final three minutes, Gary Wood threw a 40-yard touchdown strike to Oldham and a five-yard TD strike to Dave Pivec with 14 seconds remaining. With the crowd in an absolute frenzy, Ottawa place-kicker Gerry Organ attempted an onside –kick in an attempt to give the Rough Riders one final shot at the win. But the Argo special teams came up with the ball to preserve a 30-28 win that was narrower than it perhaps should have been.

The crowd left CNE Stadium in a daze. This had been one of the most exciting regular-season games in recent history, and the hometown boys had pulled it out! McQuay rushed for 95 yards and a touchdown on 12 carries. Symons, used mainly in a blocking capacity, added 25 yards on eight carries and scored a touchdown as well. Bill also did a solid job as a receiver out of the backfield, making four catches for 57 yards. Mike Eben had a tremendous game, hauling in seven passes for 76 yards. Through the air, Theismann was nine of 15 for 179 yards, a touchdown and an interception, while Greg Barton went eight of 14 for 84 yards. For the second game in a row, both Marv Luster and Dick Aldridge came up with an interception to slam the door on Ottawa drives.

The Argos were now sitting on a perfect record of 4-0 as they boarded a flight to Vancouver on their way to battle the B.C. Lions at Empire Stadium, which would play host to the Grey Cup game at the end of the season. After four weeks, it was apparent that the Argonauts defence was quite strong. The new additions, Stillwagon and Mack, had blended in well and were playing with intensity. Dave Raimey was doing a solid job at his new defensive back position. On offence, Leon McQuay had dazzled fans, opposing players and the media, yet unbeknownst to those outside the organization, he was despised by many of his teammates.

There was some bad news to temper all the good. Ed Harrington was finished for the year because of a very severe thigh injury. George Wells, a brilliant but sometimes erratic performer, would take Harrington's place in the lineup.

Joe Theismann and Greg Barton had been alternating at quarterback, but most observers felt that Joe would eventually become the No. 1 guy. Greg had been the steadier of the two, but Joe had been more spectacular. When a long drive occurred, it was usually Greg who engineered it. When a big play took place, Joe was usually behind centre.

Barton's style seemed to be working against him. He was a very disciplined, methodical quarterback who liked to establish the running game before taking to the air. But he had little chance of settling into any sort of rhythm when he was playing only on every second series. Theismann's gambling, wide-open style was far better suited to Leo's system of alternating pivots. It allowed Joe to show what he could do, while seeming to punish Greg.

The Argos headed into Vancouver full of confidence. Undefeated and taking on one of the weaker teams in the CFL, they were positive they would be 5-0 late in the afternoon.

The Double Blue jumped into a fast 10-0 lead on a 23-yard MacMillan field goal and a three-yard plunge by rookie running back Harry Abofs. The Lions fought back with a major in the second when centre Bob Howes recovered a fumble and ran it in to the Toronto end zone from three yards out. The Argos countered as Joe Theismann hit Bill Symons with a 20-yard strike for a touchdown, but the Lions came back with two field goals and a major on a 54-yard run by running back Josh Ashton. Early in the fourth quarter, quarterback Paul Brothers moved the B.C. offence down field and dived in from a yard out to increase the Lions' lead to 27-17. With less then two minutes to go in the game, Theismann capped off a desperation drive with a 13-yard TD strike to back-up tight end Tony Moro, but the Argos got no closer and suffered their first defeat of the season.

The Toronto running attack had again been strong. Leon McQuay churned out 102 yards on 13 carries and caught three passes. Symons carried seven times for 54 yards and brought the crowd to its feet with a spectacular 43-yard burst up the middle. Mel Profit was the Argos' leading receiver with five receptions. Dick Thornton had the longest reception of the game when he hauled in a 45-yard bomb from Barton. Theismann was good on nine of 18 passes for 157 yards, two touchdowns and an interception. Barton hit on eight of 11 for 151 yards and an interception.

Toronto now headed off to Edmonton with hopes of bouncing back from their first defeat of the season.

As was the case through much of the year, the Argos got on the scoreboard first when Ivan MacMillan connected on a 14-yard field goal after a drive stalled inside the Edmonton 10. But from that point on, the offence just could not score. Theismann was wracking up a lot of yards through the air but MacMillan missed two field-goal attempts and Theismann and Barton both had drives stopped with interceptions. Early in the fourth quarter, the Eskimos were ahead 14-4. With less than three minutes to go, Bill Symons closed the gap with a three-yard run for the major on a drive engineered by Barton. A two-point conversion attempt failed, leaving Toronto behind 14-9.

On the Eskimos' ensuing possession, Toronto caught a break. Edmonton quarterback Larry Lawrence threw a very poor pass and Dave Raimey made a leaping interception. Leo sent Joe Theismann in and he drove the Argos downfield with time running out. With just 57 seconds left, Theismann hit Mike Eben in the end zone for a go-ahead touchdown.

Edmonton refused to give up, however. Lawrence swiftly drove the Eskimos down field and with no time left on the clock, Dave Cutler lined up to try a 50-yard field goal for the win. The Clarke Stadium crowd was deafening. Cutler (who 10 years later would win the 1981 Grey Cup for Edmonton with a last-second field goal) booted the ball towards the goal posts. All eyes were glued to it as it sailed through the night sky, but it sailed wide. Argonaut players and coaches jumped for joy as the ball bounced through the end zone. It was good for a single point, so the Argos pulled out a 16-15 victory to bump their season record to 5-1.

Leon McQuay was kept in check by the Edmonton defence, picking up only 35 yards on nine carries although he did add five receptions to help the cause. Theismann led the Argo rushers, picking up 49 yards on seven carries, and also threw for 305 yards on 18 completions in 26 pass attempts. Mel Profit had another huge game, catching eight passes for 172 yards.

The Argos headed back home but had another road game to play, at the newly renamed Ivor Wynne Stadium in Hamilton. Two ex-Argos were now playing for Hamilton and waiting eagerly for a crack at Leo's boys. Bobby Taylor, the great receiver, and linebacker Mike Blum were now Tiger-Cats and desperately wanted to get even with their former team.

Less than four minutes into the game, it looked as if Toronto should have stayed home. Scrimmaging from their own two-yard line, Hamilton's Joe Zuger and Dave Fleming thrilled the crowd and stunned the Argo defence by linking up on a spectacular 108-yard pass-and-run touchdown. By the middle of the second quarter, Hamilton was ahead 12-0 and the Argo offence was looking awful. But Barton finally gave the Argos some life when he engineered a drive, finishing it off with an eight-yard TD pass to Mel Profit just before halftime.

In the third quarter, Toronto pulled ahead when the Argo defence pinned the Ticats back deep in their own zone. Zuger tried a quick little swing pass that cornerback Dave Raimey anticipated beautifully. He stepped in front of the receiver and bolted six yards into the Hamilton end zone. MacMillan missed the convert but the Argos had pulled ahead 14-13. MacMillan connected on a 14-yard field goal to push the lead to 17-13 going into the fourth, but that's when the nightmare began. Hamilton erupted for 17 unanswered points (including a touchdown by offensive lineman Ed Chalupka on a fumble recovery) and rolled over Toronto 30-17 at the final whistle.

One moment of levity in the game occurred when Leo spotted Bobby Taylor lining up on the sidelines (feet in bounds) with his helmet off. Cahill went crazy, as Gord Walker described in the *Globe and Mail*: "At one stage of the final quarter, coach Leo Cahill came roaring down the sidelines to yell that Hamilton's Bobby Taylor was standing, helmet off, in front of the Ticat bench as a sleeper. The play worked but because there had been a substitution on the play, it was ruled illegal."

The game was a brutal introduction to the savage Toronto/Hamilton rivalry for Joe Theismann. He completed less than half of his passes and threw four interceptions. Greg Barton looked more poised but had only marginally more success. Leon McQuay had a huge game, picking up 144 yards on 19 carries against a very tough defence. Symons added another 27 yards along the ground on eight carries.

The ex-Argos looked good for Hamilton. Bobby Taylor made two catches for 27 yards, and Mike Blum victimized Joe Theismann on one of the four interceptions. Rookie defensive back Al Brenner, who was having a great season, picked off two Theismann passes and veteran John Williams got the other.

So the Argos had reached the halfway point of the 1971 season. They had come flying out of the gate winning their first four, but had now lost two of the last three. Leo decided to make a couple of personnel moves to try to shore things up. Wanting to get highly touted rookie Tim Anderson into the lineup, Cahill released safety Gerry Sternberg (who was quickly picked up by Hamilton). He also traded defensive back Jim Tomlin to British Columbia for future considerations. (Tomlin, an Eastern all-star the year before, had requested the trade. His wife, a certified school teacher from Texas, was unable to find a school board in the Toronto area that would hire her.) Anderson would take Sternberg's place, and Dick Thornton, who had done a terrific job at wide receiver, would move back to defensive back to replace Tomlin.

Toronto and Hamilton had a rematch the following week, this time at CNE Stadium. Once again the Ticats broke out early, scoring a major less than three minutes into the game. But the Argos countered when Greg Barton moved the offence down the field and fired an 11-yard strike to Jim Henderson. In the second quarter, Henderson put Toronto ahead 14-7 when he caught a Joe Theismann pass for six points.

In the third, Leon McQuay again brought the sellout crowd to its feet when he took a handoff from Barton and exploded for a 64-yard touchdown run to pad the lead to 21-7. The Ticats picked up another major in the fourth while the Argo defence added a safety, sacking Joe Zuger in the end zone and making the final score 23-14 in favor of Toronto.

This time, it was the Argo defence coming up with the interceptions. Tim Anderson, Dave Raimey (with his third in three games) and Gene Mack all picked off Ticat passes. The Argonaut defence overall was superb, with Jim Stillwagon and Jim Corrigall wreaking havoc in the Ticats backfield. They were the big factor as Toronto sacked Zuger five times and Gabler once.

McQuay broke the 100-yard barrier again, running for 105 yards on 14 carries. Theismann struggled, completing only three of eight passes for

64 yards, one major and one interception, but Barton was simply outstanding, completing 13 of 15 for 81 yards with a touchdown and an interception. Greg was totally in control; his passing was sharp and he used the running attack brilliantly to set up the passing game. Barton may not have looked as spectacular as Theismann at times, but his star was starting to shine. Signing two big-name quarterbacks was looking like an act of genius on Leo's part.

The Argos hit the road again for the ninth game of the season. This time they'd be taking their show into Lansdowne Park to battle the young but up and coming Rough Riders. Ottawa broke out in front when quarterback Rick Cassata rolled out to pass, saw a seam in the Argo defence and took off, racing 58 yards for a major. Three minutes later, Tricky Dick Thornton evened things up when he stepped in front of a Cassata pass and returned it 43 yards for a touchdown.

In the second quarter, the Argos pulled ahead on touchdown receptions by Leon McQuay and Tony Moro. The Toronto offence stalled through much of the second half only getting five points off the toes of MacMillan and Andrusyshyn, but it was all the Argos needed as they picked up their seventh win of the year, 26-17 over the Rough Riders.

Ottawa had apparently decided to test Thornton., assuming he might be rusty at the defensive back position since he had played the first half of the year at wide receiver. How wrong that was. This game turned out to be one of the finest in Thornton's long and brilliant career. He intercepted three Cassata passes, returning one for a major, and made several spectacular tackles. Tim Anderson was clearly showing he had no problems making the jump to pro ball as he also picked off a Cassata pass and played solidly overall.
After two poor games, Joe Theismann bounced back with a strong effort, completing seven of 11 attempts for 82 yards and a touchdown. His solid performance became very important as Greg Barton suffered a broken finger on his throwing hand and would be gone for the remainder of the regular season. Before his injury, Greg completed four of 10 for 114 yards, a touchdown and an interception. So now the Grey Cup hopes of the Argos would rest, to a great extent, on the shoulders of rookie Joe Theismann. If he failed or went down, wily old Dick Thornton would have to move into the quarterbacking role.

Joe's first opponent as the undisputed No. 1 quarterback was the Calgary Stampeders. The Stamps, Grey Cup finalists in 1970, were having another strong season and were looking to get back to the national title game and win it for the first time since 1948. They had started the season even stronger than Toronto, with seven straight victories, before stumbling when quarterback Jerry Keeling went down with a separated shoulder. But even with Keeling out, Calgary's defence was as strong as ever and the offence still dangerous.

The Argonauts won the game of division leaders handily, 18-7. Theismann came up with a strong performance, completing 16 of 26 passes and throwing two touchdown strikes to Mel Profit, but he also tossed two interceptions. Joe was aided by a strong Toronto running attack as Leo had decided to run the ball right at Calgary's magnificent middle linebacker, Wayne Harris. Harris was unbelievably fast side to side and killed most sweeps before they got started, but he was not that big and Leo felt he was vulnerable to big running backs running right at him. That is exactly what Toronto did after McQuay left the game early with an injury. Bill Symons took over and ran the ball 10 times for 60 yards. Cahill also used Harry Abofs, Mike Eben and Dave Cranmer as ball carriers, and Theismann ran 11 times as well. All in all, Argo runners netted 183 yards.

The Toronto defence was simply tremendous. Led by Jim Stillwagon, who exploded into the Calgary backfield seemingly on every play, the Argos almost completely nullified the Stampeders' running attack, holding it to 60 yards.

Jim Lindsey, the Stamps' backup quarterback, was sacked three times and completed only 18 of 38 passes. Pete Martin and Dick Thornton made interceptions. Thornton, after just two games at his old DB position, had already picked off four passes and returned one for a touchdown. Trix was back with a vengeance, and if you dared throw into his zone, it was at your own risk.

This was a huge win for The Argos. They had proven they could beat the best teams in the West. They had whipped Winnipeg, Saskatchewan and now Calgary. If they could finally get out of the East, their chances in the Grey Cup looked good.

The win over Calgary was costly, however. After the game, it was revealed that McQuay had suffered torn knee cartilage. He would be out for a while and it uncertain if he would return at all this season. Dave Knechtel had suffered a dislocated elbow and rookie offensive lineman John Trainor tore up his knee. Add to that the earlier injuries to Greg Barton and Ed Harrington and despite a 8-2 record, the situation was not rosy.

A bizarre scheduling anomaly saw Toronto head back to Ottawa for the second time in three weeks for the next game. It turned out to be a game dominated by defence, as neither offence had much success.

At the nine-minute mark of the first quarter, Joe Theismann hit Mike Eben with a 23-yard touchdown pass, but that would be the only time Toronto got into the Ottawa end zone all game. The Argos' other points came off a 38-yard field goal from Ivan MacMillan in the second quarter and two singles from Zenon Andrusyshyn in the second half. Ottawa was held even more under control, as its offence came up with just a third-quarter single to go along with a safety touch scored by the Ottawa defence. The final score was 12-3 for the Argonauts.

With McQuay out of the lineup, most observers figured Cahill would turn the running attack back over to Bill Symons. Instead, Joe Theismann led the attack, scrambling 12 times for 62 yards. Symons carried the ball only nine times for 16 yards. Joe completed 12 of 19 passes for 118 yards and for one of the few times all year did not throw an interception. The game was an absolute disaster for Ottawa quarterbacks Rick Cassata and Paul Brothers. In total they threw four interceptions and completed only 12 of 30 passes. Tim Anderson, Marv Luster, Chip Barrett and Dave Raimey all came up with interceptions.

The Argos now headed to Montreal to battle the defending Grey Cup champion Montreal Alouettes, who were falling out of playoff contention as injuries devastated them. Toronto roared to an early lead as Theismann and Eben linked up on a 77-yard pass and run for a touchdown at the one-minute mark of the first quarter. Shortly afterwards, Toronto was moving the ball again when Theismann hit Eben with a 26-yard strike. Mike was stretched out making the catch when Montreal's Gene Gaines slammed into his rib cage, shattering a number of bones. Eben somehow hung onto the ball but he crashed to the field unconscious. It was a big play for the Argos, but it cost them one of the league's finest receivers.

In the third quarter, with the Argos up 12-3, Dick Thornton made professional football history. He picked off a Sonny Wade pass (one of five pickoffs Wade and Jim Chasey would throw that day and one of three Dick would grab) and returned it 23 yards for a touchdown. That was the eighth time in his career he had taken an interception back all the way, the most of any player in all of professional football.

In the fourth quarter, Harry Abofs caught a 34-yard Theismann pass for a touchdown and Gene Mack imitated Tricky Dick, picking off a Chasey pass and returning it 22 yards for a touchdown. The final score was 32-5 for the Argonauts and the victory clinched first place. For the first time since Tobin Rote had been their leader a decade earlier, Toronto would finish atop the Eastern Conference.

The Argonaut defence at this point was playing unbelievable football. In their last three games, they had given up only one touchdown, a single, and a field goal. That was it! The defence was certainly of championship calibre. In the Montreal game, the Alouettes had been held to 143 yards along the ground and 75 yards through the air. Thornton picked off three passes while Mack and Marv Luster each came up with one. The defence had also scored 14 points with the Thornton and Mack touchdowns plus a safety.

The offence, however, was prompting concern. The running attack without Leon McQuay was looking confused. For some reason, Bill Symons was not being utilized as much as he could be. In the Montreal game, he carried the ball only eight times. Harry Abofs rushed four times and Theismann picked up 46 yards on seven carries. Joe had a shaky game through the air, however, completing just 14 of 31 passes although two went for touchdowns and he did amass 331 yards passing.

The Toronto Argonauts, while battered and bruised, now had a record of 10-2 and had wrapped up first place. It was time to prepare for the Eastern Final, try to get healthy and pray that they suffered no more injuries.

But more bad news awaited. One of Mike Eben's lungs had been punctured by his broken ribs. He almost died on the flight home when the altitude and pressurization in the plane affected the lung and caused him to go into deep distress. It was not over when they got the plane on the ground, either.

Mike recalled the entire sequence of events: "I was having a great game and had caught a couple of passes. Gene Gaines hit me with a knee that went under the breastplate of my shoulder pads and broke a couple of ribs. One of the ribs punctured a lung. That was worsened when we flew home and the altitude caused problems. I was taken off the plane in an ambulance. After I got out of the hospital I had a homemade sausage at my mother's house and the natural bacteria in the sausage reacted with the antibiotics I had been given for the lung and I came down with a major staph infection. I remember weaving across St. George and Bloor looking like I was drunk. I got home and my head was swimming. I was taken to Women's College Hospital where I spent a week in Intensive Care."

Missing Eben, Harrington, McQuay, Knechtel, and Trainor, the Argos went lurching into a rematch at home against Montreal. Globe and Mail columnist Rex MacLeod, tongue in cheek, suggested the injuries were getting so bad that Argo general manager John Barrow might have to make a comeback. Such a development would have led to some lively practice sessions considering the low esteem Barrow was held in by the players! The only bright spot on the injury front was that Greg Barton was back and would see some playing time in the penultimate regular-season game.

Montreal moved out to a 9-0 lead by the end of the first half although the Argo defence was hanging tough. The offence, however, was still struggling. In the third quarter, Profit hauled in a seven-yard pass from Theismann for a touchdown but Toronto would get no closer. On the Argos' next drive, Montreal's all-star linebacker Mark Kosmos stepped in front of a Barton pass and returned it 46 yards for a touchdown. Montreal added 12 more points in the fourth quarter with a safety, touchdown (off a fumble recovery) and field goal, and coasted to a 28-7 victory.

Offensively, the Argos were bordering on hopeless as the playoffs approached. Theismann was their leading rusher with 41 yards on four carries. Bill Symons was simply not being used. H carried the ball just three times for a total of nine yards. Dick Thornton tried to figure out why Leo didn't use Bill more in this situation. "Leo had always been a 'throwing' coach anyway and loved to put points on the board. He was never that fond of the running game until he brought Leon on board, thinking he was God's gift to scampering for TDs – which he did in games that didn't mean shit. So when Leon went down, Leo went back to winging it."

Bill had a different opinion. "Ever since my big year in 1968, there was conflict between Leo and myself. He was on my back all though 1969 and 1970. The problem was, when I almost went to the Denver Broncos, I ended up staying out of loyalty to Blackie Johnston. Leo decided he couldn't count on me and benched me for the final game in 1969. That cost me 1,000 yards on the season. My toe was bad but I could have played. He was on me all of 1970 even though I was an all-Canadian all-star that year. Then as soon as he signed Leon, he forgot all about me. When Leon got hurt, I think Leo was afraid of being wrong. In his mind I couldn't do the job, and he didn't want to be proven wrong."

Dave Raimey feels Cahill simply lost sight of what Symons could contribute. "Leo was a wonderful man. He treated me great and I think the world of him. But I never agreed with how he treated Sy. Bill was a great back and a great leader. He always put the team first. Everything with him was the team. He would have these wonderful parties at his house for the team, and wives and children were always included. But when we got Leon, Leo just forgot about him. He used him just as a blocking back. He slowly broke Sy's spirit and it was terrible to watch."

Through the air, Theismann completed 11 of 23 passes for a touchdown and an interception against Montreal. Barton naturally looked rusty, completing only four of nine for 25 yards and an interception. The best-looking pass of the day came from Mel Profit, who took a pitchout and fired a strike to Dave Cranmer that led to a 46-yard gain.

The 1971 regular season would end the following week at CNE Stadium with the Hamilton Tiger-Cats coming to town. A couple of days before the game, Leo made an important phone call to Danny Nykoluk, who had retired after the 1970 season, ending a magnificent 15-year career with the Double Blue. He had done everything in that career except play in a Grey Cup game. Leo, looking at the Argos' depleted injury list, decided Danny could help.

With a week off while the Semifinal was played, there was a chance Mike Eben would be able to return for the Final. But with the loss of John Trainor, the offensive line was a huge concern. Montreal had sacked Theismann five times and got through to punter Zenon Andrusyshyn once. You could not win playoff games giving up that many sacks. Leo felt if Nykoluk was in any sort of decent shape, he could be a big help.

Leo recalls the phone conversation: "I said to the coaches, 'I'm going to get Nykoluk.' They all said, 'There's no way he'll play.' 'Well, you just listen to this conversation.' I called Nykoluk and said, 'Danny?' 'Yeah, coach.' 'How're you doing? You know what I'm calling for.' 'Yeah, I think I do.' 'What do you say?' 'What time do you want me there?' "

Once again, Leo had shown that he could be creative when it was necessary to find a key player.

The season-ending game against Hamilton didn't exactly inspire confidence about the post-season. Hamilton jumped in front early and never looked back. By early in the fourth quarter, the Ticats were ahead 23-1 as the Toronto offence was once again doing nothing. Theismann threw four interceptions and saw two of them returned for touchdowns. Hamilton defensive back Al Brenner picked off two passes, taking one back 50 yards for a score. Mike Eben remembers Brenner's eagerness to face the rookie. "Before a game Al Brenner would ask me if Joe was starting. When I said Yes, he practically jumped for joy."

The offence finally got some life when Theismann and McQuay connected on an 81-yard passing play for a touchdown. With less than a minute to go in the game, Joe hit Dick Thornton, who was doing double duty at wide receiver and defensive back, with a five-yard pass for a touchdown, but all that did was make the final score a more respectable 23-15.

In his return from injury, McQuay was a shadow of his former self other than the one big play. He carried the ball 11 times for just 17 yards. Bill Symons never carried the ball once, although he did catch five passes coming out of the backfield. Theismann filled the air with passes, throwing 40 times and completing 22 for 376 yards. Danny Nykoluk, although understandably not in great shape, did play well and was a big help on the offensive line.

The Ticats were extremely pleased with their convincing victory over the team they expected to face in the Eastern Final, but also suffered a huge blow in the game. Joe Zuger, their great veteran quarterback, was gang-tackled by the relentless Toronto defence onto the asphalt running track that circled the CNE Stadium field. He was driven shoulder first into the track, practically destroying the joint. Hamilton's Grey Cup hopes would now rest squarely on the shoulders of ex-Argo Wally Gabler.

Toronto, after finishing with a league-best record of 10-4, now waited for the winner of the Hamilton/Ottawa semifinal. In the Western Conference, Calgary and Saskatchewan both finished with a record of 9-6-1, with the Stampeders awarded first place in a tie-breaker. The Roughriders would battle Don Jonas's Winnipeg Blue Bombers in the Western Semifinal. Jonas, like Gabler an ex-Argo, had led the league in passing and would go on to be named the CFL's most outstanding player of 1971.

In the semifinals, Hamilton – led by a superb performance from Wally Gabler –thumped Ottawa 23-4 while Saskatchewan outlasted Winnipeg in a shootout, 34-23. The Argos now prepared for the two-game final, starting with a trip to the Steel City against their most hated rivals.

Days before the game, Leo decided to make a huge change on defence in an effort to keep Hamilton off-balance. He removed Pete Martin, who had played very well in the middle linebacker position all year, replacing him with rookie Larry Brame, who was cut in training camp and been on and off the roster all season. The team was stunned by the move. "Pete had played great all year," says Bill Symons. "Larry was the better athlete, but Pete was much smarter on the field. It didn't make sense to do it."

Dick Thornton was also baffled. "I have no idea why Leo moved Brame to middle linebacker. I've always said, don't break up a winning combination that has worked all year long. Could be that American/Canadian syndrome again. I just don't know, but it did upset Pete and the rest of the defensive unit. Like I've said before, I'll take brains over athletic ability any time."

Leo, when asked about the move, simply said: "Pete was a student of the game. He would stand beside me during games and point out things I didn't know. He was a great leader on and off the field. But Larry Brame was a better player."

Regardless of the uproar it caused, the move was made and the team headed into Hamilton to battle the very confident Tiger-Cats. Although Toronto had finished with the league's best record, Hamilton had whipped the Argos twice and Toronto had sagged badly at the end of the year. Toronto looked ripe for an upset.

But all was not well in Hamilton. Head Coach Al Dorow had become involved in an off-field incident that greatly upset and embarrassed Tiger-Cats management. General manager Ralph Sazio had decided that Dorow would be gone at the end of the season regardless of what happened in the playoffs. He would still be on the sidelines in the meantime, but would do little coaching. The players, led by Wally Gabler, would take that over. Wally explains: "Myself, Garney Henley and a couple of other players got together at a Burlington restaurant and figured out what plays we would use and put together a game plan. Al actually hung around as a figurehead but it was clear he was gone at the end of the year and he really didn't do any serious coaching."

Wally spoke about the Ticats' preparation for Toronto: "I loved playing the Argos, as Leo used a lot of man-to-man defence, which is a quarterback's dream if you can read it correctly. I burned Toronto the year before when I was in Winnipeg, hitting Ken Neilsen with a TD when he was isolated on Tricky man to man. Toronto had much more talent than we did and based simply on that, we knew we shouldn't have even been close. Our defence, though, felt we could take Leon out of the game by getting on him quickly. We knew if we gang-tackled him and hit him hard early, then he would take himself out of the game. He didn't like to get hit."

Along with the switch from Martin to Brame, Leo also decided to go the distance with Joe Theismann at quarterback in an effort to get the offence back on track. Cahill decided that with McQuay back in the lineup, the Argonauts would revert to a more conservative running game. McQuay and Bill Symons would get a lot of work chugging the ball downfield. This had worked early in the year and Leo hoped it would be successful again.

Ivor Wynne Stadium was packed for the game. The Argos struck first and took the crowd out of the game for a while. The defensive "blue and white wall" came through to score the points. Zenon Andrusyshyn drove a rocket of a punt down to the Ticats' one-yard line and on two plays later, Gabler dropped back into his end zone to pass. The front four of Jim Corrigall, Dave Knechtel, Jim Stillwagon and George Wells blasted through the Hamilton offensive line. Gabler vanished beneath Knechtel on the artificial turf.

The safety put Toronto up 2-0. Less than five minutes later, the Argos struck again. From the Toronto 50, Theismann rolled right with Angelo Mosca in hot pursuit. Before reaching the right sideline, Joe suddenly stopped, pivoted left and launched a missile of a pass all the way back across the other side of the field. The ball sailed 52 yards to Jim Henderson at the Hamilton eight. He made the catch and sprinted unmolested into the end zone. It was an incredible throw, not unlike something Russ Jackson would have done against Toronto in the late 1960s. Ivan MacMillan's convert moved the Argonaut lead to 9-0 and the crowd at Ivor Wynne was quiet. This Argo team was obviously far different from the one Hamilton had beaten so badly two weeks before.

Before the first quarter ended, the Argos were back on the board with MacMillan hammering a 41-yard field goal to stretch the lead to 12-0. Hamilton's offence finally showed some life on their next possession when Gabler, from his own 40, threw deep to Dave Buchanan. Dave Raimey gambled and tried for the interception but missed and Buchanan, who had slipped in behind him, made the catch and turned it into a 50-

yard gain The Argo defence then came up big, forcing Tommy-Joe Coffey to kick a 25-yard field goal that got Hamilton on the board.

In the second quarter Theismann's season-long penchant for throwing interceptions cropped up again. He had passes picked off by Al Brenner (for the fifth time that year) and Bob Krause deep in Toronto territory. But great play by the Toronto defence, some stupid penalties by Hamilton (including a careless offside and a roughing penalty caused by an idiotic punch) cost the Ticats dearly. And Coffey missed three field-goal attempts, keeping Toronto in the lead at the half 12-6.

The Argos increased the lead to 16-6 in the third quarter on a single off an Andrusyshyn punt and a 29-yard MacMillan field goal. Those points were set up when Hamilton took two unnecessary roughness penalties that kept Argo drives alive. Late in the third, Theismann marched the offence 60 yards in seven plays, with the big one a 34-yard bootleg run by the QB. The drive ended when Bill Symons plowed into the Ticat end zone on a third-down gamble from the Hamilton one. The final scoring in the game came in the fourth quarter when Hamilton punter Paul McKay drove 55- and 45-yard punts through the Toronto end zone for singles, making the final score 23-8 in favour of the Argonauts. That meant a 15-point lead in the two-game, total-points series. To get to the Grey Cup, all Toronto needed to do the following week at home was win, tie or lose by less than 15 points.

The Argo offence looked much more effective in Game 1, with Leo reverting to a ground-oriented attack. Leon McQuay, getting his heaviest workload of the year, carried the ball 20 times for 71 yards and seemed to have recovered from his knee injury. Symons, getting more work as well, ran nine times for 42 yards and caught two passes. Theismann, working with a very conservative game plan, picked up 38 yards along the ground on five carries. Through the air, Joe completed six of 18 passes for 112 yards. He had the TD strike to Henderson but also had three passes intercepted.

The Hamilton offence had little success along the ground and was held to 95 yards. Wally Gabler was harassed throughout the game, sacked twice and under constant pressure otherwise. He had passes intercepted by Chip Barrett (who also made two bone-crunching tackles on Ticat receivers when they made receptions deep in Toronto territory) and Tim Anderson, who was continuing the brilliant form he had exhibited since joining the squad back in August. Leo's gamble on Larry Brame had not hurt the defence. The linebacking corps of Brame, Gene Mack and Dick Aldridge played extremely well and was a huge factor in nullifying the Tiger-Cats' ground attack. The other Argo question marks, Mike Eben and Danny Nykoluk, were answered in the affirmative. Nykoluk was rounding into shape and did a solid job on the offensive line, while Eben – playing with heavily wrapped ribs – made one catch and clobbered a couple of Ticats with strong blocks.

The Argos began preparation for the second game with the entire city of Toronto gripped in a championship frenzy. After the disheartening losses to Ottawa in 1968 and 1969, though, there was almost a sense amongst the Argo faithful that they would find yet another way to blow a critical game. Feelings were mixed among the players, too. Mel Profit, among others, felt the tension. "Preparing for the second game against Hamilton in 1971 was the most pressure-filled week of football I've ever experienced," he wrote later. "The big problem was overcoming the Argonaut jinx, the long-established habit of blowing the important game." Mike Eben looked at it differently: "There were a lot of new guys on the team who were not around against Ottawa. We knew Hamilton was not Ottawa and felt with our defence, if we didn't make any bonehead plays we would beat them."

Newcomers like Jim Stillwagon never gave the so-called Argo jinx a second thought. "I had no recollection of the past Argonauts. We were focused as a team on the situation at hand."

Along with talking about his feelings of trepidation, Profit was also hinting to the press about retirement. His battles with John Barrow and his overall distaste for the world of professional sports were really beginning to nag him. In an interview in the *Toronto Star* published on November 20, 1971, which was conducted at his boutique on Wellesley Street, Profit spoke frankly:

"If you wrote that the second game could be my last before Toronto fans, I could not challenge you. For one thing, it's become harder and harder for me to justify some of the things about football that happen to me.

There are dehumanizing things about the game, things you don't justify by saying that we're well paid. That's the typical public reaction. For one thing, it's not normal not to know from one day to the next where your home is. There are things in life more important than $15-20,000 a year. I think I proved my principle on that last year. I took a chance and I won, so I guess I must have been right."

That was a reference to his contract dispute the previous December, when Profit threatened to retire on a point of principle. Intervention by board chairman John Bassett salvaged the situation.

Preparing for Game 2, Leo was determined to stick with the same game plan he had used in the first game. Keep it conservative on offence by running the ball and managing the clock. Cahill emphasized the importance of hanging onto the pigskin, and pointed out that all the pressure was now on Hamilton. The Ticats were down by 15 and had to come back against the tremendous Toronto defence.

The second game of the 1971 Eastern Final was played on a chilly day. The temperature was 38 degrees F and the field at CNE Stadium was muddy. This would be the final game ever played on natural turf at CNE Stadium as the City of Toronto had made plans to install artificial turf the following season.

Hamilton quieted the sellout crowd early. With the Argo offence scrimmaging inside its own five-yard line, defensive lineman Gary Inskeep (an ex-Argo) blasted into offensive guard Joe Vijuk and knocked him back into Joe Theismann, who stumbled and fell in the end zone, giving a quick safety to the Ticats.

It was a bizarre way to start and left Argo fans wondering if this was a foreshadowing of the rest of the game. But this was not the old Argos. They were not going to fold up or give up. Four minutes later, Jim Corrigall, who would play the game of his life, sacked Wally Gabler inside the Hamilton 20 and stripped the ball loose. Gene Mack, barreling in from his outside linebacker position, recovered on the 12-yard line. On the next offensive play, Theismann handed off to Bill Symons who shot through a gaping hole created by centre Paul Desjardins and guard Joe Vijuk in the Hamilton defensive line to score easily. Ivan MacMillan's convert made the score 7-2 and the hill the Ticats had to climb was that much higher, with an aggregate series score of 30-10.

In the second quarter, Wally Gabler moved the Cats 63 yards on 11 plays and finished off by sending running back Max Anderson, on a third-down gamble, crashing into the Argo end zone from four yards out to get the lead back at 9-7. Later in the quarter, Tommy-Joe Coffey missed a 24-yard field goal and got a single point out of it, so the Argos' overall lead was down to 12 at 30-18.

Theismann didn't panic and brought the offence roaring back. He marched the Argos 85 yards with the big plays a 27-yard scramble on his part and a 14-yard completion to Mike Eben. From the Hamilton 13, Joe dropped back and fired for Mel Profit in the end zone. Garney Henley went for the interception but unintentionally tipped the ball right into Profit's hands. Mel juggled it and then pulled it into his body for the score. If Henley had made the interception, there was nobody between him and the Argonaut end zone 110 yards away. The old Argo "bounce," rarely seen since 1953, seemed to be back. The convert made the score 14-10 in the game and 37-18 overall.

The Argos took their 19-point series lead into the locker room at halftime. Leo emphasized the need to play it close to the vest. He told punt returners Harry Abofs and Peter Paquette to forget about runbacks – simply catch the punts and don't risk a fumble. He told Theismann to hand the ball off to Symons and McQuay as much as possible. "Hamilton will be desperate now," he told the guys. "Gabler will have to come out throwing. Be ready for it, and just keep doing what you have been doing."

Early in the third quarter, Toronto had a huge chance to put the game way out of reach. Theismann marched the Toronto offence down to the Hamilton one-yard line. He took the snap from Desjardins and spun to hand the ball to McQuay. But Joe was in such a state of excitement that he ran into slotback Dave Cranmer, who was coming out of the backfield, and fumbled the ball with the Ticats recovering.

Wally Gabler then came out firing. The Ticats needed points and they had less than 30 minutes left to get them. They picked up a single on a

38-yard punt by Paul McKay and on their next possession, Wally drove them 61 yards on eight plays, with Dave Raimey being nailed on a pass interference call to set up a two-yard run by Dick Wesolowski for the touchdown. That narrowed the series gap to 37-25.

Hamilton had another big chance before the quarter ended but failed to capitalize as Gabler hit receiver Gord Christian, who had slipped behind the Argo pass coverage and was wide open. Christian dropped it, costing the Ticats an almost sure touchdown. That proved to be Hamilton's last offensive gasp. Early in the fourth quarter, the Toronto offence marched determinedly down the field. McQuay had a brilliant 13-yard run for one first down. Theismann connected with Eben for another 21 –yards. MacMillan ended the drive by coming through with a 29-yard field goal to give the Argos a 15-point overall lead, 40-25.

Hamilton tried everything possible to close the gap. Garney Henley went out to return punts, Gabler threw on every down and gambled on every third down, but it simply was not enough. The Blue and White Wall would not be breached again. The sellout crowd at CNE Stadium was on its feet roaring with joy as the clock ran out on the Ticats. Toronto was headed back to the Grey Cup for the first time in 19 years!

The final score in the game was 17-17 and the Argonauts won the total-points series 40-25. No longer would the Argos be known as the team that could not win the big game. At long last, a championship was in sight.

It was an impressive performance by the entire Toronto squad. Joe Theismann played a very mature game, sticking to Leo's conservative plan and not making any crucial errors. He completed just six of 16 passes but one went for a touchdown. And most importantly, he avoided throwing any interceptions. Leon McQuay, looking like his knee was fine, picked up 88 yards on 17 carries. Symons added another 45 yards on eight carries.

The Argo defence was nothing short of outstanding. It held the Tiger-Cats to only 106 yards along the ground and kept Gabler under constant pressure. Jim Corrigall was a tower of strength on the defensive line, sacking Wally twice and rocking him on two other occasions with devastating hits just after he released the ball. Hamilton did not play a bad game offensively, but Toronto was simply a better team.

Speaking to the Toronto Star's Ken McKee after the game, Dick Thornton said: "I figure we beat them because we had the better club, nothing else. Their preparation was superb."

The Argonauts did not escape the game unscathed. Larry Brame, who had been playing well at middle linebacker since replacing Pete Martin, suffered a broken hand and would have to play in the Grey Cup with his hand in a cast. Dick Aldridge suffered a badly sprained ankle and was iffy. Jim Stillwagon was labouring on a bad knee that was causing him a lot of pain.

The 1971 Grey Cup would be played on Sunday, November 28, at Empire Stadium in Vancouver. Toronto would face the Western Conference champion Calgary Stampeders, who had defeated the Saskatchewan Roughriders in the best-of-three Western Final 30-21 and 23-21.

Ever since he took over the Argonauts, Leo Cahill had for the most part been able to stay ahead of the dismal cloud that had been chasing the franchise since 1953. It had made a devastating appearance in the final game of the 1969 Eastern Final, and seemed to "hang around" the team through much of 1970. But the jinx now seemed to have vanished and the Argos were going back to the Grey Cup with the knowledge and history that the team had never lost a Grey Cup to a Western-based team.

Eight

1971 Grey Cup

The Toronto Argonauts landed in Vancouver on Tuesday, November 23, as the "bad boys" of the East. The Calgary Stampeders were the "good guys," a clean-cut squad from a very conservative town, and they were going up against the big-city Argos, with their long hair, beads and wild clothes. It was a classic East vs. West matchup.

Despite the Argonauts' 18-7 victory over Calgary in the regular season, the Stampeders were slight favourites going into the game. Calgary was a veteran squad in its third Grey Cup game in four years. The Stamps had lost the 1968 and 1970 championship games. This might be their last chance at victory, a factor that many observers felt would give them an edge. Some thought that the Argos, after all their playoff collapses in recent years, would be satisfied simply to be there.

Mike Eben confirms that even some Argos might have felt that way: "There was a feeling that we finally got the monkey off our back just getting there." Eben, who was still working towards his PhD, was stuck in his hotel room all Grey Cup week when the team wasn't practising, studying hard for a major exam the following week. There were no Grey Cup parties for him.

But there were for other players. "It was always lots of fun," remembers Dick Thornton. "Leo took the approach that we were men, not boys, and gave us free rein in Vancouver 'til the night before the game. There were actual parties for the team as a whole and we were able to take part in most of the festivities. Thinking back, though, it rained every day, so that put a big damper on the street parties."

Dick did not feel the team was satisfied just to get there, and in fact he was confident every player was ready. "Practices were crisp and short because of the rain; we all knew what we had to do. You get to the Big Dance only a few times, so we realized it was now or never. The mood of the team was of total confidence."

Jim Stillwagon agrees: "We thought we would beat them. They were a good team but we had the confidence of the Argonauts. We were the bad guys of the league, and the rest of the league loved to hate us. We respected Calgary but we did not fear them."

Toronto's offensive game plan was the same one the team had used against Calgary earlier in the season. Leo wanted to run Bill Symons and Leon McQuay right at Wayne Harris, and use short passes from Joe Theismann sprinting outside. The Argos' main concern with the Calgary defence was the front four of John Helton, Craig Koinzan, Fred James and Dick Suderman. This was the biggest, strongest and fastest defensive line in the CFL. Backed up by Harris and outsider linebackers Joe Forzani and Jim Furlong, they were capable of putting tremendous pressure on any offence. Toronto had done a good job neutralizing them in the regular season, but since then Calgary had been playing better every game. The Stampeders' defence had done a fine job shutting down Ron Lancaster and the high-powered Saskatchewan offence in the Western Final.

The Calgary offence was also strong. At quarterback, Jerry Keeling was an underrated but solid veteran quarterback who seemed to get the job done somehow. His running backs, Jesse Mims and Hugh McKinnis, were not flashy but picked up tough yardage when they had to. The receiving corps of Gerry Shaw, Jon Henderson, all-star tight end Herm Harrison and Canadian slotback Rudy Linterman were all very capable.

Nonetheless, Leo didn't install any special defensive game plan. The Calgary offence was good, but he had complete confidence in the ability of his defence to handle it.

Grey Cup Sunday was dark and gloomy, with a steady rain pounding down on the artificial turf of Empire Stadium as the temperature hovered around 40 degrees. During the warmups, players on both teams were appalled by the footing. Despite the best efforts of the grounds crew, there was more than an inch of water on the turf and it seemed to be getting deeper. The turf was slippery and would make running very difficult.

"I really thought we'd win that game until we saw the weather," recalls Eben. "It rained every day we were there. We liked to pass and that type of weather took that away from our game."

The Argonauts came out for the game in their road uniforms: white jerseys, dark blue pants. The Stamps were in their home red jerseys.

Toronto won the coin toss and elected to receive the ball. Larry Robinson kicked off to Dave Raimey. From the Toronto seven-yard line, he took the ball out to the Argonaut 26. On the Argos' first play from scrimmage, Theismann handed off to Symons, who slashed for six yards. On second down Theismann dropped to pass. The Argo offensive line seemed to collapse as the Calgary front four swarmed in, and Theismann crashed to the turf enveloped in the arms of Fred James for a loss of 10 yards. Zenon Andrusyshyn then hammered a punt that was returned by Jim Silye to the Stampeder 53.

Figure 8-1: *"Joe Theismann barks the signals as the Argo offence prepares for action."*

"In the picture are Mel Profit # 75, Danny Nykoluk # 60, Charlie Bray # 57, Paul Desjardins # 44, and Jim Henderson, # 72. Jim Furlong # 70 is visible for Calgary."

On Calgary's first play, quarterback Jerry Keeling, who had not played in the regular-season meeting between the clubs, fumbled the snap, got it back and watched the Argo defence pour in on him. He cocked his arm to fire just as he was drilled by Marv Luster, swarming in from his safety position. Luster knocked the ball loose and the Argos recovered at the Calgary 34-yard line. The Argos were jubilant until they saw that the officials had ruled it an incomplete pass. They ruled that Keeling's arm had been in motion before he was hit. TV replays suggested it should have been ruled a fumble with the Argos taking over the ball deep in Calgary territory. Leo could only curse this early bit of bad luck. Despite the disappointing turn of events, the Toronto defence held. Calgary was forced to punt, giving the ball back to the Argos.

The resulting Toronto series began with an incomplete pass from Theismann. On second down, Dick Suderman came charging in and Leon McQuay failed to block him. Theismann was buried again, the second sack series-ending sack in a row. Andrusyshyn punted to the Calgary 54 and Jim Silye returned it the Argo 52.

Keeling now got the Stampeders moving. After a five-yard run by Mims that was stopped by Jim Stillwagon, the veteran QB connected with Rudy Linterman for a 17-yard gain to the Argo 30, where Tim Anderson made a desperate tackle to drag him down. Two more runs moved the Stamps to the Toronto 14. Then Keeling dropped back to pass and hit Herm Harrison, who had slipped behind Larry Brame and between Pete Martin and Chip Barrett, for the first touchdown of the game. Robinson's convert made the score 7-0 for Calgary.

Toronto lost linebacker Dick Aldridge for the rest of the game on this series. A Stampeder inadvertently kicked Aldridge's sprained ankle, finishing him for the day, so Pete Martin replaced him at outside linebacker. Martin, although happy to be playing again after being benched for Brame a few weeks earlier, felt terrible for Aldridge. "Dick is still a great friend of mine. We both joined the Argos in 1965 and to work so hard and for so long to get to the Grey Cup. To get hurt after just a couple of plays – it was really too bad. I felt terrible for him."

Robinson's kickoff came down to Raimey at the Argonaut five. Dave quickly lateralled to McQuay, who danced, slipped and skidded his way across the water-covered turf to the Toronto 40-yard line. Leon then took a handoff from Theismann and picked up another four yards. On the next play Joe dropped to pass, ducked away from heavy Calgary pressure and scrambled for 12 yards to pick up Toronto's initial first down of the game. Two more McQuay runs gained just six yards and Andrusyshyn came in to blast a punt down inside the Calgary five. Silye fielded the punt, dropped it, then picked it back up at the goal line just as Tony Moro, streaking down on the punt coverage team, rocked him with a tremendous hit that sent Silye flying five yards back into the end zone. It appeared Silye had been knocked into the end zone by Moro, which would have meant a two-point safety. But the officials ruled Silye was tackled at the one-yard line, so no points were awarded. Had it been called a safety, it would have been two important points for Toronto. Instead, the Stamps scrimmaged at the one, from where Keeling moved them to their own 32 before the Argo defence stiffened and forced a Furlong punt.

In *The Argo Bounce*, Jay Teitel described the scene when the Argo offence came back on the field: "Joe Theismann walked over to the referee with the ball and started remonstrating with him passionately, as though he wanted to return it for flaws. Whatever Joe was asking, the referee looked bemused and slightly troubled." What he was doing, it turned out, was asking the officials to place the ball on a towel before they put it down on the sodden turf, a common practice in the U.S. but one that the Grey Cup refs apparently couldn't grasp. "They just looked at me when I asked them," Joe would report later.

Theismann was having trouble handling the wet ball on the snap from Paul Desjardins, which was making it difficult to execute handoffs and passes. The officials were using a dry ball on every play, but the ball was being placed on the soaked turf and would then be pushed down into the field by the centre. By the time Theismann got the ball, it was waterlogged and slick. Placing it on a towel would have prevented this situation but the rules didn't allow for it.

The resulting Argo series picked up seven yards and Andrusyshyn was forced to punt again. Calgary could not move it and punted the ball back to the Argo 51. Theismann then connected with McQuay on a screen pass for 16 yards, but it was called back on a clipping call. On first and 20, Leon churned for three yards and the first quarter then ended.

The second quarter opened with Toronto trailing 7-0 and sitting on second down, 17 yards to go at their own 44-yard line. Theismann dropped back to throw, hung on until the last possible second and, just before being hammered by a defender, unloaded a rocket. It was an incredible throw considering the soggy state of the football and it sailed through the rain, deep down the left sideline to Mel Profit, who had cut clear across the field. Mel hauled it in around the 22-yard line and made it as far as the Calgary 11 before being knocked out of bounds by defensive back Terry Wilson after a gain of 55 yards. As it had so many times through the season, the Argo offence had moved the ball with a big play. Profit had long been considered the Argonauts' best receiver in the clutch, and he had come through again.

On first down from the Calgary 11, Theismann dropped back to throw and fired again for Profit at the goal line, but the pass was a bit too high. On second down, Joe threw to McQuay deep in the end zone, but Terry Wilson knocked it down. Ivan MacMillan trotted out and booted an 18-yard field goal to get the Argos on the scoreboard at 7-3.

Rather than accept a kickoff, Calgary elected to scrimmage from its own 35. On second and 10, Keeling fired deep for Herm Harrison at the Toronto 41, but Tim Anderson leaped in front of the receiver and picked off the pass. Harrison dragged him to the ground immediately, but the Toronto offence was getting a chance to go right back on the field. A screen pass to McQuay picked up 13 yards, but Theismann then fumbled a snap and Calgary's Dave Crabbe recovered.

Neither team was moving the ball offensively. Another exchange of punts gave the ball back to Calgary at the Toronto 51. Keeling completed a quick six-yard pass to Jon Henderson, who slipped out of bounds before Dick Thornton could hit him. Keeling then rolled out and fired to Rudy Linterman, who was being covered by Anderson. Tim slipped slightly on the wet turf and went sprawling as Linterman made a leaping catch. He spun away from Dave Raimey and headed downfield until Marv Luster finally dragged him down at the Argo 5 after a gain of 40 yards. On first and goal, Hugh McKinnis was thrown for a loss of one by

Jim Corrigall. On second down, Jesse Mims shot through the Argo line and scored easily. The convert pushed the Calgary lead to 14-3.

Figure 8-2: *"The Blue and White Wall smothers Jesse Mims." Visible are Gene Mack # 76, George Wells # 53, Larry Brame #52, Dick Thornton # 25, and Marv Luster # 27."*

A deep sense of concern was entering the hearts of the Argos and their fans. The Toronto defence was playing well, but with the exception of that one big play by Mel Profit, the Argos had shown little on offence.

Tony Moro fielded the kickoff after the touchdown and fumbled the wet ball out of bounds at the Argo 38. A run by Symons picked up a yard and then Theismann went back to Mel Profit for a gain of 12. A pass to Eben picked up 15 valuable yards, to the Stampeder 44. Symons plowed for three to the 41. Finally Toronto was putting a drive together.

What happened next was one of the more bizarre plays in Grey Cup. Rolling right, Theismann was clobbered by Craig Koinzan and fumbled. Offensive tackle Ellison Kelly, charging to recover the ball, accidentally kicked it and sent it rolling backwards deep into Argo territory. A mass of players chased it down until Kelly finally fell on it at the Toronto 29 for a staggering loss of 40 yards. On third and 47, Andrusyshyn punted. Calgary's rush was aggressive and at the height of his kick, Zenon got knocked down. On the same play, Toronto was hit with a penalty for rough play. Contacting the kicker resulted in an automatic first down for the kicking team, so the Argos retained possession. But after the rough-play penalty was applied, they were back at their own 14 on a drive that had started on their 38. In six plays, the Argos had gained 31 yards, lost 40 on the broken play and lost 15 on a penalty. They were 24 yards back from where they started, yet they still had a first down!

Theismann began another drive, highlighted by a 15-yard rough-play penalty against Calgary, a completion to McQuay, and a 26-yard pass to Eben. Joe then scrambled for 13 yards to the Calgary 43, where defensive back Reggie Holmes dropped him. Following this play, Theismann had to leave the field with blood pouring from a broken nose courtesy of the Holmes hit. The Argos' forgotten second quarterback, Greg Barton, was forced into the game. On first down, he dropped to throw. Bill Symons went flying out of the backfield and down the left sidelines. He was behind the Calgary secondary when Greg let loose with a high floater. The ball sailed towards Symons, who was wide open at the Calgary goal line. Defensive back Reggie Holmes was racing towards the play and when the ball dropped short, he was able to get a hand on it, deflecting it away from the diving Symons. Bill pounded the turf in frustration as he had lost a sure touchdown. After the game, in an interview with the *Toronto Star,* Greg attributed the incomplete pass to the wet ball: "I saw Bill behind his man but I underthrew him. As soon as I threw I knew I wouldn't get him. I was throwing a 90-pound ball . . . The referee had put it down, it had rolled over and was just so damned wet."

A short completion to Eben netted three yards and MacMillan trotted out to attempt a 47-yard field goal with Dick Thornton holding. Ivan had the range but was wide. Calgary ran the ball out to avoid giving up a single point. The Stampeders then kept the ball on the ground, running out the first half. They entered intermission with a 14-3 lead.

In the Toronto locker room, the Argos tried to regroup. Offensively, they were struggling and their game plan of running right at Harris had been abandoned early. Sweeps were being stopped easily by the star middle linebacker before they gained much yardage. The only thing working with any consistency was the short passing game.

Charlie Bray and Danny Nykoluk on the right side of the offensive line were holding their own after a tough first quarter. Joe Vijuk and Ellison Kelly, though, had been having a very rough time containing John Helton and Dick Suderman.

Leo told his players they were going back to their original game plan. Symons and McQuay were going to run straight ahead. Before coming out for the second half, Leo got angry at league officials over the playing conditions. "Because of the halftime show, the CFL decided not to squeegee off the field. There was so much water on the field. I guess they felt it was more important to have the bands play than to have a good field for the players. It just got more slippery as the game went on."

Zenon Andrusyshyn kicked off to start the third quarter. Two runs by the Stampeders netted only eight yards, so they punted. But now, instead of reverting to the game plan as discussed, Leo (who called most of the offensive plays) had Theismann go back to the air. A pass to Profit was incomplete and a scramble by Joe netted only six yards. Big Z, who had been hammering the ball on punts, got off a poor kick this time. Jim Silye, expecting a much deeper punt, tried to make a running catch at the Stampeder 36-yard line but the wet ball bounced off his hands and skidded away. Joe Vijuk, part of the punt coverage team for Toronto, scooped the ball up, took a couple of steps, was grabbed by a Calgary player and started to fall. But before he hit the turf, Vijuk alertly pitched the ball laterally to backup offensive lineman Roger Scales. Scales tucked the ball under his arm and began sprinting for the end zone, escorted by Gene Mack, Peter Martin and Paul Desjardins. No Stampeder was even close as Scales completed a lineman's dream by running 33 yards for a touchdown. MacMillan's convert was good, making the score 14-10 for Calgary. The Argonauts were back in the game!

The defences for both teams now stepped it up. The "Blue and White Wall" in particular gave a simply awe-inspiring performance throughout the second half.

After yet another exchange of punts, Calgary took over on its own 51. Keeling went back to pass and fired a sideline pass to Gerry Shaw. But Thornton stepped in front and almost made an interception. Dick was furious with himself for not hanging onto the ball as there was a clear path down the sideline. After a punt, the Argos took over on their 18. Leon McQuay picked up nine yards on a sweep. But instead of playing it safe and going up the middle for a first down, Leo elected to pass. Joe threw down the middle for Eben, who dropped the pass.

The Stamps took over on their own 42 after the ensuing Toronto punt. Keeling tried Linterman on a sweep left, only to have Marv Luster charge in and dump him for an eight-yard loss. Another run was also stopped by Luster, forcing Calgary to punt again, this time to the Argonaut 26.

Leo now called for a trick play. Symons ran a sweep to the right, turned and threw the ball back to Theismann. An opportunity to make good yardage was there, but the throw fell short and was incomplete.

Dick Thornton then ran in from the sideline to go in at flanker. Theismann dropped back and, just before being buried by the Calgary pass rush, threw a strike to Tricky Dick, who made a sensational diving catch at the Toronto 40-yard line for a first down to keep the drive alive. Joe then went back to throw again. He spotted Jim Henderson deep down field and hit him for a 43-yard gain to the Calgary 27. Henderson made a great catch, going up between two Calgary defenders to pull it in.

The hopes of Argo fans rose again with that huge play. Symons then busted up the middle to pick up three yards. Theismann threw for Tony Moro at the 15-yard line but the pass was incomplete, so MacMillan came out again. He was wide on a 31-yard field goal attempt. It scored a single point and brought Toronto to within a field goal at 14-11, with 2:39 to go in the quarter.

Neither team could do anything offensively for the rest of the third quarter. Calgary opened the fourth quarter with a contacting-the-kicker penalty handing Toronto a gift first down at its own 25. Cahill, desperate to get the offence moving, sent Greg Barton in at quarterback but his first series accomplished little. Two runs by Bill Symons netted only three yards and Andrusyshyn was punting again. Calgary's offence took over at its own 53 and Keeling fired for Herm Harrison, only to see Pete Martin leap in front of the Calgary tight end and pick it off. That gave the ball back to the Argos at their own 41-yard line. Barton completed a screen pass to Symons for no yards and then threw deep for Dave Cranmer, the first time all day the Argos had gone to him. The pass failed to connect and Andrusyshyn came on again to punt.

The game was now settling into a kicking duel between Andrusyshyn and Jim Furlong, with Zenon clearly outkicking his Calgary counterpart. On every exchange of punts, Toronto drove Calgary deeper into its own zone as neither offence could move the ball.

With less than five minutes to go in the fourth quarter Toronto got the ball at mid-field. A couple of first downs would put them in position to tie the game with a field goal. A screen pass went incomplete but on second down, Symons took a handoff and broke off tackle to the right. Terry Wilson hit him, knocking the ball loose, and Wayne Harris recovered. The hopes of the Toronto players, coaches and fans were quickly beginning to fade. It was becoming apparent in these last few desperate minutes that if the Toronto Argonauts were to win the Grey Cup, their proud defence would have to do it for them.

That defence was getting angry, as Dave Raimey recalls: "We were mad. We were giving it our all and almost felt like the offence wasn't trying. We knew they were, but when we were playing so well and they were accomplishing nothing, well, it was very frustrating."

Again the Toronto defence held, with Brame and Mack coming up with big tackles. A Furlong punt drove the Argos back to their own 23. Leon McQuay scampered for nine yards, but Wayne Harris then stuffed Symons up the middle for no gain. On third and one, in an effort to confuse the defence, Joe Theismann was sent on the field instead of Zenon Andrusyshyn. Joe had punted in high school and college, and Leo wanted to see if he could induce the Stampeders to jump offside. Calgary, however, showed good discipline and stayed onside. Theismann got off a good punt, aided by a huge bounce, to drive the Stampeders back to their own 27-yard line with about three minutes to go.

As Jerry Keeling led his offence onto the field, he had to be worried. With the complete inability of the Stamps to move the ball and the way Andrusyshyn (and now Theismann) were punting, he knew that another exchange of punts would allow Toronto to take the ball over within field-goal range. Keeling absolutely had to get something going now. He ran a sweep with Linterman to the right, only to see Chip Barrett charge up from his rover position and nail him after only a two-yard gain. Keeling then decided on a huge gamble. If he could complete just one deep pass, Toronto would be finished.

On the defensive side, Dick Thornton knew in his heart that if he could get his hands on the ball somehow, he could turn the Argos' fortunes around. He taunted Keeling at the line, daring him to throw in his direction. Jerry took the snap and dropped back to throw as the Argonaut defensive line stormed in. Keeling threw deep to Jon Henderson, who was being covered at the Toronto 40-yard line by Marv Luster with Thornton lurking in the shadows.

"As soon as the ball was snapped, I sprinted back full speed for 25 yards, then coasted near the receiver, turned and looked for the ball. Sure enough, here came this floater right to me and I just gathered it in and took off running for the end zone."

Dick made the interception at the Toronto 42-yard line. In a split second, the Argonaut players knew they had got the break they so desperately needed. If they could have chosen any player in the history of professional football to cover a pass at this stage, with their season on the line, they probably would have picked Dick Thornton. He was known for his sure hands and his propensity for making big plays, and he had come through again.

The Argonaut defenders began clearing a path for Tricky Dick. Chip Barrett cut down one Stampeder who was homing in on Thornton like a heat-seeking missile. Pete Martin sprang Dick loose with a ferocious block that destroyed a trio of Stampeders who had been closing in as a group. Thornton shot past the carnage created by Barrett and Martin. Other Stampeders were being cut down all over the field by Toronto blockers. Dick exploded down the right sideline towards the end zone. Jon Henderson was in hot pursuit but had no chance of catching him.

Figure 8-3: *"The interception of the decade. Dick Thornton takes off with Jerry Keelings' pass late in the 1971 Grey Cup."*

In the foreground Pete Martin blasts Tricky free with a big block while Chip Barrett # 30 moves in to throw another. Jon Henderson is in pursuit.

Closing in on the Calgary end zone, Thornton had one Stampeder left to beat: quarterback Jerry Keeling. Most quarterbacks are not trained to tackle and wouldn't be much of an obstacle to a star like Dick. But Keeling was a former star defensive back before he replaced Pete Liske at the helm of the Calgary offence. He knew exactly what he had to do. He kept backpedalling to avoid Jim Stillwagon, who was the final blocker between himself and Dick. Stillwagon, who was nothing short of magnificent in this game, describes what happened: "In the series before, I got hit hard on my thigh. I didn't wear thigh pads, and could hardly move my leg. I was also playing with a bad knee. Keeling kept 'dancing' and would not commit. I could not get a good shot at him and as Dick came down the sidelines he was kind of weaving. I glanced over my shoulder to see what he was doing but he'd weave one way and I'd go the other."

Dick knew he would have to get past Keeling to score, but to do that he would have to slow down. "I would have much preferred facing Jerry one on one in the open field going full speed, but because he was so balanced and using Wagon as sort of a shield, I had to slow down. I then quickly decided to cut inside left because the sideline was fairly close on the right and didn't want to get knocked out of bounds. But because of my lost acceleration just as I cut, someone from behind (Jon Henderson) dove, caught my heel and I began to stumble. Keeling then spun around and brought me down at the 11-yard line."

Thornton, Keeling and Stillwagon all went down in a huge spray of water. Although disappointed that Dick didn't score, the Argos and their fans were ecstatic over the sudden turn of events. In a matter of seconds, despair and defeat had turned into a great shot at victory.

Randy Beatty, the young ball boy, was standing on the Argo sideline when Dick made the interception. "The bench just exploded when Dick picked that pass off. We knew we had the game won at that point."

Leo sent the offence onto the field under the command of Joe Theismann. Bill Symons remembered the mood of the offence. "There was a slight sense of panic as we had not done anything all day. This is where we needed Tom Wilkinson. Tom was a calm veteran who would have said something like, 'There is lots of time. We are going to score here. Just whatever you do, hang onto the ball.' Joe, to be fair, was just a rookie and was very excited. That added to the feeling of fear."

Leo ordered Joe to keep the ball on the ground. On first down, Leon McQuay broke off tackle to the right, following blocks by Bray and Nykoluk. Dick Suderman made an outstanding stop, diving across the line to bring Leon down at the seven-yard line. On the sidelines, Thornton was begging Leo to put him in the game. "I went to Leo on the sidelines and told him to put me back in at wide receiver. I knew Calgary would be playing the run and blitzing, so I could have easily beaten the corner man on man with an out-and-up pattern. All Joe would have had to do was float it into my hands, but Leo just looked at me and never said a word."

Theismann also wanted to throw. But Leo, remembering the many interceptions Joe had thrown throughout the season, was reluctant to risk a pass. He also considered the field position. The Argos were seven years from the goal-line and the ball was placed far to the right. If a pass failed it would mean a terrible angle for MacMillan to try a possible game-tying field goal. So Leo elected to call another running play, this time a sweep to the left with McQuay. If the rookie scored, the Grey Cup was Toronto's. If he was stopped, the ball would be perfectly centred for MacMillan to kick the field goal and tie the game. The way his defence was playing, Leo would have been content to take his chances in overtime. Go into overtime and simply have Zenon Andrusyshyn drive a couple of punts through the end zone for singles – that would finish Calgary.

Mike Eben agreed with Leo's strategy to run the ball. "Look at the two backs we had. Surely to God, when you are that close you should score. Our sweeps had worked all year. And yes, Leo was concerned about Joe's interceptions."

Joe barked the signals, took the snap from Desjardins and handed off to McQuay. Linemen from both teams exploded together in a violent collision of power and strength. As Leon swept to the left, he likely spotted two things. The first was Wayne Harris charging up from his middle linebacker's position towards him. The other was a slight hole in the line, with a clear path to the end zone. Leon headed for that hole but as he made his cut, his right foot slipped on the drenched turf, went out from underneath him and he crashed to the turf onto his right elbow.

McQuay had just violated one of the cardinal rules of football. A player is taught from his earliest days to always carry the ball in his outside arm to protect it from an inside hit. Players are instructed on how to switch the ball to the other arm if necessary to ensure it will be protected. Leon either forgot or ignored that fundamental principle. He was carrying the ball in his right or inside hand while running left. When he landed on his right elbow, the wet ball shot out and skidded away.

Figure 8-4: *"As Joe Vijuk # 59 battles Calgary's Reggie Holmes, Leon McQuay slips on the Empire Stadium turf and the Argos 1971 Grey Cup dreams come to an end."*

Ever since the 1971 Grey Cup game, that fateful play has been discussed and debated. Cahill has always pointed out that under the rules of football, the ground can't cause a fumble. The ball has to be knocked away by another player. Yet the ground is what Leon's elbow hit, causing the ball to squirt away.

But before the debate could begin on the merits of that non-call, the play was still unfolding. Any player's first instinct should be to try to pounce on a loose ball. But instead of scrambling to recover his own fumble, Leon grabbed his knee as if he was hurt. Joe Vijuk, the Toronto guard, made a frantic dive for the ball but was beaten to it by defensive back Reggie Holmes, who recovered at the 12-yard line.

Dave Raimey is still furious when he sees the replay of Leon's fumble. "I think he was faking it when he grabbed his knee instead of trying to get the ball. To me that was one of the phoniest things I ever saw."

Neither team could believe their luck. The Stampeders were jumping for joy while the Argos were stunned. The Toronto defence ran onto the field, absolutely livid. What more could they do? They had done everything humanly possible to win. They had given the offence a golden opportunity to wrap it up, and it had failed again.

With a little more than a minute to go, Keeling handed off to Jesse Mims. Dave Knechtel, playing in a frenzy, flung a Calgary blocker off and smothered Mims for a loss of one. Larry Brame then stopped Hugh McKinnis after a gain of four yards. With 42 seconds to go, Jim Furlong stood near his goal-line ready to punt. The Argos still had life. They should get the ball back in decent field position. There was still a chance to get into Ivan MacMillan's field-goal range and send the game into overtime.

Leo ordered his players to try to block the kick. Thornton disagreed with the strategy. "You never block a punt in that circumstance. The line knows they have to hold you and the kicker knows he has to get the ball away fast. You block a punt when the other team gets sloppy. That was not the case here. It would have been better to have a third returner back."

Don Jonas, writing in the *Toronto Star*, agreed that there should have been a third returner back to ensure no mixups in fielding the kick. "Then no matter where Jim Furlong kicked the ball, someone would be in position to run it back."

Furlong, facing a heavy Toronto rush, got an excellent kick away through the rain-filled air. It came arcing down away from the two punt returners, Harry Abofs and Peter Paquette. Abofs had to run a great distance for the ball, which was taking a "Calgary bounce" and rolling into Toronto territory.

Harry caught up to it at the Argo 48-yard line and, frantic to stop the clock, kicked the ball out of bounds. He could not have chosen a worse course of action. According to the CFL rulebook, a player who kicks a punted ball has in fact punted the ball back to the opponent. It was now Calgary ball at the Toronto 48-yard line with less than a minute to go. The Argos had completely thrown away the magnificent opportunity Dick Thornton's interception had given them.

Marv Luster, who simply refused to give up, stopped two runs by McKinnis. With scant seconds left, Furlong punted again. Leo sent McQuay and Symons out to return it this time. "It was total desperation at that point," remembers Symons. "Remember, in that era you were not allowed to block on a punt return. There was almost no chance of being able to run a punt back but if anyone could do it, it would be Leon with those quick feet of his."

Furlong made sure his punt went to Symons to avoid the slim chance of McQuay getting any running room. Bill took it at the Toronto 23 and was brought down at the 28-yard line. Theismann led the offence out again with time for one more play. He went back to throw as every eligible receiver Toronto had raced downfield for the "Hail Mary"pass. But before Joe could even get set to throw, John Helton streaked in and buried him behind the line of scrimmage. It was over and the Toronto Argonauts had lost the 1971 Grey Cup 14-11.

In the Argonauts dressing room, there was a sense of shock. Mel Profit was obviously shattered, belying the image some people had of him, that he didn't care about football. Gene Mack, whose play had been outstanding, was shaking the door of his locker in rage. Dick Thornton remembered Leon McQuay looking quite nonplussed. "His attitude was nonchalant in the locker room afterwards. I do not think he ever fully realized the impact of his mistake".

Ball boy Randy Beatty said the dressing room "was dead quiet. We were so disappointed. Leon, however, looked very composed."

The game statistics were interesting. Offensively, they showed just how poorly Toronto had played. Theismann had completed eight of 14 passes for 189 yards. Barton completed only two of five for three yards. Jerry Keeling on the Calgary side had not had a good day, either. He was six of sixteen for 111 yards, one touchdown and three interceptions. Along the ground, McQuay had just 39 yards on 12 carries, Symons added 33 and Theismann carried 10 times for minus-10 yards. Calgary was held to 103 yards along the ground, with Hugh McKinnis the leading rusher with 50 yards on 12 carries. The Argonauts' top receiver was Profit, with 67 yards on two receptions. While the Calgary defence had been outstanding the entire game, Toronto's defensive effort had been truly stifling in the second half, holding the Stampeders to a single first down (and that was as a result of an offside penalty). It was a simply unbelievable performance and yet it was to no avail.

Three Argonaut defenders in particular had been superb. Jim Stillwagon played the game of his life at defensive tackle. Calgary Coach Jim Duncan commented afterwards in the *Toronto Star*: "That damned Stillwagon pushed our guards back so much we never got a thing going." Marv Luster, playing in his first Grey Cup after 11 magnificent years in the CFL, did a superb job calling the defensive signals, keeping Keeling off balance, and made tackles all over the field. And, of course, there was Dick Thornton. Calgary seldom threw anywhere near Tricky Dick. On the two occasions when they did, he almost picked one off and then made the interception should have won the game. Thornton also made a huge catch as a wide receiver in the third quarter.

But the knowledge that the defence had played an outstanding game was little consolation. Nineteen years after their last Grey Cup appearance, the Toronto Argonauts had fumbled away a golden opportunity to return to championship glory.

Nine

1972

Although the Calgary Stampeders won the Grey Cup in 1971, few football fans doubted that the team of the future in the CFL would be the Toronto Argonauts. They were loaded with great young talent and experienced veterans – and Leo Cahill was determined to add more unique players to the mix.

His first goal was to improve his offence and in particular the line, which had clearly been overpowered by Calgary in the Grey Cup. Danny Nykoluk had retired again and Ellison Kelly was near the end of his career.

To rectify this situation, Leo headed back to the University of Tampa, where the previous year he had scooped up Leon McQuay. This time he walked away with the two best offensive linemen at the school: Ron Mikolajczyk and Noah Jackson. The university, livid because both players were juniors with a year of eligibility left, announced that no CFL more scouts would be allowed on campus. Pete Martin remembers Leo saying, "I could never fly over Tampa again because if the city knew I was in a plane above them they'd shoot me down with anti-aircraft fire!"

That was not the only big-name signing by the Argos that off-season. Leo had his sights set on Michigan State star Eric "The Flea" Allen. He was the leading rusher in the history of the school and in 1971, had been voted the top player in the Big 10 conference. The only knock on Allen was size. At 162 pounds (hence his nickname "The Flea") there was some concern over his ability to take the physical pounding of pro football.

Cahill faced two challenges in getting Allen. One, of course, would be persuading him to play in Toronto instead of Baltimore, where the NFL's Colts had drafted him. The other was the fact that he was on Hamilton's exclusive negotiation list. Leo went to work. He put Dave Raimey on recallable waivers, which was a way for a team to ascertain how much interest there was in a player among other teams. If another team selected him, the original team could withdraw the waiver and try to work out a deal with the team that claimed him. If no deal could be worked out, the original team could either keep the player or let him go on waivers. Hamilton, seeing Raimey's name on the waiver wire, quickly put in a claim.

However, Raimey had a huge contract with a no-cut clause that Leo knew the Tiger-Cats had no inkling about. He called the new Hamilton head coach, Jerry Williams, and outlined Raimey's contract situation. Williams blanched; he was well aware of General Manager Ralph Sazio's legendary reluctance to spend money. (More than once it was said of Sazio that he "threw nickels around like manhole covers.")" Leo offered to take Williams off the hook – if Hamilton would give Toronto a player off its negotiation list, namely Eric Allen. Williams hurriedly agreed and Allen became available for Leo to pursue.

Cahill didn't use any special tactics to woo Allen. He felt no need to bring John Bassett into the negotiations, as he had with Jim Corrigall, or to threaten to call the NFL team with whom he was competing, as he had with Jim Stillwagon. This time it was simply old-fashioned bargaining. Leo convinced Eric and his agent that he would have a better career in Toronto and came up with the money needed to sign him. The Colts were livid, and Toronto now had an important new offensive weapon to throw at the opposition. Leo planned on using Allen at wide receiver, feeling he was set at running back with McQuay and Symons.

The next big announcement out of the Argonaut head office was that Mel Profit was retiring. Leo explained in *Goodbye Argos* what happened: "One problem was that to play these two Americans (Mikolajczyk and Jackson), another American player would have to become vulnerable. We looked over our personnel and finally it came down to Profit. We had two Canadians playing at tight end behind him. Tony Moro had been a regular before and Bob Hamilton looked like he was going to come along. Between them we'd get the job done at tight end."

The Argonaut players didn't buy this story. "We all felt that Barrow had released Mel outright solely because of his attitude," says Dick Thornton.

"Leo was only playing politics and covering his ass. He was blowing smoke about the new offensive linemen from Tampa. They were still unproven, anyway. Tony Moro was good, but not a Mel Profit in either leadership, size or experience."

Bill Symons also didn't believe Leo's version. "It was a political move releasing Mel. He did not get along with management and by releasing him, it really hurt the team. He was not a leader off the field but on the field he was very good."

Naturally, Leo disagrees with both Tricky and Sy. "I made the personnel decisions on the team. Nobody in the front office told me what to do. I called Mel into the office before training camp and told him that because of the Canadian/American ratio I would be looking at going with a Canadian at tight end. If things worked out, then he (Profit) would be our tight end. However, I felt he should know the direction we were going. I also offered to trade him to any team he wished, as I felt he had earned that right. He simply said, 'The hell with you,' and walked out."

Aside from his nationality, another strike against Profit was his public stance against the installation of artificial turf at CNE Stadium. He was totally opposed to the use of taxpayers' money to fund that, telling Trent Frayne of the *Toronto Star:* "There are people and projects in this town requiring $625,000 far more than pro athletes and their fans need a new floor for their playpen." Mel's social conscience angered the Argonaut front office and may have been another reason for their desire to get rid of him.

Along with the loss of Profit, Dave Cranmer had major abdominal surgery in April and would be out until at least the middle of the season.

The Argonauts hit training camp as overwhelming favorites to win the 1972 Grey Cup. But right away problems began to emerge. Jim Stillwagon still remembers that training camp with horror: "The entire coaching staff was in disarray, upper management as well. In training camp the team took on a different perspective. John Barrow showed up and there was conflict after conflict. There was so much animosity between players and management. Barrow was always talking about how great he was as a player. One day I said to him, 'If you are so fucking great, why don't you suit up?' I think we lost track as a team on what we were supposed to do."

Leon McQuay had not matured over the off-season, and Leo was still babying him. "Leon was immature and I blame Leo Cahill for that," says Stillwagon. "Leo felt Leon was bigger than the team. Leon was a 22-year-old, with a Greek god's body and a three-year-old's brain. Everyone on the team said fuck it, if Leon could do that, why should we have to follow the rules? He got Leo off focus and the team off focus."

Dave Raimey had a similar perspective. "Leon had great talent but he was immature and in love with himself. He got away with murder and I don't think Leo ever disciplined him. Maybe he did near the end, but we didn't see it. Leon wouldn't show up for a practice and Leo would tell lies and say, 'I gave him permission to take the day off,' and stuff like that. Then he would come to me quietly and say, 'Dave, go find him'. I'd take my gear off and drive to Leon's house and say, 'Come on, Leon you can't be doing this. We're waiting for you,' and convince him to return."

Most shockingly for a team that had been tightly knit and bereft of cliques, Bill Symons says the 1972 squad "started having racial problems, black and white issues. One of our leaders began to go offside with this stuff."

Amidst all this turmoil, the Argos had a decent training camp. But only days into it, outstanding young safety Tim Anderson suffered a severe broken ankle and was forced out for the entire year. Jimmy Dye, who had retired after the 1969 season, made a comeback and would have to carry the brunt of the load at safety in replacing him.

The first preseason game was the all-star game. Leo was coaching the CFL all-stars against the Grey Cup champion Calgary Stampeders. Along with Cahill, the Argos were represented by Joe Theismann, Leon McQuay, Jim Corrigall, Paul Desjardins and assistant coach Blackie Johnston. During this game, Corrigall broke his leg. So before the season had even started, the defence had suffered two huge losses. Leon McQuay also supposedly hurt his wrist during an all-star practice and saw very little action in the game.

The Argonauts staggered through the preseason as injuries continued to mount and internal problems ripped the team. Ed Harrington, who missed most of 1971 with a bad thigh, simply could not run on it and decided to sit out the year. Offensive tackle John Trainor blew his knee out again. Rookie defensive back Ward Smith broke an ankle. McQuay also missed a lot of training camp with his wrist injury and various other ailments.

There were other changes from 1971 in the works as well. Leo cut Ivan MacMillan in training camp, figuring Zenon Andrusyshyn could handle both placekicking and punting responsibilities. Middle linebacker Larry Brame was also cut and Pete Martin got his old job back. (Brame would end up returning just weeks later.)

Greg Barton and Joe Theismann staged another spirited battle for the No. 1 quarterback job during camp and the exhibition season. Most observers felt Joe had the upper hand, but with Leo, nothing was certain.

The already battered Argonauts opened the 1972 season at home against the Montreal Alouettes. Cahill still had not announced who would start at quarterback. When he did, it was memorable to say the least. "Leo had publicly stated that he was scratch the platooning and finally going to go with one QB that season," remembers Dick Thornton. "Well, Leo decides on Joe 10 minutes before the first league game at home. My locker was right in between Joe and Greg, so I witnessed this entire brief scenario. Both QBs are nervous as hell as Leo comes around the corner, never breaks stride and says, 'Joe, you're starting' and then disappears. Joe now jumps up, starts yelling and screaming and begins to make the gung-ho rounds of each player's locker, trying to assume his new leadership role. I glance over at Greg and it's like he's crying his eyes out – almost a state of semi-shock, collapse and total devastation.

"Now this is still very vivid in my mind after 30 years. I slide over close to him and say almost verbatim: 'Greg, listen man, you've got to pull yourself together. It's a long season and anything can happen. Joe got the nod tonight, but shit, he might go out and break his leg in the first quarter and then it's all up to you. You have to be mentally ready to go anytime.' But walking away, I glanced back . . . and he was still in a coma."

Leo decided to keep McQuay out of the lineup for the opener, to try and let him heal more. But instead of simply letting Bill Symons carry the brunt of the running game, Cahill decided to move Dave Raimey into the backfield from his cornerback position (moving Peter Paquette into the starting DB role to replace Raimey), and start Eric Allen in the backfield with him. Bill was moved to the slotback position (replacing the injured Dave Cranmer) where he would act more as a receiver than as a ball carrier. It was an odd move and one that upset Bill as well as many of his teammates, but he refused to make a scene. "Leo really hurt my career after Leon joined the team. Many of the guys urged me to speak out, but I was a captain and figured the team was bigger then myself. I thought I had to try and make it work."

CNE Stadium was jammed to capacity on opening night as the Argonauts and Alouettes hit the field. Battered though they were, the team soon got the crowd roaring. Less than six minutes into the game, Theismann marched the offence right down the field before sprinting around right end for a seven-yard touchdown run.

On the next series, disaster struck. Theismann rolled out of the pocket on a designed quarterback run, got gang-tackled and had to be helped off the field. On the sidelines, the team doctor told Leo that Joe's leg was broken. The entire team was in disbelief. Dick Thornton's premonition had come true. Greg Barton was now the man.

In the second quarter, Montreal moved ahead on a Moses Denson touchdown run and a single off a missed field-goal attempt by Don Sweet. The Argo offence was foundering as under Barton seemed uncertain and confused. Several offensive players told Cahill that Greg looked scared in the huddle and was not taking charge as any quarterback is expected to.
Barton even seemed hesitant to throw safe passes. He was sticking solely to the ground game. At one point, Leo pulled him aside on the sideline and screamed, "Goddamnit, you've got to throw the football deep! We gotta get back in the game! Our players have gotta know that you are taking charge!" Greg looked at Leo and said no, Montreal coach Sam Etcheverry was yelling at his defence to defend the pass. Leo felt his heart sink at Greg's response. A coach yells that kind of stuff all the

time! Cahill started seriously questioning whether Greg could handle the responsibility of leading his team.

At halftime, Dick Thornton went to Leo with an idea. "I remember clearly, during that first game when Barton tanked it, I went to Leo in the locker room and told him to put me in. Despite my sore arm and not having played there much, anyone could have done better. I still had the speed and shiftiness, plus our offence was geared around what we called the sprint out attack with quick, short passes in the flat area to either the flanker, tight end or slotback, whoever was open. However, I got the same old answer. Trick, you stick to playing and I'll do the coaching."

Things got no better for Toronto in the second half. Barton simply couldn't hit his receivers. Some of his passes were so off the mark that at times, no one even knew to whom he was throwing. Rex MacLeod of the *Globe and Mail* described it well: "Although normally an accurate passer, his throws were horrible. In bowling, he would have been throwing down the wrong alley."

The Toronto defence, as was normally the case, played very well but it was not enough. The final score was 19-8 in favor of Montreal.

The passing stats told the sad tale for Toronto. Barton completed five of 19 passes for a grand total of 10 yards, and threw two interceptions. His longest completion of the game was a nine-yard pass to Raimey. Before getting hurt, Joe had been good on one of five for 33 yards. The running attack was not that bad but could not compensate for the lack of a passing game. Eric Allen, in his first regular-season professional game, carried 11 times for 53 yards and Raimey added 32 yards on seven carries.

Heading into the second game of the year in Regina against the powerful Roughriders, Leo was not about to give up on Barton. Greg played well at times in 1971 and had looked good in training camp. Leo felt Greg had choked in the opener but rationalized that it had been a number of years since he had been the No. 1 QB on any team. He needed time to adjust. Cahill felt Barton had far too much talent not to bounce back. After all, Greg had signed with Toronto in the first place because he felt he would be given a good chance to be the starting quarterback. Now was his big chance. Leon McQuay would also be back in the lineup for the second game and would provide Greg with a deadly weapon to ease the pressure.

Early on, Barton moved the offence into field-goal range where Zenon Andrusyshyn was good on a 27-yard attempt. In the third quarter, trailing 8-3, Greg moved the Argos inside the Roughrider 10 before the drive stalled. Big Z came through again with a 13-yard field goal. However, the Boatmen never got any closer. In the second half, an undermanned defence played valiantly, keeping them within two points, but the offence simply couldn't score. Peter Paquette, now a regular with Tim Anderson injured, stepped in front of a Ron Lancaster pass and returned the interception 25 yards to stop a Saskatchewan drive. Greg made a couple of outstanding passes, including a 40-yard completion to Allen, and Eben had a huge game with six receptions, but the offence simply could not get any type of sustained drive going. Barton had three drives stopped by interceptions. Early in the fourth quarter, Lancaster hit Bobby Thompson with a 40-yard scoring strike that finished the Argos. The final was 15-6 for Saskatchewan.

Barton had been better in this game, completing 14 of 30 passes for 179 yards, but he hurt the team badly by throwing too many interceptions. McQuay didn't provide the offence with the answer, either. He was only average at best, rushing for 44 yards on 11 carries.

Moving back and forth between running back and wide receiver, Eric Allen had a good day. He carried seven times for 34 yards and made five receptions. Bill Symons, who had yet to carry the ball this season, did make one reception for 14 yards.

The bewildered Argos now headed back to Toronto to take on the Ottawa Rough Riders. Surely, fans thought, Greg Barton would finally come up big in this third game. Much to their horror, he failed again.

Though Ottawa beat Toronto 14-8, the Argo defence was again superb. Ottawa was held to 71 yards along the ground and 137 yards through the air as quarterback Rick Cassata was kept under constant pressure. He was sacked once and completed only 12 of his 23 passes. Marv Luster came up with a big interception and Jim Corrigall, already back from his broken leg, stopped a drive by recovering a fumble. But the offence simply did not produce. Barton completed only nine of 26 passes for 112 yards, was intercepted twice and fumbled once. Leon McQuay carried 16 times but managed only 69 yards and Eric Allen, who now had replaced Bill Symons in the backfield, carried 13 times for 65 yards. Bill actually got one carry, but was stacked up for no gain.

Ottawa had taken a 7-0 lead into the half, courtesy of two Gerry Organ field goals and a single. In the third quarter, rookie defender Dick Adams picked off a Barton pass and returned it 41 yards for a touchdown. Late in the third, Zenon Andrusyshyn missed two field goals but picked up singles on both. In the fourth, he connected on two three-pointers to close the gap to 14-8. In the final minutes, Barton finally got a drive going, moving the offence down to the Ottawa 10-yard line. But he threw two incomplete passes as time ran out. The once mighty Argonauts had dropped to 0-3 on the year, and incredibly had scored only 22 points.

Under heavy pressure, Leo made a move at the quarterback slot. Montreal released QB Jim Chasey and Leo wasted no time signing him. Chasey had good mobility (in contrast to Greg, who had none) and a solid arm. The plan was to start Greg and slowly work Jim into the system in the next game against a very good Blue Bombers team in Winnipeg.

Days before the game, Leo cut defensive lineman George Wells, who had been inconsistent at best. The Argos also lost wide receiver Jim Henderson. A steady player for Toronto since 1969, Henderson became tired of the turmoil surrounding the team as well as his lack of playing time. Leo blew up at him during a practice and Jim decided enough was enough. He walked off the field and quit.

The Argos went into Winnipeg desperate for a victory. Barton moved the offence down the field on the opening drive, but a pass into the end zone was picked off. He got another drive going but saw it, too, end with an interception. Fed up, Leo sent Jim Chasey into the ballgame on the next series. Just before the first quarter came to a close, Chasey fired a 10-yard strike into the end zone to rookie receiver Bruce Bergey for the Argos' first touchdown since Joe Theismann scored in the first quarter of the first game.

Early in the second quarter, Chasey again moved the team into scoring position and scrambled five yards for a touchdown to give Toronto a 14-1 lead. Ex-Argo Don Jonas then went to work for the Bombers, leading them to 10 points before the end of the half.

The third quarter of this game sadly marked the end of Greg Barton's CFL career. Leo had been alternating Chasey and Greg every series, but at one critical point Leo noticed Greg on the bench when it should have been his turn to be in the game. Leo abruptly asked him why he wasn't out there, and Greg mumbled something to the effect of "Jim is playing well." Leo turned away in disgust – it was obvious to the coach that Barton didn't want to play.

The game ended in complete frustration for Leo and the Argonauts. Andrusyshyn missed field goals from 24 and 27 yards and the Double Blue went down to a 21-19 defeat. They also lost Bruce Bergey with a lung injury. The 1972 season was becoming a never-ending nightmare for the Toronto Argonauts.

Jim Chasey had at least given the Argonauts competent quarterbacking, completing eight of 15 for 86 yards and a touchdown. He also picked up 26 yards along the ground and scored a TD. Greg Barton, in his final appearance in a Toronto uniform, went four for seven for 34 yards and two interceptions. Neither Leon McQuay nor Eric Allen had much success along the ground and Leo continued to act as if Bill Symons didn't exist. Dick Thornton, though, had a great game in his former home stadium, picking off two Jonas passes and returning one of them 39 yards.

When the Argos returned home after the game, Greg Barton was given his outright release – a move that hurt Leo's credibility with Barrow and the rest of the Argonauts management team. After all, the team was still on the hook for Barton's big salary.

Nobody was quite sure why Greg failed so badly, but Mike Eben feels Barton may simply have lacked the necessary talent, notwithstanding his reputation before his arrival in Toronto. "I never really thought Greg was a great athlete. Width of the field and lack of mobility all worked against him. He came here with this great reputation of having a rifle of an arm but there were QBs in the league with a much better throwing arm than him."

Leo has his own thoughts on Barton: "He all kinds of ability but I don't think he had the mental toughness to be a football player. He could go in and alternate with Joe knowing that if he failed Joe would be right back in there on the next series. He just couldn't handle being the No. 1 guy, though."

Dick Thornton adds: "I roomed with Greg in training camp so I knew his mental state of mind from Day 1. He was so positive he would get to start that first game. When Joe got the call, something just snapped in his head, never to be retrieved. His confidence never came back."

Panic was beginning to set in among Argo management after the 0-4 start. Rumours were rampant that John Barrow was talking privately about firing Cahill. When the players heard this, all they could do was shake their heads. They knew that the defence was playing as well, if not better, than the year before. At some point the offence had to come around, they felt.

Needing a second quarterback, Leo went to the phone and swung another deal. Wally Gabler had been traded by Hamilton to Edmonton but he refused to report. Gabler called Leo to tell him he'd come back to Toronto. Leo felt Gabler was the best quarterback available so he traded offensive lineman Roger Scales to the Esks for Wally's rights. Gabler was no Joe Theismann but was a capable professional quarterback who knew Leo and understood the Argo offensive system. With a good supporting cast, Wally had proven in the past he could be a winner. The Argos, if they could avoid any more injuries, still seemed to have enough talent to win.

Wally spoke to the *Toronto Star's* Ken McKee after rejoining Toronto: "My home is in Burlington. My job is in Hamilton. I still have the drive, the desire to prove myself, and the only place I can do it, since Hamilton didn't want me, was Toronto. That's why I called coach Cahill."

Leo then described why he made the deal: "We had to do something. He was the best available at the time and as soon as I found out he'd come, I started working on it."

Wally had only two days of practice with Toronto before the Argos headed up to Ottawa for their next contest. Jim Chasey would start, giving Wally a chance to watch and learn more of the game plan from the sidelines.

Minutes into the game, the black cloud that seemed to have been hovering over the Argos since Leon McQuay's fumble in the previous year's Grey Cup showed itself again. Chasey drove the Argos deep into Ottawa territory, then got knocked out cold. When he regained consciousness, he couldn't remember any of the plays so Wally had to get in there much sooner than expected.

Leo could only watch in shock. What more could happen? On Gabler's first play, he dropped to pass, spotted McQuay wide open in the Rough Rider end zone and fired a pass that hit Leon right in the numbers. Leon dropped the ball, costing Toronto an easy touchdown.

Wally gave it his best shot in this game. He threw 33 times and completed 17, including a touchdown strike to Tony Moro, but gave up two interceptions. He also ran four times for 20 yards and was Toronto's best offensive weapon. This might have been Wally's bravest performance in an Argonaut uniform. With little preparation, he put the team into position to win, but it was not to be. In the second half Gabler spotted Bill Symons wide open deep down field and hit Bill right in the hands with the pass. Just as McQuay had earlier, Sy dropped it. The two dropped passes cost the Argos a sure 12 points. To add to the agony, Andrusyshyn missed the convert after Tony Moro's touchdown, and Ottawa won the game 14-13.

For the fifth straight game, the Toronto defence had played more than well enough to give the team a victory, yet the Argos were still winless. Ottawa was held to only 102 yards along the ground. Rick Cassata completed only seven of 23 passes and gave up interceptions to Marv Luster and Chip Barrett. Dave Knechtel recovered a fumble. It didn't seem possible that the D could play any better, but it wasn't enough.

On offence, Leon McQuay was sub-par once again, rushing for just 28 yards on 11 carries. He also got into an argument with Wally Gabler on the sidelines and Leo finally had to step between the two men to calm things down. Eric Allen picked up 24 yards on seven carries, and snared four passes. Symons carried once for two yards.

The *Globe and Mail's* Gord Walker pointed out another odd moment in the game: "While complete cohesion was not to be expected in view of Gabler's short time with the team, it was rather astounding to note that he frequently needed to direct his backfielders to where they should be stationed."

Was Gabler simply not understanding the offence, or was there so much confusion that he really needed to correctly position his backs? Wally comments: "Leon was not lining up properly. I knew Leo's offence cold and knew where people should be. Later I told Leon in the huddle, 'If you don't want to play, get the fuck off the field!' and I sent him off. Leo backed me up there."

The injury bug cropped up again with Pete Martin, who had never missed a game since joining the Argos in 1965, dislocating an elbow. He would be out at least a couple of games.

Leo Cahill no longer had any idea of what he could do to turn things around. His defence could not play any better. He had thought decent quarterbacking would change the team's fortunes. Well, both Wally and to a lesser extent Jim Chasey had given the Argos that – and still they were losing. How could they win a game when wide-open receivers dropped perfectly thrown passes and the kicker missed converts?

The buzz around town that Leo was about to be – or should be – fired drove the coach nuts. What did injuries, dropped passes or missed kicks have to do with the coaching staff?

"Leo was very mature as a coach when I got back in 1972," recalls Gabler. "What was going on there had nothing to do with his coaching ability, however. Leo was preparing us well for games. It was almost as if it were simply not meant to be."

The desperate Argonauts headed into Molson Stadium in Montreal in what was virtually a must-win situation even though the season was not yet half done. If they were to have any shot at the playoffs, they would have to finish ahead of the Alouettes and they certainly could not afford another loss to them now. In fact, they could not afford another loss, period.

There was more turmoil before the game. Leon McQuay missed the flight to Montreal after a heated verbal encounter with the head coach at practice that carried over into a violent argument with Dave Raimey in the locker room. There was talk McQuay had quit the team, just as Jim Henderson had done earlier in the season. Leo called Leon's agent and told him to find the missing running back and get him to Montreal. Bill Symons remembers the scene in the dressing room when Leon arrived. "Leo ordered us to cheer when Leon came in. We were livid!" The players' dislike of McQuay and their resentment towards Leo for how he treated Leon were growing.

Ball boy Randy Beatty, when asked how the other Argo players viewed Leon by this point, remarked: "Leon was considered a member of the team, but most of the players simply ignored him. He was also incredibly moody and difficult to get along with. One time during a practice he asked me for something from our toolbox and when I wouldn't give it to him he picked a fight with me! We got into a brawl and Lew Hayman, who was watching the practice, had to break it up. Another time, Leon came into the dressing room cursing and told the equipment manager (Tommy Bowen, Randy's uncle) that his helmet was too tight. My uncle said, 'No problem, Leon, I'll fix it'. He put the helmet on a shelf and the following day when Leon came in, my uncle said, 'Here you go.' Leon put it on and said, 'That's perfect.' Of course, my uncle hadn't done anything to the helmet at all."

If the previous game was perhaps Wally Gabler's guttiest performance in a Toronto uniform, the battle in Montreal might have been his best, period. He played his heart out and led Toronto to its first win of the 1972 season.

Early in the first quarter, Gabler marched the Argos down the field. Leon, actually playing with some desire, scored on an 18-yard run. Montreal tied it on a Peter Dalla Riva touchdown and then pulled ahead, but Mike Eben hauled in a 16-yard pass for a touchdown to tie the score by halftime.

At the start of the second half, Wally hit Eric Allen with a 52-yard bomb for a major. In the fourth quarter, Allen scored again on an eight-yard pass and McQuay pulled in a 43-yard pass for another. Andrusyshyn added a single and Ivan MacMillan – who had been resurrected by Cahill after the Big Z's earlier failures – came through with two field goals and a single. The Argos ended up blasting Montreal 43-21.

Wally was outstanding, completing 17 of 34 passes for 247 yards, four touchdowns and only two interceptions. Bill Symons remembers Gabler's play in 1972: "Wally had really matured when he came back to us. He was a much better quarterback in 1972 then he was in his first stint on the team."

Jim Chasey saw a bit of playing time as well and completed three of four for 58 yards and a major. Leon was brilliant, for once, picking up 129 yards on 14 carries and scoring two touchdowns. The Toronto defence played solidly, sacking Montreal quarterback George Mira three times and holding the Als to 96 yards along the ground. Marv Luster, Dave Raimey and Peter Paquette all came up with interceptions to help the cause.

CNE Stadium was packed the following week to see the newly rejuvenated Argonauts battle the Hamilton Tiger-Cats. Hamilton was playing very well as rookie quarterback Chuck Ealey was tearing the league apart. The Ticats were still as mean as ever, with Angelo Mosca, Dave Fleming, Garney Henley and Tommy Joe Coffey leading the way as usual.

The hope among Argo faithful was that the victory in Montreal would be the catalyst to turn the season around. Dave Cranmer would be returning to the lineup for the first time all year. To make room, Harry Abofs, one of the goats of the 1971 Grey Cup loss who had seen little playing time this season, was released. With Wally providing good quarterbacking, the injured players starting to return and Leon running well, the feeling in town was that the Argos just might be able to turn the season around despite the dismal start.

Despite the importance of the game to the Argos, the team was not the main focus of the sports pages. September 1972 marked the first meeting between the Soviet national hockey team, considered the finest "amateur" team on the planet, and the finest Canadians in the National Hockey League. Going into the series, Canadians expected Team Canada to win the eight-game series easily. But after a shocking 7-3 loss on opening night, Canada found itself heading into the second half of the series in Moscow trailing. The country was in shock. The focus on the historic hockey series might have eased some of the media pressure on Leo and his struggling team.

Toronto started the game fast in the first quarter with a 43-yard field goal from Ivan MacMillan. Six minutes later, a 65-yard punt by Zenon Andrusyshyn went for a single. In the dying seconds of the quarter, Gabler hit Eric Allen with a 62-yard bomb for a major to push Toronto ahead 11-0. CNE Stadium was practically shaking with the roars of the Argo fans.

But disaster struck early in the second quarter. First year Argo Elmars Sprogis fumbled a Ticats punt on the Toronto 10-yard line. He picked it, circling back into the end zone where he was hit by Hamilton tight end Tony Gabriel. Sprogis fumbled again, with Gabriel falling on the ball for an easy touchdown.

Hamilton pulled ahead in the third quarter on a one-yard run by Dave Fleming, but Toronto came back less then two minutes later. Gabler drove the Argos down field and hit Leon McQuay with an 18-yard scoring strike to move Toronto back into the lead, 18-14.

The Toronto defence now dug in. This was what Leo was hoping for. He wanted to be in a situation where he had the lead and could turn it over to the defence to protect it. Jim Stillwagon left the game twice with injuries (a split-open chin and a leg problem) only to return and lead the charge on Ealey. The quarterback would be dropped three times for losses by the fired-up Boatmen. Marv Luster and Dick Aldridge, who picked off Ealey passes, were also conspicuous with their great play.

Midway through the fourth quarter though, the Argos found another way to self-destruct, though. Penned deep in their zone on second and 10, Cahill ordered Gabler to quick-kick. Wally took the snap, dropped back and suddenly changed his mind. He threw to McQuay only to see the pass bounce off Leon's outstretched hands and into the hands of defensive tackle Bruce Smith. Smith took the interception back to the Argonaut six-yard line, where he was brought down by Charlie Bray and Noah Jackson. On the next play, Dave Fleming ran in for a touchdown. Moments later a Hamilton punt sailed through the Toronto end zone for a single, pushing Hamilton ahead 22-18.

The strangeness wasn't quite over. With less than two minutes to go, Gabler started moving Toronto downfield. On second and long, he lateralled to Dick Thornton, who had gone into the game on offence. The crowd gasped in shock as Dick immediately punted the ball. While no one realized it immediately, there was a method to Leo's madness. "It was obviously a passing situation and we needed a first down," the coach says. "Dick was a good punter. I told Dick to simply nudge the ball across the line of scrimmage and then fall on it. If it got across the line of scrimmage it would count as a punt, and as the punter he could recover it. That would give us a first down. We also had Bill Symons lined up onside so he could recover it as well. Nobody had ever thought of that play before and I don't think it has been used since."

Leo explains what happened next. "Gerry Sternberg was the DB, and seeing as it was an obvious passing down, he should have been playing off the line. Instead, he was right up on the line of scrimmage. Wally flipped the ball to Dick and Sternberg charged. I think Dick panicked when Sternberg rushed him, and he kicked the ball out of bounds."

Kicking the ball out of bounds simply turned the ball back over to Hamilton with little time left on the clock. Not knowing the logic behind Leo's call, fans were outraged. Boos and catcalls began to fill CNE Stadium. The Argo offence got the ball back with time for one final desperation play. Gabler threw deep only to see Al Brenner intercept the pass to end the game.

After the game, Leo spoke to Al Sokol, who had moved to the *Toronto Star* after the *Telegram* folded the year before. "We needed this game so badly, it was so vitally important to us, and there was no reason for us to lose it."
Gabler had a rough day, going 11 of 32 for 251 yards, two touchdowns and three interceptions. Leon McQuay played well, churning out 79

yards on 13 carries and catching four passes. Symons again saw little action, and the Toronto media were openly questioning his lack of use as a ball carrier. The Toronto coaches acted as if the great back was washed up, but Wally Gabler certainly didn't feel that way. "I didn't notice any drop in his performance. Heck, when Sy dropped that pass on me against Ottawa, he was at least 30 yards behind the secondary. He still had the speed to get open."

The Toronto defence was again outstanding, shutting down Chuck Ealey with surprising ease. Ealey completed only four of 12 passes for 45 yards and was kept under fierce pressure all game. But the defensive effort was wasted by the woeful offence and special teams.

Next up for the staggering Argonauts would be the British Columbia Lions. The Lions were struggling themselves, giving Toronto an opportunity to regain the momentum they had lost after the Hamilton game. Leo, desperate to change the team's luck, decided (finally!) to move Bill Symons into the backfield. He had been absolutely wasted as a slotback so far this year.

Before yet another sellout at CNE Stadium, the Argos jumped in front when Ivan MacMillan missed a 49-yard field goal but picked up a single.

Minutes later they were on the move again. Wally Gabler handed off to Symons for the first time in the game and Bill roared around the right end for 29 yards. The crowd went crazy and Leo could sense that fans and reporters were saying "told you so." Two plays later, Leon McQuay shot 31 yards up the middle for a touchdown. The convert gave Toronto an 8-0 lead.

Early in the third quarter, with Toronto clinging to an 8-6 lead, B.C. quarterback Don Moorhead threw deep to all-star receiver Jim Young. Young made the catch, broke the desperate tackle of Dave Raimey and took it all the way for a 72-yard scoring play. To add to the misery, the score came after the Argos forced the Lions into a punting situation but jumped offside, giving B.C. a first down. Four minutes later, the Lions had more points when fullback Johnny Musso smashed his way into the Toronto end zone from one yard out.

That was it for Toronto. For the first time ever, an Argonaut team coached by Leo Cahill simply gave up. Receivers dropped seven passes, there were four fumbles lost and Gabler threw three interceptions. As the fourth quarter started, the crowd at CNE Stadium began to serenade Leo with the song (sung to the tune of *Goodnight, Ladies*) "Goodbye, Leo, we're glad to see you go." Leo tried to ignore the chant, but it was terribly embarrassing for him and his family attending the game.

The final score was 23-9 for the Lions. Leon McQuay rushed for 101 yards on 11 carries but also fumbled twice. Bill Symons, finally seeing some action in the backfield, picked up 54 yards on eight carries and caught three passes.

Wally Gabler had an erratic night, completing 15 of 32 passes for 185 yards. After the game, Leo told *Toronto Sun* reporter Eaton Howitt: "We were absolutely abominable. I can make no excuses for myself, the coaches or the players."

Toronto was now sitting on a horrific record of 1-7 and the 1972 season appeared to be a lost cause when the Boatmen headed into Hamilton. Ivor Wynne Stadium was jammed with Ticats faithful eager to see the Argos get beaten up again.

Wally Gabler started again at quarterback. Midway through the first quarter, he moved the Argos down field and Bill Symons drove in from a yard out for a touchdown. Hamilton responded with two field goals from rookie Ian Sunter, but the Argo defence was hanging tough and not giving the Ticat offence much room to manoeuvre.

As was the pattern all year, though, the Argos then suffered a dreadful break. Late in the second quarter, Gabler dropped back deep in Argo territory. The ball was greasy and as he directed a pass to Mike Eben, it slipped out of his hand and sort of hung in the air. Hamilton's all-star defensive back John Williams gathered it in and took it back 21 yards for a touchdown, putting Hamilton on top 13-7.

Things got no better in the second quarter. Then, in the first minute of the third quarter, Chuck Ealey threw deep to Dave Buchanan. When the ball arrived, both Luster and Barrett got their hands on it and it deflected off both of them right into the hands of Buchanan. He spun around, started running toward the end zone and scored easily.

Late in the third quarter, trailing 27-7, Cahill sent Chasey into the game. Gabler had already thrown three interceptions. On his first pass, Chasey connected with Dave Cranmer on a 48-yard pass-and-run play for a touchdown, narrowing the gap to 27-14. But Toronto could get no closer and the final score was 41-14 for the Tiger-Cats.

The game had been yet another disaster for Toronto. The Argonauts had given up five interceptions and fumbled three times. The last fumble seemed like a direct shot at Leo. Gabler was sacked by ex-Argo Gary Inskeep, who stripped the ball, which was recovered by another ex-Argo, George Wells. Leo had released both of them.

Wally completed nine of 20 passes and Chasey was a horrific two for 10. The Argo running attack was no factor, either. Leon McQuay carried eight times for 28 yards and Symons rushed eight times for only three yards. The Hamilton front four of Inskeep, Wells, Bruce Smith and Angelo Mosca completely dominated the Toronto offensive line.

The nightmare season would continue against the Edmonton Eskimos the following week before the usual sellout crowd at CNE Stadium. The only ray of hope for Toronto was the news that Joe Theismann would be in uniform. Gabler would start with Joe ready to go in if needed. This game generated plenty of interest around the league as Tom Wilkinson, another Argo castoff, was now the starting QB in Edmonton and was having an outstanding season. This would be his first appearance against old teammates and one of Wilkie's receivers was none other than Bobby Taylor, who had gone over to the Eskimos from Hamilton.

Edmonton jumped in front on a one-yard run by Calvin Harrell. In the second quarter with the Argos trailing 7-4, the crowd roared at the sight of Theismann running onto the field. The first time Joe got his hands on the ball, he moved the offence down the field and finished off by firing an 11-yard TD strike to Eric Allen. Before the quarter ended, Joe had them on the move again, and with no time left on the clock, he hit Eben with a scoring strike to give Toronto a lead of 18-7 going into halftime.

The crowd was going nuts and the Toronto players were suddenly full of confidence. This might be the turning point in their season. With Joe back, maybe they could finally begin winning again.

Early in the third, the Eskimos narrowed the gap to 18-14. Toronto replied with a single off a missed field goal from MacMillan to increase the lead to 19-14. Shortly afterwards, Theismann left the game with soreness in his bad ankle, and a deep sense of foreboding entered the hearts of Argo fans and players. However, Wally Gabler came back in and led the Argos on a march that finished with Bill Symons slamming into the Eskimo end zone from a yard out early in the fourth quarter. Argo hearts were calm for now.

Now came one of the wildest finishes in CFL history. Trailing 26-14, Wilkinson marched the Eskimos downfield and threw a TD strike to his star receiver George McGowan, cutting the Argos' lead to 26-21. Wally promptly moved Toronto downfield close enough for an Ivan MacMillan field goal to increase the lead to 29-21, but less than three minutes later, Wilkinson came right back with a 27-yard TD pass to Bobby Taylor. Argo fans could only stare at the sight of their old passing combination now wreaking havoc on the home team.

With Toronto hanging on to a 29-28 lead, Wilkinson started the Eskimos moving once again. With 1:39 left on the clock, he moved them into position for a 40-yard Dave Cutler field goal that gave Edmonton a 31-29 lead. But Wally refused to give up, and led the Argo offence back downfield. With no time left on the clock, MacMillan trotted out to try a long field goal. A successful attempt would give Toronto the victory. All eyes in CNE Stadium were on the ball as it sailed towards the Edmonton goal posts. It went wide. Toronto picked up a useless single and Edmonton won 31-30.

What was so frustrating to the Argo faithful was that for once the offence had produced. They scored 30 points, which in most games should be enough to win. And yet, that night and perhaps for the first time all season, the defence let them down. The magnificent Blue and White Wall that had provided the Argos with hope all season had finally cracked.

The game statistics showed how valuable Joe Theismann was. In a little more than one quarter of play, he completed 13 of 16 passes for 201 yards, two touchdowns and one interception. Wally was also better than he had been, hitting on 15 of 25 for 284 yards but with two interceptions. He had done an excellent job replacing Joe, but it was clear the offence worked best with Theismann at the controls. The running attack was weak, though; McQuay had 45 yards on 10 carries and Symons, ran six times for just 14 yards. MacMillan missed three of five field-goal attempts, essentially costing Toronto a victory.

There was one strange scenario in this game that few people knew about. It was indicative of the weird happenings that befell the Argos during the 1972 season. Dick Thornton explains:

"Leo sent me in at running back with a pass play for Joe. We were already in position on about the 15- yard line for a chip-shot field goal, but we wanted a touchdown. The play I brought in was a middle screen, but Edmonton had it smothered, so Joe throws the ball away. However, in doing so, he threw it with such force and at such an angle into the ground that it skipped right back up and into the chest of Harry Abofs (whom Edmonton picked up after his release by the Argos). He takes off running in the other direction. I had a perfect angle and saw it hit the ground and jump back up, but none of the refs did, and they ruled it an interception. Thus, on a harmless incomplete pass, Edmonton got the ball back and we got no points at all."

The following day, Al Sokol of the *Toronto Star* dropped a bombshell on the Argonauts faithful. His post-game story began: "Toronto Argonauts lost much more than yet another football game at CNE Stadium Saturday night. The decision has been made to replace head coach Leo Cahill at the end of this season."

Sokol wrote that Toronto management was talking to ex- Montreal Alouette assistant coach Bob Ward, who was a favorite of Barrow. The Argos denied the story but there was no doubt that Leo was in deep trouble. John Barrow didn't like him, period, and the horrible 1-9 record gave Barrow plenty of ammunition in persuading John Bassett to fire the coach.

Leo had one slim hope left. Because Montreal was having a very erratic season, there was still a longshot chance at the playoffs. If Toronto could win its last four games and Montreal lost all of its games, the Argos would make the playoffs. And if they got into the post season, they still had enough talent and experience to be considered a threat to any team.

The Argonauts hosted the Alouettes the following week in a crucial game for both teams. For the first time all season, CNE Stadium was not sold out. With Theismann still hobbled by his bad ankle, Wally Gabler started. The Argo offence sputtered, though, and Leo gave Wally the hook in the second quarter with Toronto trailing 2-0. Theismann, bad ankle and all, came into the game.

Minutes later, Joe hit Eric Allen in the end zone for a touchdown to move Toronto ahead 7-2. Midway through the third quarter, Theismann led a drive down field that finished off with Leon McQuay diving into the Montreal end zone from a yard out.

The Argos were now in complete control, harassing Alouettes quarterback Sonny Wade without mercy. Wade had a game reminiscent of the one he suffered back in 1970 where he threw six interceptions. This time he threw five. Gene Mack, Marv Luster, Dave Raimey, Dick Thornton and Peter Paquette all stopped Montreal drives with pickoffs.

In the fourth quarter, Toronto finished things off with two Ivan MacMillan field goals and a single from Andrusyshyn to win the game 21-3.

The Argonaut defence was at its overpowering best in this game. It held Wade to only five completions in 18 attempts. Moses Denson, the great Montreal running back, picked up just 54 yards on 11 carries and Terry Evanshen was not a factor, being held to just one reception.

For the Argo offence, Joe Theismann had a strong game. He completed 10 of 16 passes for 130 yards, a touchdown and an interception. Bill Symons, getting his most work since 1970, carried 15 times for 98 yards. This performance made it perfectly clear that Sy was still an outstanding running back, making Leo's decision not to use him most of the season even more baffling.

"A Slip in the Rain"

Barely alive in the hunt for the last playoff spot, the Double Blue headed west for a rematch of the 1971 Grey Cup game. The defending champion Calgary Stampeders, like the Argos, were having a rough season and battling just to make it into the post-season. Star middle linebacker Wayne Harris had missed most of the year due to injuries, and his loss had torn the heart out of an otherwise brilliant defence.

Calgary started off the game quickly when all-star tight end Herm Harrison scored on a 46-yard TD strike from Jerry Keeling. The lead was increased to 10-0 early in the second quarter with a Larry Robinson field goal. But Theismann, starting his first game since the season opener, brought the Argos roaring back. He marched the team downfield and finished it off with a 27-yard touchdown pass to Bill Symons, who had gone racing out of the backfield. Minutes later, Theismann connected with Tony Moro on a nine-yard TD strike to give Toronto a 14-10 lead.

Calgary was now being directed by Jim Lindsey, who replaced an injured Jerry Keeling. The Stamps picked up another Robinson field goal before the half to narrow the Toronto lead to 14-13.

A long kickoff return by Eric Allen to open the second half set up a Theismann-to-Eben touchdown play, pushing Toronto ahead 21-13. Before the quarter ended, Toronto got another three points off the foot of Ivan MacMillan. Lindsey then drove the Stampeders downfield and capped off the drive by scoring on a five-yard run to make the score 25-20 for the Argos heading into the last quarter.

Theismann engineered another long drive that climaxed with Symons blasting his way through the Calgary front four for a major, pushing the lead to 31-20. The Stampeders, seeing their own playoff hopes fading, gamely fought back with Rudy Linterman hauling in a 28-yard pass from Lindsey for a touchdown with less than three minutes to go. But Calgary got no closer. John Senst was tackled in his own end zone with 20 seconds left for a safety, making the final score 33-27 in favor of the Argonauts.

Joe Theismann's return as the No. 1 quarterback had been a great success. He completed 21 of 29 for three touchdowns. Joe, being Joe, did give up three interceptions, including two to Terry Wilson, who had played so well against Toronto in the Grey Cup the previous year. Leon

McQuay led Argo rushers with just 34 yards on eight carries, and caught three passes. Symons carried seven times for 33 yards, caught four passes and scored two touchdowns.

Figure 9-1: *"Eric Allen brings down Larry Robinson after a Joe Theismann interception in 1972."*

Calgary ran the ball well, picking up 193 yards along the ground, but Toronto stopped the Stamps when it had to. Both Marv Luster and Chip Barrett came up with big interceptions to halt Calgary drives.

Since Al Sokol's story suggesting Leo would be fired after the season, the Argos had rallied for two consecutive victories. The Toronto players actually seemed to be trying to save Leo's job. Montreal had lost again and now had a record of only 4-8. With two games to go in the regular season, Toronto trailed the Alouettes by two points. If the Argos could even tie in the standings with Montreal, they would get the final playoff position on the basis of two head-to-head victories. There was still hope.

The Argos' desperate run for the playoffs would continue at home against the surprisingly strong Ottawa Rough Riders. Jack Gotta, who had replaced Frank Clair as Ottawa head coach in 1970, had wasted little time rebuilding the Eastern Riders into a very strong team. They were now neck and neck with Hamilton for first place in the Eastern Conference.

CNE Stadium was sold out for the Argos' final home game of the year, and the crowd was rocking early when Toronto moved out in front. Mike Eben snared a short pass from Joe Theismann to give the Argos a 7-0 lead. Ottawa closed the gap to 7-6 over the next 15 minutes on a field goal, single and safety. Then Theismann hit Eric Allen on a 62-yard pass-and-run touchdown to increase the Toronto lead to 14-6 at half time.

In the third quarter, the Argos added a safety, but that was the extent of the scoring in that quarter. Theismann, despite his two TD strikes, was having an awful game. He would end up throwing five interceptions and complete less than 50 per cent of his passes.

In the fourth quarter, Gerry Organ added a single on a missed field goal to cut the Toronto lead to 16-7. With less than five minutes to go, quarterback Rick Cassata threw deep to his all-star flanker Hugh Oldham (who had stunned Toronto with that 100-yard pass and run play in 1971). Jimmy Dye, covering Oldham, slipped and fell, leaving the Ottawa star wide open. Dick Thornton, seeing Dye helpless on the field, made a superhuman effort to reach Oldham and almost got his fingertips on Cassata's pass. An inch closer and Dick might have saved the day, but it was not to be. He arrived a fraction of a second too late and barely missed an interception. Instead, Oldham took the pass and went all the way for a 60-yard touchdown. CNE Stadium was suddenly silent.

In the final minute, trailing 16-14 and backed up at the Toronto 50-yard line, Ottawa lined up for what everyone in the stadium knew would be a pass. The defensive call was made and Dick Thornton flipped. "In the huddle, Luster gets the sign from the bench to go man-to-man. I screamed at him to overrule the call and go into a three-deep zone, but he wouldn't do it." Pete Martin, who was back in the lineup after suffering a dislocated elbow, adds: "Dick was begging Marv to ignore the decision. 'Don't do it,' he yelled. 'We have to go zone.' "

Cassata went back to pass and fired to Oldham. Thornton outlines what happened: "I played Oldham to the inside and when he caught the ball, Jimmy Dye came over to help on the tackle. We both knocked each other out of the play and Oldham pranced into the end zone. If we had been in an umbrella zone, I could have maybe disguised the setup and possibly got an interception. It was just typical of shit like that which happened all year."

Argo fan and coaches could only stare at the field in stunned silence. If there was one player you would want covering a pass in a crucial occasion, it was Dick Thornton. No. 25 was right there and yet still got burned twice in less than five minutes. It could only have happened in 1972!

The shock wore off quickly, and again the fans began to serenade Leo with that haunting tune *Goodbye, Leo*. Cahill felt ill as the fans taunted and ridiculed him. This was truly a season everyone wanted to forget.

Theismann's last desperate pass was picked off to end the game, leaving Toronto on the short end of a 21-16 score and dropping its record to 3-10.

Theismann had his worst game as a professional. He completed only 12 of 28 passes for 170 yards, two touchdowns and a horrific five interceptions. Along the ground, Leon McQuay turned in a decent effort with 60 yards on nine carries, while Bill Symons added 22 yards on seven carries. The injury bug also cropped up again as Raimey suffered a broken hand and was gone for the rest of the year.

Montreal helped Toronto out by rolling over and dying in a 29-3 loss to Saskatchewan to finish its season at 4-10. If Toronto could beat Hamilton at Ivor Wynne Stadium in the final game of the regular season, the Argos would remarkably still make the playoffs.

In the week leading up to the big game, Herb Solway, a close friend of John Bassett and a member of the Argonaut management team, tipped Leo off about his long-term status with the team. A victory over Hamilton and the resulting playoff spot would save his job. A loss would guarantee his firing.

The Argos received some good news when Tim Anderson, who had been out of the lineup since training camp, told Leo he was ready to go. With the loss of Raimey, Anderson's return would be a big boost to the defensive backfield.

Several veteran players approached the coaching staff during the week to suggest that Wally Gabler start at quarterback. It was obvious that Joe Theismann wasn't 100 per cent. His ankle was still bad, in the last two games he had thrown eight interceptions and he had looked simply abysmal against Ottawa. Wally was a tough, battle-hardened veteran. He might not have the pure physical ability of Joe but he had a decent arm, good mobility and veteran savvy. With everything on the line, many of the vets felt he should get the call and lobbied hard for him to start. But Cahill, stubborn as ever, stuck to his faith in No. 7.

A capacity crowd jammed Ivor Wynne Stadium for the final regular-season game of 1972. The Ticats, with a record of 10-3, were trying to hold off Ottawa for first place and would be going all out against Leo's desperate Argonauts.

Leo had his team whipped into a frenzy for the game. After all, his career as Argo coach hinged on winning this contest. The Argos came out flying early as Theismann marched them down the field and hit Eric Allen with an eight-yard touchdown pass. Hamilton fought back with a single off a missed field goal, and then the Ticats caught a huge break.

Dick Thornton describes it: "There were a couple of really strange officiating calls against us early in the game and Leo immediately began verbally blasting the refs, calling them every name in the book. I was covering Garney Henley on a deep fly pattern down the sideline and we were running side by side when the ball clearly sailed over both our heads by a good 10 yards. We never touched each other, either. There was no contact and the ball was uncatchable anyway. I turn around and there was a flag on the ground: pass interference. Hamilton ball in the red zone. I asked the ref walking back to the huddle what the hell was that call for? He said, 'Tell your coach to keep his fucking mouth shut.' So now the officials were against us, too."

Dave Fleming finished off the drive by catching a short pass from Chuck Ealey for the major. Early in the second quarter, Hamilton came right back with Ealey hitting Tommy-Joe Coffey with a 22-yard TD pass, sending the Ticats ahead 15-7. Leo's players, though would not roll over and die. Theismann moved them into Hamilton territory and threw deep to Allen. Eric leaped up and over Hamilton's great veteran defensive back Lewis Porter and made a diving, twisting catch for a touchdown. MacMillan missed the convert so the score was 15-13. The Cats came right back on the ensuing kickoff when Porter took the Big Z's kick at the Ticat 12-yard line. Following his blockers upfield, he spotted a gap in the coverage team and roared through it. Andrusyshyn made a frantic diving attempt to bring Porter down, but Argo fans watched helplessly as the returner took it back 98 yards for a touchdown.

Before the half ended, Ian Sunter added to the Hamilton lead with a 38-yard field goal, giving the Ticats a 25-13 cushion.

The second half was wild. The Argo defence dug in and refused to give an inch to the Hamilton offence. Jim Stillwagon, playing what Argo assistant coach Bob Gibson described as his finest game as a pro, was all over the field making tackles. The defensive line, led by Stillwagon, dropped Ealey for losses seven times. Allen and McQuay both had to be restrained by teammates as they got into taunting matches with several Hamilton players. Noah Jackson was thrown out of the game for fighting. Meanwhile, Cahill paced the sidelines and continued yelling at the officials.

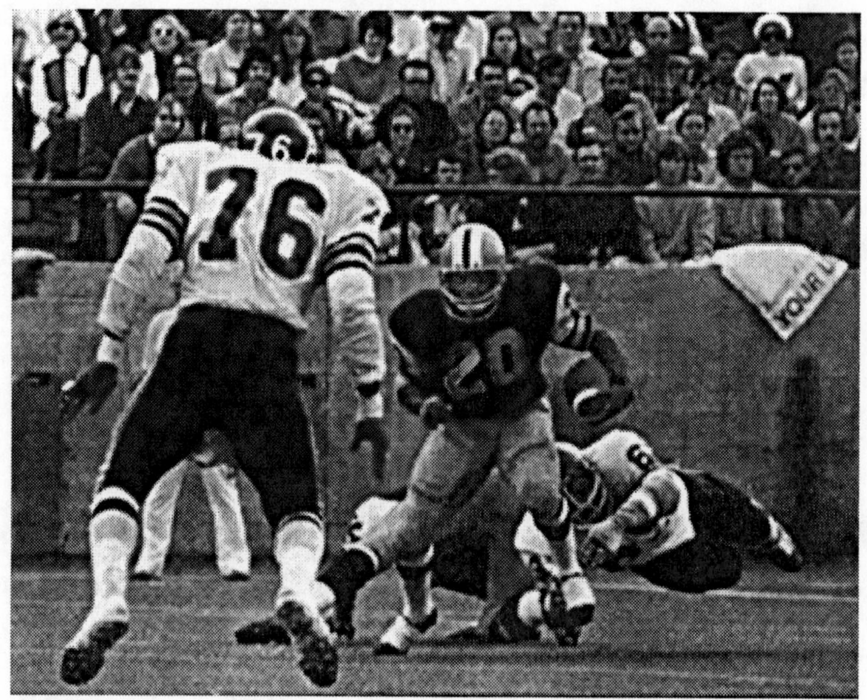

Figure 9-2: *"Final game action in 1972. Gene Mack braces for a hit."*

Amidst all this, there was still some scoring. MacMillan missed two field-goal attempts that went for singles, and in the fourth quarter, Andrusyshyn drove a 60-yard punt through the Ticat end zone for another point. Toronto got no closer, however. Hamilton safety Al Brenner set a CFL record by intercepting four passes in this game. Wally Gabler and many of the veteran Argos seethed at the fact that Gabler remained on the sidelines despite Theismann's poor performance.

Ian Sunter hammered another single on a missed 30-yard field-goal attempt late in the game. The Hamilton crowd began singing *Goodbye, Leo* as the clock ran down. When the final gun sounded, Hamilton had won 26-16. The 1972 season was over for the Toronto Argonauts.

After the game Ticats defensive legend Angelo Mosca told the *Toronto Star's* Al Sokol: "I've never seen a team want a game as much as Argos, but we just wouldn't give it to them. There's no doubt in my mind it was our toughest game this season; those guys were absolutely wild."

Hamilton coach Jerry Williams, whose team finished the year at 11-3 and would go on to defeat Saskatchewan 13-10 in the Grey Cup game, added: "Leo did an outstanding job getting his team ready for this game considering his injury problems. You can strap all the blame for a 3-11 season on a head coach, but it's not very helpful as far as the team is concerned."

So what should have been a Grey Cup season had turned out to be a dismal failure. The Argos headed back to Toronto and Leo Cahill braced himself for what was to come about in the next few days.

The chop came the following week when John Bassett, Sr., called Leo to his office and fired him and as all of the assistant coaches. The media was saying that John Barrow and the Argonauts board had pressured Bassett into the move, but the owner told *Globe and Mail* reporter Rex MacLeod: "This was my decision as chairman of the board. I also want to make it clear that apart from closing the *Telegram*, it was the hardest job I had to do."

The Argo players on the whole were upset over the firing. Mel Profit, who now hosted a talk show on City-TV, interviewed Dick Thornton,

Dave Raimey and Jim Stillwagon just days after the firing. These three players truly defended Leo. "We had a lot of unnecessary internal problems, injuries and bad luck," said Thornton. "In '64 a similar scenario took place in Winnipeg but no one panicked and we were back in the Grey Cup the following year." Dave Raimey added: "I don't think you can blame a whole season on one man." Mel, however was critical of Leo. He referred to Cahill's handling of Bill Symons as "the worst use of talent I've ever seen in football. The best running back in the game was relegated to a spectator's role."

Should Leo Cahill have been fired? Clearly he had made some errors along the way, but what coach does not? His use of Bill Symons was definitely questionable. His unorthodox rotation at the quarterback position in 1970 and 1971 never worked out as he thought it would. Leo should have learned his lesson in 1970 when Tom Wilkinson and Don Jonas struggled under this approach. Instead, he did it again the following year with Greg Barton and Joe Theismann. Yet in late 1972, as Theismann played terribly, Cahill kept Wally Gabler on the bench, wasting his veteran skills and knowledge. It was as if Leo was saying, "You criticized me for switching quarterbacks so we'll live and die with Joe."

Certainly his greatest and perhaps most fatal error was his handling of Leon McQuay. By pampering and babying the immature young star, Cahill lost the respect of his players and in some ways tore the team apart emotionally. Bill Symons, looking back, remembers a specific instance: "We were practicing in Port Credit and Leon was late. We waited two hours, just standing around for Leon to show up. Leo would not go on without him. Finally Leon arrived, with some story about how he had all four tires stolen off his car. We couldn't believe that Leo would have 31 players standing around (and being paid) waiting for one guy. If you did that in business you'd be fired.

"People used to ask why, after Leon had run a play and was knocked down, I would always go over, pick him up and lead him back to the huddle. If I didn't do it, he'd leave the field! He had unbelievable talent, and the heart of a pea."

On the other hand, Leo had taken a franchise that was the longstanding laughingstock of the CFL and turned it into a consistent winner. By 1972, the Argos were the hottest ticket in Canadian football. They played before consistent sellouts both at home and on the road and were the league's biggest drawing card. Sometimes people would show up at airports across Canada just to watch the colourful Argonauts get off the plane and walk through the terminal. Leo had turned them into the team the rest of the league loved to hate.

He had also brought many of the game's most exciting and talented players to Toronto. While society was being racked with disputes over racism, long hair and anti-establishment feelings, Leo treated his players like men. Dave Raimey once said: "Leo was colour blind." By that he meant Leo never cared about the colour of a player's skin. He only judged his players by their ability.

Dick Thornton says Cahill "treated us like the mature adults that we were. You could wear your hair as long as you liked, say what you wanted to the media and stay out all night if that's what you wanted to do. We just had to be ready to play when the band was playing, the crowd was roaring and the whistle blew. His only firm edict was to stay out of trouble."

Why did John Bassett fire Leo after a season in which the team had been devastated by injuries? No team could have recovered from the set backs Toronto had suffered all year long. Bill Symons speculates the axe fell because "Leo burned a lot of his bridges with management." Dick Thornton agrees and adds: "I believe Leo ruffled too many front-office feathers. I don't know what went on behind closed doors but Leo could be very sarcastic and he always had to have the last word. You cannot buck the power in corporate business today nor could you do it back then. Anybody in professional sport is always just pencilled in anyway. They can easily be erased when no longer needed or wanted."

Today, Leo looks back and says: "It was a good lesson for me. When you look at coaches who last a long time like Bud Grant, they were not spokesmen like I was. When you do the things that I did and things are going well, the people love you. When it went bad, they turned on me. I had become the Argos and was 10 times more popular in Toronto then Don Cherry ever was."

Epilogue

Rightly or wrongly, the Leo Cahill era of Toronto football came to an end after the 1972 season. What happened next stands in retrospect as evidence that the decision to fire him was wrong. The 1973 season marked the beginning of another dark period of futility for the team that just two years earlier had been the unquestioned flagship of Canadian football.

Enormous changes had to be made to justify the decision to fire Cahill. General manager John Barrow replaced the coach with John Rauch, a former head coach of the Oakland Raiders and Buffalo Bills who had no Canadian football experience. At the same time, the playing personnel fell victim to a revolving-door syndrome. To start the changes, Marv Luster was traded in the off-season to the Montreal Alouettes and Chip Barrett was sent to the B.C. Lions. Barrett, however, decided to go back to university to finish his degree in architecture rather than report to the Lions.

When training camp opened, John Rauch made little effort to bond with the players. "Rauch was very aloof, which was initially a bad sign," says Dick Thornton. "If I had been in his position, I would have courted the veterans for their thoughts and opinions on what the CFL was all about and on how to get the team back on a winning track. Instead, he ignored all of us, especially me.

"During training camp, he seldom said one word and left all the coaching to the assistants, whereas Leo was always running the show, in the heart of all the action and totally involved with the team on a daily basis."

Rauch wasted little time getting rid of Thornton. The way he did it was almost beyond belief. "When I only played a few minutes in the first exhibition game, I figured I was history. I came in the next day to practice and found my locker totally empty and all my personal stuff, like my cleats, special pads, shaving gear, pictures, etc., thrown into a green garbage bag. The equipment manager couldn't look me in the eye as he told me to 'see the coach and bring your playbook.'

"I walked into Rauch's office, dropped the book on his desk and waited. Rauch never looked up from his desk or said one word, so I said, 'You're making a big mistake,' and walked out. Not one of my teammates said anything, either, which was understandable as I grabbed the garbage bag and departed the eerie, totally silent locker room, got in my car and drove away from CNE Stadium for the last time."

Before the exhibition season finished, Pete Martin lost his desire to play under the new Argo regime and abruptly quit. Wally Gabler was released as well. Gabler, too, was extremely angry at how he got his walking papers. "I had my best camp ever. Rauch told me I was the best quarterback they had in the exhibition season and then he releases me. He said that Joe Theismann and (rookie) Mike Rae had no-cut contracts so they could not get rid of them. I felt it was pretty dishonest to bring me in when I had no chance at all of ever making the team."

One game into the regular season, Rauch suspended Leon McQuay for insubordination, and Barrow quickly shipped the mercurial running back to Calgary. The troublemaker who had caused so many problems in the past was now gone for good. Leo's team was being disassembled, piece by piece.

Still, there were some encouraging signs. The Argos finished the 1973 season with a record of 7-5-2, a huge improvement over the previous year's 3-11, and good enough for second place in the Eastern Conference. Toronto played host to the Montreal Alouettes in the Eastern Semifinal but was trounced 32-10. To add injury to insult, Jim Stillwagon suffered a career-ending injury in that playoff game.

After the season, Bill Symons decided he's had enough and retired. Joe Theismann, a free agent, signed with the NFL's Washington Redskins. Barrow and Rauch continued to break up the team that only two years before had been within seven yards of winning the Grey Cup. Other players who were traded, released or retired after the 1973 season included Paul Desjardins, Dick Aldridge, Charlie Bray and Ron Mikolajczyk.

Leo Cahill was back in the news in the early winter months of 1974. The new World Football League was going to start play that summer and one of its franchises was owned by John F. Bassett, Jr., son of the Argonauts owner. He announced his team would be based in Toronto and wasted little time in hiring Leo to be his general manager. Leo quickly signed Dick Thornton, who was working as a sportswriter for the *Toronto Sun* at the time, as well as Charlie Bray and Ron Mikolajczyk.

Alas, Leo's dream of once again leading a Toronto football franchise was not to be. The Canadian government, concerned that the WFL would drive the CFL out of business, threatened to pass legislation that would ban the league from Canada, so the Toronto Northmen became the Memphis Southmen before ever playing a game. The Southmen were one of the most successful teams in the league that year, winning a division championship with a 17-3 record, proving Cahill had not lost his knack for building good football teams.

Dick Thornton, at age 35, showed he could still play and had a tremendous season in the new league. He was a team captain and called all the defensive signals, made 116 individual tackles from his free safety position and intercepted five passes, returning one for a touchdown. He then retired from the game, but not before proving conclusively that Argonauts management had made a huge error in releasing him the year before.

The Argos, meanwhile, began another freefall when John Bassett, Sr., sold the team before the 1974 season to Bill Hodgson. The new owner brought in former star player Dick Shatto and J.I. Albrecht to run the front office. The Argonauts collapsed that year, missing the playoffs, Rauch was fired before the year ended and replaced by one of his assistants, Joe Moss.

Before the 1975 season, John Barrow was let go and replaced as general manager by Shatto, who brought in the Argos' old nemesis, Russ Jackson, as head coach. Despite the presence of these two former CFL greats, the Argos' fortunes did not turn around, and Toronto missed postseason play in both 1975 and 1976.

Jackson was fired in November of 1976 and Hodgson stunned the city of Toronto by rehiring Leo Cahill as head coach. Leo had been out of football after the collapse of the WFL and was working as a sportscaster for CHUM radio.

Leo's return showed he still had some of the magic touch. He took over a team with little talent (much like 1967) and led them to the playoffs for the first time in four years. Leo built a defence that was as tough as anything seen in his earlier tenure with the team, and just like 1970 and '71, once again he presided over a season-long quarterback controversy. Ex-Ticat Chuck Ealey had the job most of the time but was supplanted periodically by ex-Dallas Cowboy Clint Longley.

In the 1977 Eastern Semifinal in Ottawa, the Argos went down to defeat in a bitterly fought game that was dominated by their defence and was in doubt to the final gun. The modest success of the Toronto Argonauts in 1977 (a 6-10 record but a return to the playoffs) could be attributed in large part to the coaching and recruiting job Leo did.

Recruiting had always been Leo's strength, and he showed it again in 1977 when he rebuilt the Argo defence with a number of acquisitions. The most notable was his signing of the best cornerback in U.S. college football, Eric Harris, a first-round draft pick of the NFL's Kansas City Chiefs.

A year later, Cahill stunned the sports world by signing star NFL running back Terry Metcalf away from the St. Louis Cardinals. Metcalf was spectacular in the preseason and early in the 1978 season, but by Week 5 a disaster was starting to unfold. Despite sometimes brilliant play by Metcalf, the Argos had terrible quarterbacking and poor defence. Leo was fired halfway through the season when the Argos' record dropped to 3-6. He spent the next few years as a popular colour commentator for CBC's CFL broadcasts, working in the booth alongside Ron Lancaster and Don Wittman.

In 1986, three seasons after the Argos finally ended their 31-year Grey Cup drought, Cahill was rehired by Toronto, this time as general manager. The Argos, after their Grey Cup victory in 1983, had fallen back on hard times and missed the playoffs in 1985. Cahill, despite working under the control of former Hamilton rival Ralph Sazio, helped turn things around by recruiting stars such as linebacker Willie Pless and running back Gill (the Thrill) Fenerty. The Argos finished first in 1986, only to lose to Hamilton in a two-game, total-points Eastern Final. In 1987, they finished second but made it to the Grey Cup game where they lost to Edmonton 38-36 in one of the most exciting championship games in CFL history.

Leo was fired again after a 1988 season in which the Argonauts again finished first but failed to get past the Eastern Final. He was out of Canadian football until 1996, when he served as general manager of the Ottawa Rough Riders in their final season in the CFL before the franchise folded. In 2004, he returned to the Argonauts for the fourth time, hired by the team's new owners, Howard Sokolowski and David Cynamon, as a goodwill ambassador.

But Leo Cahill will always be associated with the Argonauts of 1967-72. That team of colourful characters and great athletes will forever live in the hearts of Toronto football fans, despite the fact that a slip in the rain cost the team its one and only chance at a Grey Cup victory. Leo Cahill and his band of mavericks and renegades played emotional, exciting football and never, ever quit, oftentimes winning or losing in dramatic fashion. They gave a lot of people a lifetime of memories. Thanks guys, Argo fans will never forget you.

Where Are They Now?

The Coaches

Leo Cahill – After an often turbulent but quite successful coaching and management career, he retired to Sarnia, Ont., and came out of retirement in 2004 to serve as a goodwill ambassador for the Toronto Argonauts.

Gordon Ackerman – Retired and now resides in Barrie, Ont.

Bob Gibson – Got out of the coaching business and moved to Florida.

Frank (Blackie) Johnston – Deceased.

Jim Rountree – "Tree" makes his home in Tamarak, Fla., where he owns a State Farm Insurance agency.

The Players

Dick Thornton – After being cut from the Argos in 1973, "Tricky Dick" resumed his pro football career as captain of the WFL's Memphis Southmen in 1974. He then served as athletic director and head football coach at Southwestern Memphis College where he won two conference championships and his team was nationally ranked in NCAA Division III. Dick had a long and successful international marketing career with Coca-Cola Co. He is now an independent contract consultant specializing in global merchandising, training and field coaching while based in Manila, the Philippines. He was inducted into the Winnipeg Blue Bombers Hall of Fame in 1988 and was named to the CFL's all-time all-star team in 1993.

Bill Symons – Bill continues a successful business career with AFA Forest Products and also operates a thriving farm near Hockley Valley, Ont. "Sy" is an active member of the Argonauts Alumni and was inducted into the Canadian Football Hall of Fame in 1997.

Wally Gabler – Wally continued on with his successful investment career after retirement and is now a vice-president with the Bank of Montreal/Nesbitt Burns in Toronto.

Peter Martin – After his football days, Pete continued his full-time teaching career. He also spent many years as the colour commentator on Argo radio broadcasts, returning to the post in 2004. He is now retired from teaching, lives in Mississauga, Ont., and serves as president of the Toronto Argonauts Alumni.

Dave Raimey – Dave worked for a while with the CFL and was involved in the insurance business. He now runs a home decorating business know as Safari Interiors in Dayton, Ohio. In 2000 he was inducted into the Canadian Football Hall of Fame.

Michael Eben – Mike got his PhD while still playing for the Argonauts and taught for many years at York University in Toronto. He is now an instructor at Upper Canada College in Toronto.

Mel Profit – After leaving the Argonauts, Mel continued to run his boutique on Wellesley Street. He hosted a popular show on City-TV for a few years, and served as the colour analyst on Argo radio broadcasts during the 1975 and' 76 seasons. Team management eventually insisted he be fired for being too critical in his comments about the team. Mel moved back to the United States and at last word was living a very private life in California.

Dick Aldridge - After leaving the game, Dick continued teaching at the high school level. Upon retirement he and his wife operated a store in Totenham, Ontario. Dick passed away after a courageous battle with cancer in the early summer of 2004.

Jim Stillwagon – Jim is the president of Stillwagon Enterprises, a firm in Hilliard, Ohio, that manufactures and sells specialty promotion items to large corporations.

Jim Tomlin – "Cricket" is an engineer working in the oil industry and a published author. He lives in San Antonio, Tex.

Bobby Taylor – Bobby still lives in Toronto and owns and operates the Black Bull pub on Queen Street.

Jim Corrigall – Served for many years as head football coach at his alma mater, Kent State University. Jim is now semi-retired and has worked as a training camp guest coach with the Hamilton Ticats. He was inducted into the Canadian Football Hall of Fame in 1990.

Gerry Sternberg – "Packrat" began his law career while still playing pro football and continues to work as a trial lawyer. His practice is located on Charles Street in downtown Toronto.

Michael Wadsworth – After his retirement in 1970, Wadsworth had a Toronto law practice and worked as a colour commentator on CFL telecasts. He spent a number of years as Canadian Ambassador to the Republic of Ireland, and served as athletic director at Notre Dame University during the 1990s. He died in 2004 after a long battle with cancer.

Gene Mack – After retirement, Gene began an acting career and worked for a time in the Argonauts front office. He continues to live in the Toronto area.

Marv Luster – Since retiring from football in 1974 after finally winning a Grey Cup as a member of the Montreal Alouettes, "Stickman" has lived a quiet and very private life in the Los Angeles area. Marv was inducted in 1990 to the Canadian Football Hall of Fame.

Joe Theismann – Joe departed the Argonauts after the 1973 season and joined the NFL's Washington Redskins. He had a long and outstanding career in the U.S. capital city, leading the Redskins to a Super Bowl victory in 1983. He retired after suffering a gruesome broken leg in a nationally televised Monday Night Football game. Theismann now works as a football analyst for ESPN and makes his home in Arlington, Va.

Chip Barrett – Chip is living in White Rock, B.C., and works as an architect.

Ed Harrington – Ed lives near North Bay, Ontario and works as the Patient Advocate at a local hospital.

Dave Knechtel – Dave is a high school teacher and football coach in Winnipeg.

Dave Cranmer – Lives in the western suburbs of Toronto and works as a high school teacher.

Peter Paquette – Peter lives in Pickering, Ont., works in financial planning and is an active member of the Argonauts Alumni.

Ed Learn – After retiring, "Rope" settled in Welland, Ont., and became owner of Ed Learn Ford, one of Ontario's most successful new car dealerships.

Paul Desjardins – At last word, Desjardins was living in Winnipeg and teaching at the University of Manitoba.

Ellison Kelly – "Elly" is retired and living in Hamilton. He was inducted into the Canadian Football Hall of Fame in 1991.

Jim Dillard – Jim returned home to Oklahoma and had a successful career with State Farm Insurance.

Tom Wilkinson – After leaving Toronto, "Wilkie's" career took off in Edmonton. He was voted CFL MVP in 1974, started 6 Grey Cups winning 3 and finished off his career by replacing Warren Moon in the 1981 Grey Cup and rallying the Eskimos to a thrilling 26-23 victory over Ottawa. After retirement Tom spent some time as the Head Football Coach at the University of Alberta. Today he is in the carpet business and still lives in Edmonton. He was elected to the Canadian Football Hall of Fame in 1987.

Jim Henderson – After retirement in 1972, Jim focused on his high school teaching career. He taught for many years in the Toronto suburb of Scarborough, and still lives in the Toronto area.

Leon McQuay – "X-Ray" didn't last long in Calgary. The Stampeders released him before the end of the 1973 season. He bounced around the NFL for 3 seasons and in 1977 was brought back to the Argos by Leo Cahill. Leon performed solidly for Leo that year but was released before training camp in 1978 when the Argos signed Terry Metcalf. After his football career ended he experienced some hard times back in Tampa and died in 1995.

Harry Abofs – deceased.

Index of Photos

Figure 2-1: "Leo Cahill" *20*

Figure 3-1: "Wally Gabler grimly watches the Toronto defense in action, during the 1967 season." *28*

Figure 3-2: "Wally Gabler sends Bill Symons into the B.C. line, during the Argos 18-17 win over the Lions." *29*

Figure 4-1: "Bill Symons faces tough going during 1968 action in Ottawa." *58*

Figure 4-2: "Wally Gabler gets off a pass under heavy pressure in the 2nd game of the 1968 Eastern Final." *71*

Figure 5-1: "Pete Martin #77 fails to prevent Russ Jackson # 12 from getting off a pass during action in Ottawa in 1969." .86

Figure 6-1: "Mel Profit hauls in a pass against Montreal in 1970."119

Figure 6-2: "Bill Symons heads up field during 1970 action at C.N.E. Stadium." *124*

Figure -7-1: "Mike Eben makes a big gain against Montreal in 1971." *152*

Figure 8-1: "Joe Theismann barks the signals as the Argo offence prepares for action." *178*

Figure 8-2: "The Blue and White Wall smothers Jesse Mims." ... *183*

Figure 8-3: "The interception of the decade. Dick Thornton takes off with Jerry Keelings' pass late in the 1971 Grey Cup."190

Figure 8-4: "As Joe Vijuk # 59 battles Calgary's Reggie Holmes, Leon McQuay slips on the Empire Stadium turf and the Argos 1971 Grey Cup dreams come to and end." *194*

Figure 9-1: "Eric Allen brings down Larry Robinson after a Joe Theismann interception in 1972." *224*

Figure 9-2: "Final game action in 1972. Gene Mack braces for a hit." *229*

Photo Credits

All photos courtesy of Canadian Football Hall of Fame and Canadian Football League with the exception of:

1. Dick Thornton 1971 Grey Cup Interception (Figure 8.3) – Photo courtesy of *Vancouver Province.*
2. Leon McQuay 1971 Grey Cup fumble (Figure 8.4) – Photo courtesy of *Toronto Star*
3. Back Cover inspired by a photograph taken by *Terry Hancey.*

Bibliography

1. Cahill, Leo, with Young, Scott, Goodbye Argos. McClelland and Stewart Ltd., 1973.
2. Profit, Mel, For Love, Money, and Future Considerations. D.C Heath Canada Ltd., 1972.
3. Teitel, Jay, The Argo Bounce. Lester & Orpen Dennys Ltd., 1982.

The author conducted numerous interviews, in person and by e-mail, with key figures in the book, in particular Dick Thornton, Leo Cahill, Bill Symons, Dave Raimey, Jim Tomlin, Pete Martin, Mike Eben and Wally Gabler.

In addition to quotes from interviews with Leo Cahill, some comments attributed came from his book with Scott Young, *Goodbye Argos.* All quotes from Mel Profit came from his book, *For Love, Money, and Future Considerations* as well as various newspaper articles. The author did not interview Mel Profit.

Considerable background information came through the author's review of stories published by the *Toronto Telegram, Toronto Star, Globe and Mail* and *Toronto Sun.* Some stories published by those newspapers were quoted in brief, with attribution.

CPSIA information can be obtained at www.ICGtesting.com
Printed in the USA
LVOW061928270911

248103LV00002B/242/A